T0303857

INCLUSIVE LEADERSHIP

This book breaks important new ground in describing the enhancements to employers, employees and customers that Inclusive Leadership can bring. For an employer, it can bring greater profitability, for an employee, increased productivity, motivation and mental well-being and for customers, products and services that are finely tuned to their needs and preferences. Illustrating these benefits through theory and practical examples, the book contrasts this style with Command and Control, Transactional leadership, a style that still holds sway in many organisations, with leaders focused on mistakes rather than achievements, and internal rather than external dynamics.

Inclusive Leadership will transport you through time and geography – from the UK, US and Australia to France and Norway – showing how much more positive an environment inclusive leadership provides than traditional transactional leadership. Read how inclusive leadership complements a strategy of innovation and how it dominates in four organisations – Royal Mail Sales, the PageGroup, Sevenoaks School and APAM – spanning sales, recruitment, secondary education and real estate. The chapters also cover the worlds of football, retailing, the army, finance, commercial aviation, and Higher Education and show the strong associations between inclusive leadership and enhanced performance, motivation and well-being in employees as well as students.

With a unique combination of both theoretical and practical perspectives, this book is a useful tool for established, and also emerging leaders in the public and private sectors in both industry and education. It will moreover be of interest to students of business, management and leadership students.

Inclusive Leadership has a foreword by Loraine Martins MBE, Director of Diversity and Inclusion, Network Rail. There is also an accompanying video featuring Case Study organisations as well as Network Rail, Queen Mary College London and Buckinghamshire New University.

Gloria Moss is Professor of Management and Marketing at Buckinghamshire New University and Fellow of the Chartered Institute of Personnel and Development (FCIPD). She is the author of six books, over seventy peer-reviewed journal articles and conference papers and has a background as a Training and Development Manager for Courtaulds and Eurotunnel, and as a consultant working on management and marketing issues.

INCLUSIVE LEADERSHIP

Gloria Moss

Routledge
Taylor & Francis Group

LONDON AND NEW YORK

First published 2019
by Routledge
2 Park Square, Milton Park, Abingdon, Oxon OX14 4RN

and by Routledge
52 Vanderbilt Avenue, New York, NY 10017

Routledge is an imprint of the Taylor & Francis Group, an informa business

British Library Cataloguing-in-Publication Data
A catalogue record for this book is available from the British Library

Library of Congress Cataloging-in-Publication Data
A catalog record for this book has been requested

ISBN: 978-1-138-09057-6 (hbk)
ISBN: 978-1-315-10857-5 (ebk)

Typeset in Bembo
by Apex CoVantage, LLC

Printed in the United Kingdom
by Henry Ling Limited

CONTENTS

FOREWORD: INCLUSIVE LEADERSHIP

Background

I am dedicated to inclusive leadership since for me it is a way of being. I work for Network Rail, which is responsible for the rail infrastructure in the UK. This includes 2,500 stations, 30,000 bridges, 700 tunnels and 800 retail units. Ours is the fastest growing and safest railway in Europe, with some 4 million passengers daily. Network Rail has over 39,000 employees up and down the country, of whom 82% are men; 8% are from a black, Asian and minority ethnic background; 2% are disabled people, and 1% are from the Lesbian, Bi-sexual, Gay and Trans community (LBGT+). The rail sector has an ageing workforce, a skills shortage and faces significant demands. Network Rail became a public sector company in 2014 and is moving from a centralised to more devolved business in which each route is empowered to run in a way that best meets the needs of its passengers and train operator customers. The onset of digitalisation and new and safer ways of working are requiring different competencies.

These are times of major change. To move an organisation and its culture to be able to identify talent in all its rich and varied forms and then benefit from that, requires institutions, businesses, functions, teams and people managers and employees to have the discipline that is inclusive leadership.

Moss's book sets out the components of inclusive leadership and its benefits. Using case studies and comparing approaches of different companies, it helps to illustrate and amplify why inclusive leadership is so important, and Moss does this well. You will come away from this book realising that inclusive leadership, at its core, is an effective way of building capacity and innovation within teams and across companies. What is interesting about Moss' work is the clear demonstration that the competencies of inclusive leaders are ones to be adopted by all leaders.

A further feature of Moss' book is that leadership is not solely about position or hierarchy within an organisation, it is about behaviours which cultivate engagement and creativity, such as in the example in the book of Royal Mail.

Benefits of inclusive leadership

At Network Rail, those leaders who are inclusive, who listen to their employees, show empathy, act on their suggestions and value their people, are reporting far better engagement scores than those leaders who maintain the more traditional one-dimensional leadership styles.

Inclusive leaders flex with their people and environment. They seek out talent and are prepared to do things differently and we have seen this amply at Network Rail. For example, in our focus on continuous improvement, part of the 'Better every day' initiatives, leaders were tasked with encouraging everyone to identify those small incremental changes that would make a positive difference to performance be it efficiencies through cutting out unnecessary activities or reducing waste to new ways of doing things. The inclusive style of inclusive leadership being developed within the organisation has seen people throughout the business stimulated to identify areas that they knew could be improved yet had previously felt discouraged from speaking up about.

The benefits of inclusive leadership can be seen daily and Moss' book is a helpful catalyst to encourage us all to be much more deliberate in making the features of inclusive leaders a more sought after and valued aspects of behaviour.

Employees have become more confident to challenge inappropriate behaviour, excited to be inclusive and less willing to accept 'old-school' leadership styles.

How has inclusive leadership been achieved

There have been several initiatives. One is the creation of diversity and inclusion champions who have a job description which contains three aspects to the role: to be a role model; to be a sign-post directing colleagues to resources and support; and to be challenging. The champions are provided with a pack and a menu of activities that they can undertake and can then use their initiative. Starting in small numbers across the company in 2014, by 2017 the company boasted 960 champions and by the end of 2018 over 1,500 including the new CEO, who became a diversity and inclusion champion immediately. From Signalers to the chair of Network Rail, anyone in the business can become a champion. The position has become an emblem of commitment and a demonstration of someone who is regularly using opportunities to advance inclusion in the workplace.

A champion status devoid of hierarchy has unlocked the discretionary effort of Network Rail's people who are now willing to go the extra mile because they feel that their contributions matter. An inclusive style of leadership has served to remove barriers that can inhibit inclusive behaviours since people are encouraged to constructively challenge the way things are done in order to fulfil our ambitions to be a more open, inclusive and diverse company.

Then there is training that has been rolled out to 4,000 managers. The initiative started in 2012 when an inclusive leadership programme was piloted with 100 leaders with attendance after this voluntary over the next four years. The day-long programme covers the factors driving inclusion, both legal and non-legal, with the bottom line being that through an inclusive culture, Network Rail will deliver better results for employees, for the business and for the people that it serves. This has analogies with the evidence of corporate benefits evidenced in Moss's discussion of PageGroup. The final part of the programme relates to 'unconscious bias' and participants are invited to explore their own biases, whether positive or negative, identify the triggers and where possible the roots of these biases and how these might play out in the workplace. They are also given a clear steer about what Network Rail desires of its leaders, namely that they be inclusive and **not** operate from a position of bias.

The essence of the programme is to show that Network Rail intends to be an inclusive, open and diverse organisation, providing tools with which this can be achieved. So, the programme creates a common lexicon within which leadership can have conversations about their behaviours and how they can be more inclusive; how they can create spaces where different voices are heard. Leaders are now conscious of when they are reverting to type and limiting access to opportunities to those who may traditionally not be given the lead on a project, or a chance to represent the team or the business. Having a shared language enables better discussions about what it is to be inclusive and what it means for the team, and how it feels when they encounter exclusionary circumstances.

The large numbers attending, and a waiting list for perspective attendance, was unheard of for a 'non-technical' programme in Network Rail but participants would become advocates of the programme and share their experience with their teams and peers. In time, the language and behaviours of the 'Inclusive Leadership at Network Rail programme' began to take hold and were supplemented by regular examples of diversity and inclusion in action. All this has happened since leaders are encouraged to be positively curious about their colleagues, their team members, exploring that which makes them different and that which makes them the same. This helps to create environments of respect and team work.

Being inclusive takes time, discipline and commitment, all elements reinforced by Moss in this book. In terms of the experience of Network Rail, as well as providing an inclusive leadership programme, six employee networks were established each focused on people with shared identities and affinities. Between them, these employee networks now have over 3,000 members.

Impacts on a Diversity Mindset

The inclusion that results from these initiatives creates room for people to shine and gives teams a chance to share the load and build on the sum of its parts. This benefit is exhibited well in the book through the example provided by Sevenoaks School. For, Moss uses the school to illustrate how inclusive leadership can benefit educational communities by empowering teachers to identify optimal methods for delivering learning to pupils and by providing an environment in which their skills and expertise are sought and harnessed.

With the greater focus on inclusion comes a heightened awareness of the benefits of a "Diversity Mindset" in which people are viewed as individuals and in which similarities and differences are recognised and valued. For members of majority/ or authority groups (those with influence and power), this can be confusing as they work out how to be inclusive – "What do I need to do to me more inclusive?" It is fair to say that some 'old style' leaders have found a consideration of inclusion and diversity to be rather while others have embraced this, bringing as Moss describes, new attitudes to the way that employees and customers are considered.

A standout example is the way that the inclusive leadership at Network Rail has been engaging with disabled passengers to improve the physical infrastructure. The leadership there has established a Built Environment Accessibility Panel (BEAP) comprised of access consultants who are also disabled people, with experience of using the railway and this panel reviews the designs for stations, level crossings, and footbridges to improve the accessibility of Network Rail's facilities. From assessing projects and building plans, to site visits, the Panel has an essential role in enhancing Network Rail's stations by considering the impacts on disabled people of seating, lighting, gradients, signage or the location of quiet spaces. All of this assessment is conducted from the perspective of diverse health conditions and impairments.

This approach has improved the skills and knowledge of project teams and designers and provided validation of the input of disabled people whilst improving the company's reputation for implementing more inclusive designs. What is more, the company has created a better customer service approach by having employees trained by disabled people. As a result, customer-facing employees are improving their support of disabled people by focusing less on the health condition of passengers than on the barriers to travelling created by the company. Network Rail has also been able to influence its supply chain by offering information on initiatives and encouraging suppliers to participate so that results can be compared, lessons shared and a higher standard of customer service achieved. The company still has a way to go in achieving a universally reliable service but by understanding its customers and focusing on disabled passenger in particular, it is improving its ability to anticipate needs and provide a better travelling experience.

Final reflections

By introducing inclusive leadership training, inclusion champions and employee networks, Network Rail has succeeded in embedding inclusive leadership within its business. The company is now more conscious of the environments that it creates, for example in its managed stations and new builds. It is now more thoughtful about providing enough seating, inclusive facilities, and quiet spaces. It is growing in confidence in recognising adapting its practice and environment to accommodate people. For example, the company's inclusive leadership has helped in the introduction of assistive technology for colleagues who are neuro-diverse (ie who have dyslexia, dyspraxia and dyscalculia) and this provision has helped neuro-diverse colleagues to read and write reports. What is more, the purchase of a corporate license has made the resource available to all employees, producing savings on individual licences and allowing everyone to feel included, even those who had not shared that they were disabled.

'Inclusive leadership' by Moss provides critical examples of why inclusive leadership is important to business. In listening to individuals talking about the negative effects of transactional leadership and the motivational, energising impacts of inclusive leadership, and by studying different sectors and varied approaches, Moss identifies the many advantages of inclusive leadership for organisations, employees and customers. For, not only does this style of leadership enhance employee productivity, creativity, wellbeing and motivation, but it also brings multiple benefits too for customer-centricity, with a greater understanding of customer needs and an enhanced ability to satisfy them. Moss also shows the gains for learning environments with University students achieving improved results, motivation and wellbeing in institutions with inclusive leaders at all levels.

The book discusses how inclusive leadership can be implemented and instead of offering rigid formulae, identifies the, common threads that allow different organisations to meet the needs of their own specific circumstances. This is evident in the four case studies, each of which has a different context, global or local, small or large; yet each of which has benefitted from the core elements of inclusive leadership. For, they present us with environments in which employees are engaged, encouraged to use their initiative and be creative; in which the contributions of employees are listened to; and in which employees and their contributions are valued. So, by stepping into these organisations we can see the value that has been derived from a style of leadership that is not only under-utilised and under-sung but more productive and inspiring than the traditional transactional or command and control leadership.

In addition to the many practical guidance provided by the book it also presents research evidence that offers a solid foundation for our understanding of inclusive leadership. So, this is a helpful addition to the burgeoning body of work that illustrates how modern businesses performance and people can be greatly improved through inclusive leadership. What is more, there is an accompanying video that illuminates the many themes and organisations presented in this book.

Loraine Martins MBE FRSA
Director of Diversity and Inclusion,
Network Rail,
March 2019

1

THE EVOLVING STUDY OF LEADERSHIP

The critical role of leadership

This is a book about leadership, something that, in the words of a report by the UK's Department for Business, Innovation and Skills (2012) can transform the fortunes of an organisation. They are not alone in this view since according to Ken Blanchard, Visiting Professor at Cornell University, excellent leaders can turn a good organisation into a great one and poor leaders can "send a great organization downhill" (Blanchard, 2011).

Blanchard's words make chilling reading, and the UK government report (above) states that nearly three-quarters of organisations in England report a deficit of management and leadership, with 43% of UK managers rating their own line manager as ineffective. The effects? According to the UK government report, this deficit contributes to the UK's productivity gap with countries such as the US, Germany, Canada, Sweden and Japan. Moreover, it is said to cost UK businesses over £19 billion per year in lost working hours and to be the cause of 56% of corporate failures.

The critical role played by leadership is the reason for yet another book about the all-important topic of leadership. This one puts the spotlight on a new style of leadership that could improve management significantly and cast poor management into the annals of history. What is more, it is tried and tested, and case studies in this book, taken from the recruitment, sales, property and education sectors, show how easily it can be adapted to different sectors and different-sized organisations, from large corporates to small and medium-sized enterprises (SMEs).

Before we look at those organisations, we will consider what we mean by leadership and how it has been defined over time. We investigate two well-known and contrasting systems, transactional and transformational leadership, and in Chapters 3 and 4 compare the largely negative experiences produced by transactional leadership, contrasting these with the more energising effects of inclusive leadership, an element of which is transformational leadership. We then compare these styles through historical examples as well as through the voices of those who have experienced these approaches.

In Chapter 5, we move on to a large-scale study examining the impacts of inclusive leadership on employees, with a large volume of quantitative and quantitative data from which to judge its effects. In Chapters 6 and 7, we look at studies examining the effects of inclusive leadership on university student attainment, motivation and well-being, and in the next four chapters, we see its effects in four different sectors – Sales, Education, Recruitment and Property Asset Management. In the penultimate Chapter 12, we examine the effects of inclusive leadership on customer centricity, exploring the extent to which it allows organisations to be more focused on customer needs. In the final chapter, we look at the tools needed to implement an inclusive style of leadership.

Ahead of this exhilarating trip into new territories, an understanding of what we mean by leadership is useful, so we explore this briefly now.

What is leadership?

Although we may all have a sense of what a good leader looks like, it is one of those concepts that is very hard to define. We are not alone in having these thoughts. As Silva tells us (2016, p. 1), more than four decades ago, Stogdill (1974) affirmed that "there are almost as many different definitions of leadership as there are persons who have attempted to define the concept" (p. 7). At the end of the last century, Bennis estimated that there were at least 650 published definitions of leadership (Bennis and Townsend, 1995), and in this century the number has exploded with Barbara Kellerman, Professor of Public Leadership at the John F. Kennedy School of Government at Harvard University, referring to about 1,400 different definitions of the words leader and/or leadership (Volckmann, 2012). As Silva has pointed out, these numbers, real or exaggerated, simply mean that there is no consensus about what leadership is, and so the search for a better definition continues.

Amidst this plethora of definitions and approaches, specialists in leadership Alimo-Metcalfe *et al* (2007) chart key stages in the history of leadership studies. Readers interested in understanding the academic stepping stones that brought us to inclusive leadership should read on; meanwhile, if you are less interested in the topic, then it is better to fast-forward to Chapter 2 at this point.

Meanwhile, for those still with us, we will now sketch the main steps that brought us to inclusive leadership.

Academic stepping stones

Alimo-Metcalfe *et al* (2007) define the stages that leadership studies have progressed through since the beginning of the twentieth century, and we have reduced these down to the following four:

1   The 'trait' or 'great man' approach
2   The 'behavioural' approach, out of which the concept of managerial and later leadership competencies emerged
3   The 'situational' or 'contingency' approach

4   The 'new paradigm' approach, with its focus on 'distant' transactional, often 'heroic' leadership; the emergence of 'nearby' transformational or 'engaging' leadership, and the associated concepts of 'distributed' and 'inclusive' leadership.

We will look at each of these stages in turn, drawing extensively on Alimo-Metcalf's excellent overview. For some, this may appear somewhat academic in flavour but this overview provides a useful backdrop to the discussion that runs through the book on inclusive leadership.

1. The trait approach

Initially, the first efforts at leadership research were focused on identifying the features that differentiated leaders from non-leaders. As you can imagine, factors such as intelligence, energy and dominance emerged as differentiating features alongside hundreds of other traits, so meta-analyses – studies bringing together the findings across several studies – were conducted by Stogdill (1948) and Mann (1959) to determine recurring traits. In fact, the main finding from these studies related to a lack of consistency in the conclusions of these studies. For example, Mann's study (1959), reporting on ninety-one studies, highlighted a significant positive relationship between leadership status and intelligence in some studies but no such relationship in others, and even a negative relationship in one further study. In fact, Stogdill (1948) reached the conclusion that the qualities, characteristics and skills needed by a leader are, to a large extent, determined by the demands of the situation in which he (or she) functions and that it is therefore fruitless to look for a set of common traits.

Before writing off the trait approach, it is worth noting (Alimo-Metcalfe *et al*, 2007) that Stogdill later wrote that, while personality and situational factors are involved, a number of relatively consistent personal characteristics are associated with leader-like behaviour. These include a strong drive for responsibility and task completion, originality and initiative, self-confidence and sense of personal identity, and ability to influence others' behaviour and to structure social interaction systems. Also, some years later, a study by Church and Waclawski (1995) found that managers classified as 'motivators' were more likely to encourage risk-taking, to maintain a challenging and motivating work environment, and to take time to celebrate accomplishments; 'inventors', on the other hand, were significantly better at innovating, setting direction, and establishing a sense of mission about their work, but were no more than average at galvanising followers' hopes, enthusiasm and energy.

The contradictions in trait studies had sullied the waters, however, and so a new line of research was launched into the *behaviours* that distinguished leaders. This is the subject of the next section.

2. Behavioural approaches

Instead of a focus on personality features, the emphasis now was on looking at the behavioural characteristics of leaders. Essentially, the behaviours investigated included participative approaches, task fulfilment, consideration of others and a directive approach. A variety of combinations of these were used in studies, most famously perhaps the two-dimensional grid based on concern for people and concern for results (Blake and Mouton, 1964), with many studies conducted at the Ohio State University where Stogdill worked.

Unfortunately, while the 'consideration' behaviours of a leader (supervisor/manager) were correlated positively with employee satisfaction, they were negatively correlated with the productivity of the manager's group (Stogdill, 1974). At one point, the notion of 'managerial competencies' (McClelland, 1973) emerged, but the realisation that situational factors could play an important part shifted attention to the importance of the *situation*.

3. Situational and contingency approach

Theories emerged in the 1960s and 1970s examining the impact of situational factors in optimizing leadership. There was a veritable flurry of activity starting with Fiedler's 'contingency model' (1994) which placed specific emphasis on three situational variables: the position power of the leader, the degree to which a task is structured, and the quality of leader–member relationships. Importantly, Fiedler broke new ground in suggesting that a democratic style of leadership was most favoured in situations which were only moderately favourable.

Fiedler's work was followed by House's path-goal theory of leadership (House, 1977; House and Dressler, 1974), the Vroom and Yetton (1973) 'normative model' of leaders and finally the Hersey and Blanchard (1982) 'situational leadership model', the most practitioner-friendly of them all.

In path-goal theory, the emphasis is on the relationship between leadership style and the characteristics of both the subordinates and the work setting. The underlying assumption was that subordinate motivation would be greater if subordinates (a) thought themselves capable of doing their work, (b) believed that a certain outcome would result from their effort, and (c) regarded the payoffs as worthwhile.

The main criticisms of these approaches were that they failed to explain why some styles were more effective than others and were also, at times, confusing and difficult to apply. In this spirit, Henry Mintzberg, Professor of Management at McGill University, wrote a scathing critique (1982) of the irrelevance of leadership research to practising managers, and Hunt followed in his footsteps some years later (1999) by suggesting that leadership studies offered little concrete advice on how leaders should behave in an environment of continuous and significant change. Not surprisingly, these critiques of situational and contingency theories led to a drive for new ways of defining effective leadership.

4. New approaches: transactional, transformational leadership, distributed and inclusive leadership

It is ironic that it took a political scientist and biographer, James McGregor Burns, to formulate the all-important, oppositional concept of 'transactional' and 'transforming' leadership, the subject of a book on this topic (1978). It was then Bernard

Bass, psychologist and scholar of leadership, who took up the reins where Burns left off, reframing the second one as 'transformational' leadership and suggesting that the two styles were complementary. He also developed corresponding leadership competencies and, with Avolio, created a questionnaire (the Multifactor Leadership Questionnaire, 'MLQ') by means of which the impacts of these styles could be measured.

Burns and Bass had opposing views as to whether the two leadership styles were complementary, and you might ask which of these two approaches has prevailed. Over 20 years of research has been undertaken by psychologists adopting, most commonly, the MLQ to compare the effectiveness of transformational and transactional leadership styles (Alimo-Metcalfe *et al*, 2007), and the evidence is that the transformational style is generally more effective and satisfying than the transactional style alone (Bass, 1997, 1998; Alimo-Metcalfe *et al*, 2007), attracting great commitment from followers (Alimo-Metcalfe *et al*, 2007). Incidentally, the studies have been wide-ranging since they have involved secondary school teachers, white collar workers, supervisors of insurance company employees as well as military personnel (Bass, 1998; Alimo-Metcalfe *et al*, 2007).

Many factors in fact make transformational leadership a prime candidate to act as a building block for inclusive leadership (Echols, 2009), the subject of this book. One is the lengthy record of research on this type of leadership, another is the emphasis in this model on connecting with employees (i.e. being inclusive), and a further factor is this leadership's style proven efficacy – according to one professor of Human Resources it is the "one style, more than any other, [that] has been found to be effective" (Van Dierendonck, 2014, p. 544). More of this later.

Meanwhile, for the reader who is curious, the competencies formulated by Bass for transactional and transformational leadership are shown in Tables 1.1 and 1.2.

TABLE 1.1 Transactional competencies

Transactional leadership attributes	*What the attribute involves*
Active management by exception	With the objective of monitoring the process, leaders monitor the lack of compliance with established rules and standards, and when required undertake corrective measures.
Passive management by exception	In order to manage the process, leaders intervene only in cases in which set objectives are not achieved.
Monitoring followers' performance and correcting mistakes	Little autonomy or scope for self-control is offered to followers.
Laissez-faire management	Leaders avoid making decision and those involved in the process relinquish all responsibilities.
Contingent reward	The recognition of achievement by rewarding efforts and good performance.

Source: Bass and Avolio (1995)

TABLE 1.2 Transformational competencies

Inclusive leadership attributes	What the attribute involves
Individualised consideration	Showing individual interest and offering one-to-one support for followers
Idealised influence	Having admirable qualities that followers want to identify with
Inspirational motivation	Providing an appealing vision that inspires followers
Intellectual stimulation	Encouraging followers to develop their ideas and to be challenged

Bass's work spanned the decades of the 1980s and 1990s, and it was during this period that John Kotter, Harvard professor since the age of 33, and Konosuke Matsushita, Professor of Leadership since 1990, described *leadership* in a landmark article in the *Harvard Business Review* (Kotter, 1990). Here, Kotter described it as a future-focused activity involving "setting a vision, motivating and inspiring people" (1990, p. 104), an activity that could be performed at any level of the organisation. He contrasted *leadership* with *management* which he described as an activity that seeks to ensure that work functions in the way that it should.

In terms of detail, Kotter defined *leadership* as the process of developing a vision for the organisation, aligning people with that vision through communication and motivating people to action through empowerment and basic need fulfilment, actions that create uncertainty and change in the organisation. He contrasted this with the *management* process, which he described as rooted in planning and budgeting, organising and staffing, and controlling and problem solving, activities that reduce uncertainty and stabilise the organisation.

Kotter later warned of the negative consequences of 'over-managed and under-led organisations', pointing out that "there are very, very few organisations today that have sufficient leadership" (2013) and, as he portentously remarked, that this could "make them increasingly vulnerable in a fast-moving world" (*ibid*). He was not alone in this opinion, for just a year before Kotter penned his 1990 *Harvard Business Review* article, a book by Warren Bennis, Professor at MIT, appeared. This was entitled *On Becoming a Leader* and contrasted the activities of the leader and manager. As Bennis wrote:

- The manager administers; the leader innovates.
- The manager is a copy; the leader is an original.
- The manager maintains; the leader develops.
- The manager focuses on systems and structure; the leader focuses on people.
- The manager relies on control; the leader inspires trust.

- The manager has a short-range view; the leader has a long-range perspective.
- The manager asks how and when; the leader asks what and why.
- The manager has his or her eye always on the bottom line; the leader's eye is on the horizon.
- The manager imitates; the leader originates.
- The manager accepts the status quo; the leader challenges it.
- The manager is the classic good soldier; the leader is his or her own person.
- The manager does things right; the leader does the right thing.

Moreover, and this chimes with Kotter's thoughts just one year later, Bennis wrote:

> to survive in the twenty-first century, we are going to need a new generation of leaders – leaders, not managers. The distinction is an important one. Leaders conquer the context – the volatile, turbulent, ambiguous surroundings that sometimes seem to conspire against us and will surely suffocate us if we let them – while managers surrender to it.
>
> *(p. 7)*

One could ponder the extraordinary coincidence of two professors writing, completely independently and just a calendar year apart, on the contrasting nature of leadership and management. Bennis's book *On Becoming a Leader* was published in 1989 and Kotter's article appeared in the *Harvard Business Review* in 1990 in the May-June edition. Was the idea in the air? Did Kotter catch sight of it in Bennis's book or were one or the other or both influenced by the fascinating 1977 article in the *Harvard Business Review* by Abraham Zaleznik in which he discusses the topic of management versus leadership.

Zaleznik held the same professorship at Harvard as Kotter was to later on and, while there, contrasted the valuable but distinct contributions of leaders and managers. So, while Zaleznik considered that leaders advocate change and new approaches, he suggested that managers advocate stability and the *status quo*. Furthermore, while leaders were, in his view, concerned with understanding people's beliefs and gaining their commitment, managers were those who carried out responsibilities, exercised authority and worried about how things would be accomplished.

Zaleznik's perspective was an interesting one since he was an early contributor to the International Society for the Psychoanalytic Study of Organisations and interested in understanding the psyche of the 'manager' as against that of the 'leader', concluding that:

> The difference between managers and leaders lies in the conceptions they hold, deep in the psyches, of chaos and order. Managers embrace process, seek stability and control, and instinctively try to resolve problems quickly – sometimes before they fully understand a problem's significance. Leaders, in contrast, tolerate chaos and lack of structure and are willing to delay closure in order to understand the issues more fully.

What he goes on to say is even more extraordinary:

> Business leaders have much more in common with artists, scientists and other creative thinkers than they do with managers. Organisations need both managers and leaders to succeed but developing both requires a reduced focus on logic and strategic exercises in favour of an environment where creativity and imagination are permitted to flourish.

Fast-forward thirty years or so, and it is interesting to find Fred Lunenberg, Professor of Education at Sam Houston State University, summarising the arguments on leadership and management in an imagined continuum of activities (see Table 1.3).

What we see here is a notion of *leadership* that is essentially future-oriented, visionary, people-focused, people-serving and empowering, while the activities of *management* are more present-oriented, focused on plans rather than visions, less people-focused, more directive and more controlling. The oppositional character of leadership and management presented here highlights in a helpful way the gap between the activities of leadership and those of management, with individual commentators focusing on particular aspects of these activities. So, one commentator concentrates on the 'visionary' (Sashkin, 1988), others on the 'charismatic' (House, 1977; Conger, 1989; Conger and Kanungo, 1988), and still others on the 'transformational' aspects (Burns, 1978; Bass, 1985; Bass and Avolio, 1990).

Lunenberg's summary brings us back to the transactional and transformational leadership models, since there is much about transactional leadership that connects it with the activities that Lunenberg associate with *management*, and much about transformational leadership that connects it with his understanding of *leadership*. Moreover, the fact that MLQ results show transformational

TABLE 1.3 Comparisons between leadership and management (Lunenberg, 2011)

Category	Leadership	Management
Process	Focuses on people	Focuses on things
	Looks outward	Looks inward
Goal setting	Articulates a vision	Executes plans
	Creates the future	Improves the present
	Sees the forest	Sees the trees
Employee relations	Empowers	Controls
	Colleagues	Subordinates
	Trusts and develops	Directs and coordinates
Operation	Does the right thing	Does things right
	Creates change	Manages change
	Serves subordinates	Serves superordinates
Governance	Uses influence	Uses authority
	Uses conflict	Avoids conflict
	Acts decisively	Acts responsibly

leadership to be more effective than transactional leadership echoes Kotter's views on the vital importance of real *leadership* in organisations rather than just as *management*. In fact, as so often happens with management theories, labels can change over time, but the reader may find it useful to equate discussions of 'transactional' behaviours with discussions of 'management'; and, by the same token, discussions of 'transformational' behaviours with discussions of 'leadership'.

The territory mapped by leadership studies is not fixed at the concepts of transactional and transformational leadership and of management either. For, in the latter decades of the twentieth century and the beginning of the twenty-first century, three new theories appeared which have the potential to revolutionise our understanding of leadership. One is 'servant leadership' (Greenleaf, 1970, 1977), one is 'distributed leadership' and the third is 'inclusive leadership'. A brief word on each is necessary so that the reader can understand the thinking that has produced the concept of inclusive leadership used in this book.

Servant leadership

The phrase 'servant leadership', although based on a timeless concept, was coined by Robert Greenleaf in his essay, 'The Servant as Leader' (1970). There he wrote:

> The servant-leader is servant first . . . It begins with the natural feeling that one wants to serve, to serve first. Then conscious choice brings one to aspire to lead. That person is sharply different from one who is leader first, perhaps because of the need to assuage an unusual power drive or to acquire material possessions . . . The leader-first and the servant-first are two extreme types. Between them there are shadings and blends that are part of the infinite variety of human nature.
>
> The difference manifests itself in the care taken by the servant-first to make sure that other people's highest priority needs are being served. The best test, and difficult to administer, is: Do those served grow as persons? Do they, while being served, become healthier, wiser, freer, more autonomous, more likely themselves to become servants?

Basing our understanding on Greenleaf's original writing (1970) and that of subsequent commentators (Spears, 1995; Russell and Stone, 2002), it is possible to identify eleven attributes of a servant leader (see Table 1.4). The left-hand column, indicates the source of these attributes, showing that ten of the eleven attributes derive from Greenleaf's original writing (with the concept of 'confidence building' drawn from Greenleaf's reference to 'lifting' people up) and nine of the attributes appearing in the work of the former CEO of the Greenleaf Centre, Spears. Note that the eleventh competence of 'stewardship', a word derived from Russell and Stone's work (2002), draws on the concern that Greenleaf showed in ensuring that community is maintained. So, all eleven competencies shown in Table 1.4 draw closely on Greenleaf's work.

TABLE 1.4 Servant leadership competencies: the Roman numbers in brackets indicate the publications from which the competencies are drawn

Servant Leadership competence as defined by (i) Greenleaf, 1970 and 1977; (ii) Spears, 1995; (iii) Russell and Stone, 2002	Definition
Unqualified acceptance (i)	Being inclusive in considering followers that involves being non-judgmental and accepting each follower as a unique individual
Empathy (i) (ii)	Putting oneself mentally and emotionally into the follower's place in order to more fully understand his/her experiences and perspectives
Listening (i) (ii) (iii)	Actively listening to followers that involves not only listening to the content but also the underlying meaning and emotional significance behind followers' views and opinions
Persuasion (i) (ii) (iii)	Being able to influence followers by showing them the benevolent merits of the direction that they are being led in rather than through formal authority or force
Confidence building (i) (iii)	Providing followers with opportunities and recognition so that they see themselves as valuable contributors to the team and organisation; lifting them up
Growth (i) (ii)	Encouraging followers to reach their full potential by providing opportunities for them to make autonomous and unique contributions and to emulate servant leadership behaviours
Foresight (i) (ii)	Having the ability to see events and anticipating where they might lead, and being sensitive to warnings of potential negative events ahead of time (foreseeing the unforeseeable)
Conceptualisation (i) (ii)	Having a vision about possibilities and articulating that vision to followers (knowing the unknowable)
Awareness (i) (ii)	Being fully open and aware of environmental cues in the face of challenges; being mindful and insightful rather than allowing stress to interfere with clarity of thinking
Stewardship (iii)	Articulating the belief that the organisation's legacy is to contribute in a purposeful way to society
Healing (i) (ii)	Helping followers cope with any burdens or personal troubles in their lives

Distributed leadership

Of course, the concept of servant leader implies that two parties at least, the leader and the follower, are central to leadership, and this connects us with the views of Barbara Kellerman, Professor of Public Leadership at the John F Kennedy School of Government at Harvard University. For she has not only advocated a move from a focus on traits, but has also emphasised the importance of the leader-follower dynamic and the context in which they find themselves (Kellerman, 2015). In fact, her approach has analogies with the notion of distributed leadership (Bennett *et al*, 2003; Bolden *et al*, 2015) with its emphasis on leadership as a network of interacting individuals with expertise distributed across the many and not the few. Interestingly, distributed leadership is described by education and industry commentators (Forde *et al*, 2011; Canwell *et al*, 2014, respectively) as operating at all levels of the hierarchy and, in that sense, operates rather as Kotter had imagined of *leadership*, at any level of the organisation.

Of course, the question arises as to the consistency with which leaders will operate a system of distributed leadership (Oshagbemi and Gill 2004) and the extent to which there is a 'connectedness' of leadership across the hierarchy (Forde *et al*, 2011, p. 57) that will create a defining culture, in this case of distributed leadership (Schein, 2010; Moss et al, 2016). Moreover, since the quality of leadership at the top of an organisation has a major effect on an organisation's culture (Schein, 1996), the presence or absence of distributed leadership at the top of an organisation will have a major impact on the culture experienced within an organisation.

Inclusive leadership

Our journey brings us to inclusive leadership (IL), the concept that is at the very heart of this book. We apologise for taking a little while to reach this point, but an appreciation of the theories that preceded this makes it easier to understand this concept, particularly since, to our way of thinking, it builds substantially on these earlier theories.

In fact, it is only since around 2004 that academics and practitioners have shown any interest in this style of leadership. Academics have been writing about it since that point (Nicola and Thomas, 2004; Echols, 2009; Carmeli et al, 2010; Hollander, 2012, Allen *et al*, 2016) and practitioner organisations began to show an interest just a few years later (Deloitte, 2012; Opportunity Now, 2014; Catalyst, 2014). On visiting this diverse literature for the first time, two things become apparent. The first is that there is no obvious consensus on the relative importance of IL as a tool for enahncing workplace diversity as against the more generic benefits of workplace productivity, motivation and mental well-being. We tend to support both views, considering IL to be a tool that can facilitate both types of outcome, effectively offering organisations two sets of benefits in exchange for a single intervention, two for the price of one to use the language of sales! Secondly, there appears to be no obvious consensus on the elements that make up IL, with one study Nitu and Atewologun (2015) revealing that a mere 12% of articles on inclusive leadership refer to a theoretically established form of leadership. Of these, leader-member exchange and transformational leadership are said to be the most frequently cited theories/models. So, few articles on IL refer to a theoretically established form of leadership. We can see this from some of the earliest attempts at definition with a 2004 study referring to a six-fold behavioural description of inclusion (Nicola and Thomas, 2004) based on the leader characteristics of "respect, recognition and appreciation for others" and the process-related aspects of "participative decision making, integrity and cooperative leadership style". A second IL instrument followed (Carmeli, Reiter-Palmon & Ziv, 2010) rooted in openness, availability, and accessibility.

In the midst of these differences, it is refreshing to find one early piece of academic work (Echols, 2009) making a persuasive case for IL being the combined product of transformational (Tf) and servant leadership (SL), just a theory at that stage since it had not yet been empirically tested. However, even before empirical work was undertaken to test the extent to which over sixty industry respondents shared Echols' definition of IL (ie as rooted in Tf and SL) and the extent to which survey findings showed Tf and SL to form a common construct (for details of both see chapter 5), a mapping of the concept s of IL used in Echols (2009) against those used in other academic and practitioner studies (see table 1.5 below) shows a pretty close match (see Table 1.5 below). What is more, Tf and SL are well-respected leadership models

TABLE 1.5 Inclusive leadership components from a reading of the literature (name of scholar, practitioner or organisation offering a particular model is shown in brackets)

	Inclusive Leadership		Corresponding theories of Inclusive Leadership (from either the (i) academic or (ii) grey literatures)
	Transformational	*Servant Leader*	
1. Relationships	*Individualised consideration:* attending to individual needs; offering empathy and support; genuine concern for the needs and feelings of followers; personal attention to each follower as a key element in optimising effort (i Bass, 1990)	Unqualified acceptance of those served (i Greenleaf, pp.10–11) Empathy (ibid, pp. 10–11) Healing (ibid, p. 20)	Approachable, non-hierarchical (ii Opportunity Now, 2014); Respect (i Nicola and Thomas, 2004); availability and accessibility(i Carmeli et al, 2010); Showing genuine concern and willingness to take on board people's concerns (i Alimo-Metcalfe, 2010); Altruistic leadership (ii Catalyst, 2014); Feedback on progress (i Hollander, 2008); Authentic appreciation for the diversity of team members (ii Bilimoria, 2012)

	Inclusive Leadership		Corresponding theories of Inclusive Leadership (from either the (i) academic or (ii) grey literatures)
	Transformational	*Servant Leader*	
2. Culture	*Idealised influence*: providing high ethical values; serving as an ideal role model for followers; leader walks the talk and is admired for this (i Bass, 1990)	Persuasion (i ibid, pp. 15–17) Stewardship and community building/spirit (i ibid, pp. 20–22) Growth: power used to create opportunities and build autonomy for followers (i ibid, p. 23) Confidence building by providing opportunities (i ibid)	'Integrity (i Nicola and Thomas, 2004) 'Reognition and appreciation' (i Nicola and Thomas, 2004)' Role modelling (i Schein, 1996; i Echols, 2009; ii Opportunity Now, 2014); Authentic and open (ii Linkage, 2014); Promotes team relations that are fair rather than based on favouritism (i Pittinsky, 2010; ii Bilimoria, 2012); Uses the participation of the maximum number of people (i Echols, 2009); Shares authority, power and credit (ii Linkage, 2014); Empowers people in line with organisational goals (i Echols, 2009); Acting with integrity and being honest (i Alimo-Metcalfe, 2010); Perpetuates the morality of the worth of the individual (i Echols, 2009); Replicates inclusive leaders (i Echols, 2009); Highly collaborative (i Ryan, 2007); Evoking feelings of belongingness in followers; Modesty and humility (i Ryan, 2007);

(Continued)

TABLE 1.5 (Continued)

Inclusive Leadership		Corresponding theories of Inclusive Leadership (from either the (i) academic or (ii) grey literatures)
Transformational	Servant Leader	
		Honest communications that encourage trust and loyalty (i Hollander, 2008).
Intellectual stimulation: solicits followers' ideas; challenges followers to be innovative and creative; constantly challenge followers to higher levels of performance (i Bass, 1990)	Listening (i ibid, p. 8) Awareness (i ibid, pp. 14–15) Growth: commitment to the growth of people (i ibid, p. 11)	Listening (i Hollander, 2008); Learning from diverse perspectives (ii Bilimoria, 2012); Seeking out diverse perspectives (ii Deloitte, 2012); Openness (i Carmeli et al, 2010); Openness to the views of others (i Alimo-Metcalfe, 2010); Co-operative leadership (i Nicola and Thomas 2004); Followers know that their ideas count (ii Bilimoria, 2012); Participative decision-making (i Nicola and Thomas, 2004) Encouraging psychological safety that allows the voicing of dissent or imagination; Understanding personal biases both similarity-attraction bias and process bias and showing curiosity in relation to other people (ii Deloitte, 2012); Empowerment (ii Catalyst, 2014); Understanding biases (ii Deloitte, 2012); Empowering individuals to reach their full potential (i Echols, 2009); Creating a workplace in which diverse talent is fostered (ii Deloitte, 2012);

	Inclusive Leadership		Corresponding theories of Inclusive Leadership (from either the (i) academic or (ii) grey literatures)
	Transformational	Servant Leader	
			Encouraging women to take developmental roles or apply for promotion and giving women credit and a voice in meetings (ii Kelan, 2015); Developing talent (ii Opportunity Now, 2014).
3. Decision-making style and strategy	Inspirational motivation: articulating a vision; inspiring and motivating followers (Bass, 1990)	Foresight (i ibid, pp. 12–13) Conceptualisation (P. 18 i ibid, p.18)	Promoting a common vision based on shared values (ii Bilimoria, 2012); Engaging followers (i Hollander, 2008); Two-way communications between leader and follower (ibid); Promoting team conditions that encourage members to speak up about ideas (ii Bilimoria, 2012); Leveraging difference for competitive advantage (ii Opportunity Now, 2014).

Source: Taken from Moss et al (2016)

and ones that – like Kotter and Lunenberg's concept of *leadership* – emphasise the people element in organisations. So, one can have confidence that these two styles of leadership provide a solid foundation for the concept of inclusive leadership, and one which can garner more support than the more random definitions provided by the practitioner as well as earlier and later academic literatures on IL.

Given the somewhat random selection of attributes that has underpinned some of the earlier academic and practitioner work on IL it is important to note that the definition of IL used in studies to uncover the effects of IL in industry (Moss *et al*, 2016; Moss, 2016, and see Chapter 5), in higher education (see Chapters 6 and 7) and in the design and consultancy sectors (see Chapter 12) is underpinned by Echol's more reasoned definition of IL, rooted as it is in the well respected concepts of transformational and servant leadership. The evolution of definitions relating to IL is summarised in Table 1.6 below.

TABLE 1.6 Concepts of Inclusive Leadership used in four studies

Attributes of IL used in 3 studies and where they overlap (indicated by showing attributes from different studies on the same line)

Nicola & Thomas (2004) (empirically tested)	Carmeli *et al*, (2010) (empirically tested)	Echols (2009) (not empirically tested) and Moss *et al*, 2016 (empirically tested)
6 attributes	3 attributes	15 attributes
Respect		Individualised consideration; unqualified acceptance
Recognition		Confidence building
Appreciation		Confidence building
Participative decision-making		Intellectual stimulation
Integrity		Stewardship
Co-operative leadership		Intellectual stimulation
	Openness	Listening
	Availability	Individualised consideration
	Accessibility	Healing
		Inspirational motivation
		Idealised influence, awareness
		Empathy, persuasion, foresight
		Conceptualisation

As mentioned earlier, the decision to anchor the definition of IL in Tf and SL was validated subsequently by the definitions of IL volunteered by over sixty interview respondents in eleven organisations (see Chapter 5 for details of this study). For, 75% of the competencies that thirty-eight managers considered as defining IL corresponded with servant leadership while the remaining 25% of the competencies corresponded with transformational leadership. Moreover, the survey that was conducted alongside the interviews, measuring as it did the views of just under 1000 respondents in industry regarding their perception of Tf and SL behaviours across 11 organisations, revealed that the concepts of Tf and SL worked together, and not divergently as had been thought in a previous study (van Dierendonck *et al*, 2014) In fact, Tf and SL together accounted for 80% of the variance in performance, engagement and well-being outputs amongst employees (Moss *et al*, 2016) and since 73% of the variance in the model is accounted for by SL and Tf working together (*ibid*), these two types of leadership must be closely associated. To view these two forms of leadership as the main building blocks for inclusive leadership is therefore highly appropriate.

Incidentally, as we shall also see in Chapter 5, the survey conducted amongst employees in eleven organisations also revealed a strong association (0.87) between the perception of leaders as inclusive and employees' self-perceptions as highly productive and engaged and with a strong sense of mental well-being. A similar association of 0.85 was found in university students' perceptions as well (see Chapter 6), showing a strong link between perceptions of leadership as inclusive and self-perceptions as productive, engaged and with mental well-being in both industry and in higher education. So, these results show Tf and SL working powerfully together, with the studies reported in this book boosting an existing finding as to their joint, positive impact on employee engagement (van Dierendonck *et al*, 2014) with findings of their strong association also with enhanced productivity and mental well-being, findings that are entirely new. Note also that the association works inversely as well with the perceived *absence* of IL producing lower self-ratings of productivity, engagement and well-being (Moss *et al*, 2016; Moss, 2016).

Finally, linking to earlier points about distributed leadership, it is interesting to note that the definition selected for IL (defined as a combination of Tf and SL) maps closely to distributed leadership. We can see this by comparing a well-respected definition of distributed leadership with those competencies underpinning IL (see Table 1.7).

The close mapping of the Tf and SL competencies to this model of distributed leadership shows that the concept of inclusive leadership used in the previous two studies (Moss *et al*, 2016; Leadership Foundation for Higher Education, 2018) and used throughout this book is in fact a distributed form of leadership.

We will return to inclusive leadership in Chapter 4 and the following chapters but meanwhile will look at relevant concepts and issues such as high performance

TABLE 1.7 The way that Bolden *et al*'s (2008) and Gosling *et al*'s (2009) concepts of distributed leadership in higher education maps against transformational and servant leadership concepts

Bolden *et al*'s (2008) and Gosling *et al*'s (2009) categories	Way that the 15 Transformational (Tf) and Servant Leadership (SL) competencies map against these
Personal (vision, values, ethics, emotional intelligence, openness, authenticity, interpersonal and persuasive skills)	Conceptualisation (SL); individualised consideration (Tf); empathy (SL); listening (SL); confidence building (SL); persuasion (SL)
Social (ability to navigate social groups; networking and developing trust; mentoring; teambuilding)	Idealised influence (Tf); inspirational motivation (Tf); intellectual stimulation (Tf); unqualified acceptance (SL); empathy (SL); listening (SL); confidence building (SL); healing (SL)
Structural (devolution of responsibility)	Growth (SL)
Contextual (outer social and inner organisational contexts)	Foresight (SL); awareness (SL); healing (SL); conceptualisation (SL); stewardship (SL)
Developmental (having an impact over time and being organisational stewards)	Stewardship (SL); growth (SL)

working; gender and leadership; and the impacts of ethnicity, nationality and personality and leadership.

High performance working

We referred earlier to studies that confirmed the effectiveness of transformational leadership and so it is appropriate to discuss the concept of 'high performance working' (HPW) and the part that transformational leadership (and to some extent transactional leadership) can play in this. It is important to be aware of this, since transformational leadership is a major plank in inclusive leadership and therefore the potential benefits of transformational leadership will feature in inclusive leadership as well.

The International Labour Organisation (ILO) describes high performance working as the achievement of high levels of performance, profitability and customer satisfaction in a situation where employees enthusiastically use their skills to assist an organisation (ILO, 2002). When is this most likely to happen? According to one commentator, HPW is associated with flatter and less hierarchical structures that encourage autonomy, teamwork, trust and communications (Stevens, 2003). Such an approach is thought to provide a major source of competitive advantage (Martins *et al*, 2011), producing a motivated, skilled, empowered and loyal workforce (Gill and Meyer, 2008).

What is more, according to a joint study by the Engineering Employers Federation (EEF) and the Chartered Institute of Personnel and Development (CIPD), productivity boosts of an extraordinary 20% accompany HPW, with employee motivation critical in determining employee disposition (EEF and CIPD, 2003: Stevens, 2003). Interestingly, a similarly strong boost to productivity is associated with the combination of transformational (Tf) leadership and the contingent reward (CR) aspect of transactional leadership (Tc), a combination that rates highly on all six of the assessment measures used in an earlier and important study (Judge and Piccolo, 2004). Incidentally, to avoid a rather cumbersome combination of words, we refer to this blend of behaviours as 'Tf + TcCR' with the phrase 'contingent reward' referring to a system in which rewards dovetail with performance. Note also that while there is much in the EEF/CIPD concept of HPW that parallels elements of Tf and TcCR (Table 1.8) the non-contingent reward elements in transactional leadership (specifically passive and active management by exception) produce negative impacts on all six measures. This explains the reasons why passive and active management by exception - management styles in which employees are largely ignored until things go wrong - do not feature in Table 1.8. They just do not appear to contribute to HPW.

Why is Tf + TcCR such an effective combination? While TcCR leadership assists followers in meeting expectations, Tf leadership assists followers in moving *beyond* expectations (Bass, 1998), producing what in management jargon is known as the 'augmentation hypothesis'. Do not be put off by this technical sounding phrase since it simply means that 'contingent rewards' (ie rewards linked to performance) have a multiplier effect with Tf leadership which, as we have seen produces

TABLE 1.8 How the principles in the CIPD's 'Maximising Employee Potential' (2003) relate to element of Tf and TcCR leadership

HPW and the EEF/ CIPD's defining management principles	Transformational (Tf) and transactional (Tc) principles (Bass, 1995, 1998) that correspond to these principles	Definitions of the Tf and Tc leadership principles (Judge and Piccolo, 2004)
Employee autonomy and involvement	Intellectual stimulation (Tf)	Degree to which the leader solicits followers' ideas and acts as a mentor or coach to the follower, listening to the follower's concerns/needs Degree to which the leader challenges assumptions and solicits followers' ideas
Support for employee	Individualised consideration (Tf) Intellectual stimulation (Tf) Inspirational motivation (Tf)	Degree to which the leader solicits followers' ideas and acts as a mentor or coach to the follower, listening to the follower's concerns/needs Degree to which the leader challenges assumptions Degree to which the leader articulates a vision that is appealing and inspiring to followers
Information for employee	Inspirational motivation (Tf)	See above
Rewards for employment	Contingent reward (TcCR)	Degree to which the leader sets up constructive transactions or exchanges with followers, establishing rewards for meeting exchanges

Source: Taken from Moss *et al* (2006)

job satisfaction, commitment and low stress (Alimo-Metcalfe and Alban Metcalfe, 2003; Eagly, 2004), producing better long-term results for organisations across a wider range of sectors and continents than the non-TcCR aspects of transactional leadership. In fact, with such a plethora of studies attesting to the positive effects of Tf leadership, it is a wonder that organisations still allow the management by exception and laissez-faire aspects of transactional leadership to be used. For the curious reader, here is a note of just some of the research confirming the power of Tf plus TcCR: Ferrario and Davidson (1991), Bass *et al* (1996), Lowe and Kroeck (1996), Bass (1998), Sarros *et al* (2002), Eagly *et al* (2003), Alimo-Metcalfe and Alban-Metcalfe (2003) and Eagly (2004).

Since inclusive leadership is an extension of transformational leadership, what we have said about Tf leadership will also apply to IL but new research (beyond that presented in this book) will need to be conducted to compare the effects of IL on its own and IL with contingent reward (TcCR). Our focus in the short space left in this chapter will be on gender, national culture, ethnicity and personality.

Gender and leadership styles

You may be wondering whether men and women are equally likely to deliver a transformational and inclusive style of leadership. Unfortunately, there is no reliable evidence yet in relation to inclusive leadership, but there is evidence – a large body of it – in relation to transformational leadership, one of the elements of inclusive leadership.

So what does this research show? Although an early study found no evidence that men and women led in different ways (Kanter, 1977), a landmark article in the *Harvard Business Review* in 1990 by Rosener sketched new directions. As she explains in the abstract:

> Men are much more likely than women to view leadership as a series of transactions with subordinates, and to use their position and control of resources to motivate their followers. Women, on the other hand, are far more likely to describe themselves as transforming subordinates' self-interest into concern for the whole organization and as using personal traits such as charisma, work record and interpersonal skills to motivate others. Women leaders practice what the author calls "interactive leadership" – trying to make every interaction with co-workers positive for all involved by encouraging participation, sharing power and information, making people feel important and energizing them.

In fact, a meta-analysis thirteen years later comparing the findings over several studies (Eagly *et al*, 2003) agreed that female leaders were more transformational than male leaders in their leadership style, a conclusion mirrored by studies showing divergences between male and female leadership constructs (Sparrow and Rigg, 1993; Alimo-Metcalfe, 1995; Moss and Daunton, 2006). By contrast, male leaders have been found to score higher on the laissez-faire and management by exception (active and passive) components of transactional leadership. Interestingly, these differences are in line with observations from both Europe and the US that men and women 'manage differently' (White, 1995; Vinnicombe and Singh, 2002; Bird and Brush, 2002).

So much for *how* men and women manage. What about the value that men and women place on male and female leaders? One study (Luthar, 1996) showed that men tended to ascribe higher values to men's leadership skills than women's, and women the reverse. This suggests that men and women may exercise different criteria when evaluating leadership. The consequences? One is that the gender of those involved in leadership selection may influence the selection outcome, an important conclusion emerging from research conducted in a public sector organisation by the author (Moss and Daunton, 2006). The facts here are interesting since the female HR director had drawn up a job specification rooted largely in transformational competencies but the male interviewers, when asked about the key leadership skills needed for the high-level job in question, cited competencies that were transactional in character. The single female interviewer, on the recruitment panel, however, cited transformational competencies insetad, thereby mirroring the competencies in the original job specification. Not surprisingly, perhaps, given the greater number of men than women on the recruitment panel, a leader was appointed whose leadership style was transactional in character, even though the job specification had been firmly rooted in transformational competencies.

How to avoid these biases? A second public sector organisation required interviewers to undergo training in leadership styles before the selection process, and this may have been instrumental in ensuring that interviewers selected according to the elements in the job specification rather than in line with individual preferences (Moss et al, 2006). So, the vertical segregation and 'glass ceiling' that women encounter in private and public sector organisations in all developed countries (Burke, 2002; Burke and Nelson, 2002) could be a consequence of the failure to enforce transformational criteria in selection processes, with only those women with transactional attributes being recruited into senior positions.

The question as to which leadership criteria are adopted – both officially and in reality – is a critical one if organisations are to have leaders who can foster high performance working, something facilitated, as we have seen, by transformational rather than transactional leadership. So the process of appointing transformational leaders needs to be supported by training and work on unconscious bias to ensure that organisations and women do not lose out.

As things stand, despite dramatic increases in the number of women pursuing professional careers (Vinnicombe and Singh, 2002), women are still in a minority in managerial positions and directorships. In the US, for example, data published in 2017 showed that while women constituted nearly half (46.8%) of the labour force, only slightly over a third (39.2%) of managers in 2015 were women (Catalyst, 2017). In the UK, according to a parliamentary report on corporate governance, in the FTSE 100, only 10.4% of executive director positions were held by women (those positions held after working up the talent pipeline), compared with 33.7% of non-executive directors (Verdict, 2017).

Cultural and leadership styles

Can transformational and inclusive leadership take root in all national cultures? There are studies from the late 1990s suggesting that transformational competencies can be transferred across no fewer than sixty-two cultures (Den Hartog et al, 1999; House et al, 1999), and a study by Catalyst (2014) found that a sense of being included enhanced innovation and teamworking in the six countries (Australia, China, Germany, Mexico, India and the US) in which the research was conducted.

Incidentally, a 'sense of being included' was defined in relation to people's perceptions of being similar while distinct, a definition of inclusion that regrettably does not link to any well-known theory of leadership.

In fact, it would be surprising if Tf and IL leadership were equally likely to take root in Anglo-Saxon and non-Anglo-Saxon cultures given the differences in these cultures revealed by well-known cross-cultural studies (Hofstede *et al*, 2010; Trompenaars and Hampden-Turner, 2015). Gert Hofstede, for example, found evidence of large divergences in power distance between Anglo-Saxon (UK, US, Canada and Australia) and Scandinavian countries on the one hand and Asian and South American and Mediterranean Latin countries on the other, It is therefore hard to see how the Tf competence of 'individualised consideration', necessitating perhaps a low power distance context, could take root in a high power distance culture in which power differences between the most and least powerful employees are accentuated. Moreover, Anglo-Saxon countries may experience greater individualism than Scandinavian countries, and this poses the question as to whether Scandinavian cultures (characterised typically by low power distance and high collectivism) are more able to deliver transformational and inclusive leadership than countries with high levels of individualism.

Of course, organisational culture may influence people's innate dispositions, and it could be that organisational cultures can override national characteristics. So, the four case studies presented in this book, all British organisations with highly inclusive practices, may have acquired a culture supportive of IL despite being based in the UK with its highly individualistic and masculine culture. For, as we shall see in Chapters 8 to 11, all four organisations have taken steps to build a supportive culture in which teamwork flourishes and people feel listened to. So, perhaps a strong organisational culture can override aspects of national culture.

Ethnicity and leadership

What of ethnicity and inclusive leadership? An interesting study in a bank in South Africa (Booysen, 2000) reported on perceptions of effective leadership among male and female 'black' and 'white' managers. What this study revealed were differing perceptions of effective leadership amongst black and white staff (see Table 1.9).

TABLE 1.9 Booysen (2000): constructs of effective leadership held by white and black managers in South Africa

White managers	Black managers
• competition and work-orientation	• collaboration
• free enterprise	• consensus and group agreement
• liberal democracy	• collective solidarity
• individual self-sufficiency	• concern for people
• self-fulfilment	• inclusivity
• exclusivity	• respect and dignity
• planning and methodology	

Based on these reactions, one could imagine that transformational leadership would more likely to take root amongst black than white managers, just as it might align better with women's than with men's leadership constructs. Perhaps it is divergences in leadership constructs such as these that lie at the root of the finding that black and female managers in a UK local authority received lower ratings by their boss than white males, while receiving higher ratings by their peers and direct reports (Alban-Metcalfe and Alban-Metcalfe, 2004). Normally, ratings by peers and direct reports have been found to be more valid than those of bosses (Fletcher and Baldry, 1999; Alimo-Metcalfe et al, 2007), so biases in the leadership constructs of bosses could be skewing the results.

Leadership and personality

For some reason, only a small number of studies have investigated the links between personality and leadership traits. They have used three personality tests, namely the Big Five (measuring neuroticism, extraversion, openness to experience, agreeableness and conscientiousness), the Big Four MBTI (measuring extraversion/introversion; sensing/intuition; thinking/feeling and judgement/perception) and finally an *ad hoc* 'managerial model' distinguishing between (i) innovators for change or inventors, (ii) analytical coordinators or managers, (iii) organised pragmatists or implementers and (iv) enthusiastic idealists or motivators.

The way that the findings have been interpreted is strange to say the least. Take 'agreeableness', for example, with one study (Howard and Bray, 1988) finding it to be negatively correlated with managerial potential; a further two studies (Judge and Bono, 2000; Srivastava, 2011) linking it to overall job performance and managerial effectiveness; and a third study (Moutafi et al, 2007) finding no relationship at all with managerial level. How could three studies reach such varied conclusions concerning the role of agreeableness in managerial effectiveness?

Potentially, the problem may lie in the fact that the assumptions regarding managerial effectiveness are neither spelled out nor necessarily consistent across the three studies and since notions of managerial effectiveness can vary greatly – we have only to think of the differences between transactional and transformational leadership (Burns, 1978) – different assumptions concerning managerial effectiveness could underlie the different results. We certainly now know how divergent are the concepts of transactional and transformational leadership, something acknowledged by the originator of these concepts (Burns, 1978).

This analysis of the problem may not be so far-fetched and may explain why in one study the 'warmth' element of extraversion (part of the 'Big Five') is not correlated with managerial seniority (Moutafi et al, 2007) while the 'feeling' element of the 'Big Four' is associated with no more than an enhancement in innovation (*ibid*). For, if the researchers presuppose a transactional model of leadership, one that is heavily reliant on command and control, then 'warmth' and 'feeling' are unlikely to be at a premium. On the other hand, if a transformational model is assumed, this lack of correlation is less easy to understand.

Just one study has in fact avoided this problem since it took the important step of defining the leadership styles against which personality types were compared (Church and Waclawski, 1998). In this study conducted within a highly diversified global corporation, an *ad hoc* leadership tool, the 'managerial model', was used, and the personality features associated with this model were identified in a cohort of 253 senior executives and their direct reports. The findings? Inventors and motivators were more transformational in their leadership style than were implementers, a finding that showed the extent to which personality can be a determinant of leadership style.

The conclusion? We urgently need studies that highlight the association between personality type and those leadership styles linked to high performance working. Top of my research list would be studies investigating the personalities of transformational and inclusive leaders, since these have yet to be conducted.

Conclusion

This has been a long journey through the leadership literature, and the reader should now understand the steps that brought us to transformational and servant leadership and linked them to inclusive leadership, the subject of this book. In the next chapter, we look at some of the factors that prioritise an inclusive leadership style in the early years of the twenty-first century.

References

Alimo-Metcalfe, B. (1995). An investigation of female and male constructs of leadership and empowerment. *Women in Management Review*, 10 (2), 3–8.

Alimo-Metcalfe, B. (2010). An investigation of female and male constructs of leadership and empowerment. *Gender in Management: An International Journal*, 25 (8), 640–648.

Alimo-Metcalfe, B. and Alban-Metcalfe, J. (2004). Leadership in public sector organisations. In Storey, J. (ed.), *Leadership in organisations: Current issues and key trends*, pp. 173–202. London: Routledge.

Alimo-Metcalfe, B. and Alban-Metcalfe, J. (2003). Leadership: A masculine past, but a feminine future? paper presented at the *BPS Occupational Psychology Conference*, Bournemouth, 8–10 January.

Alimo-Metcalfe, B., Alban-Metcalfe, J., Semele, C., Bradley, M. and Mariathasan, J. (2007). *The impact of leadership factors in implementing change in complex health and social care environments: NHS plan clinical priority for mental health crises resolution teams*, www.netscc.ac.uk/hsdr/files/project/SDO_FR_08-1201-022_V01.pdf, accessed on 26 December 2017.

Allen, G., Moore, W., Moser, L., Neill, K., Sambamoorthi, U. and Bell, H. (2016). The role of servant leadership and transformational leadership in academic pharmacy. *American Journal of Pharmacological Education*, 80 (7), 113, www.ncbi.nlm.nih.gov/pubmed/27756921, accessed on 20 November 2017.

Bass, B. M. (1985). *Leadership and performance beyond expectations*. New York, NY: The Free Press.

Bass, B. M. (1990). From transactional to transformational leadership: Learning to share the vision. *Organizational Dynamics*, 18 (3), 19–31.

Bass, B. M. (1997). Does the transactional – transformational leadership paradigm transcend organizational and national boundaries? *American Psychologist*, 52 (2), 130–139, http://dx.doi.org/10.1037/0003-066X.52.2.130

Bass, B. M. (1998). *Transformational leadership: Industrial, military and educational impact.* Mahwah, NJ: Lawrence Erlbaum.

Bass, B.M. and Avolio, B.J. (1990). Developing trans-formational leadership 1992 and beyond. *Journal of European Industrial Training,* 14, 21–27.

Bass, B. M. and Avolio, B. J. (1995). *MLQ multifactor leadership questionnaire, leader form, rater form, and scoring.* Palo Alto, CA: Mind Garden, http://dx.doi.org/10.1037/0003-066X.52.2.130

Bass, B. M., Avolio, B. J. and Atwater, L. (1996). The transformational and transactional leadership of men and women. *Applied Psychology: An International Review,* 45, 5–34.

Bennett, N., Wise, C., Woods, P. and Harvey, J. (2003). *Distributed leadership,* Full Report, Nottingham: NCSL.

Bennis, W. G. (1989). *On becoming a leader.* New York, NY: Addison-Wesley.

Bennis, W. G. and Townsend, R. (1995). *Reinventing leadership: Collins business essential.* New York, NY: Collins.

Bilimoria, D. (2012). *Inclusive leadership: Effectively leading diverse teams,* 4 March, https://weatherhead.case.edu/news/2012/04/03/inclusive-leadership-effectively-leading-diverse-teams

Bird, B. and Brush, C. (2002). A gendered perspective on organization creation. *Entrepreneurship Theory and Practice,* 26, 41–65.

Blake, R. and Mouton, J. (1964). *The managerial grid: The key to leadership excellence.* Houston: Gulf Publishing Co.

Blanchard, K. (2011). *Why does leadership matter,* 8 October, http://howwelead.org/2011/10/08/why-does-leadership-matter/, accessed on 18 December 2015.

Bolden, R., Jones, S., Davis, H. and Gentle, P. (2015). *Developing and sustaining shared leadership in higher education: Stimulus paper.* London: Leadership Foundation for Higher Education, in collaboration with LH Martin Institute.

Bolden, R., Petrov, G. and Gosling, J. (2008). Tensions in higher education leadership: Towards a multi-level model of leadership practice. *Higher Education Quarterly,* 62, 358–376.

Booysen, L. (2000). Cultural differences between African black and white managers in South Africa. Paper presented at the *12th Annual Conference of Southern Africa Institute for Management Scientists,* 31 October–2 November.

Burke, R. (2002). Career development of managerial women. In Burke, R. and Nelson, D. (eds.), *Advancing women's careers.* Oxford: Blackwell.

Burke, R. and Nelson, D. (2002). Advancing women in management: Progress and prospects. In Burke, R. and Nelson, D. (eds.), *Advancing women's careers.* Oxford: Blackwell.

Burns, J. M. (1978). *Leadership.* New York, NY: Harper & Row.

Canwell, A., Dongrie, V., Neveras, N. and Stockton, H. (2014). *Leaders at all levels: Close the gap between hype and readiness.* Deloitte University Press, 7 March, https://dupress.deloitte.com/dup-us-en/focus/human-capital-trends/2014/hc-trends-2014-leaders-at-all-levels.html, accessed on 20 November 2017.

Carmeli, A., Reiter-Palmon, R. and Ziv, E. (2010). Inclusive leadership and employee involvement in creative tasks in the workplace: The mediating role of psychological safety. *Creativity Research Journal,* 22 (3), 250–260.

Catalyst. (2014). *Inclusive leadership: The view from six countries,* www.catalyst.org/system/files/inclusive_leadership_the_view_from_six_countries_0.pdf, accessed on 1 October 2015.

Catalyst. (2017). *Women in management,* www.catalyst.org/knowledge/women-management, accessed on 22 December 2017.

Church, A. H. and Waclawski, J. (1995). The effects of personality orientation and executive behavior on subordinate perceptions of workgroup enablement. *International Journal of Organizational Analysis,* 3, 20–51.

Church, A. H. and Waclawski, J. (1998). The relationship between individual personality orientation and executive leadership behaviour. *Journal of Occupational and Organisational Psychology*, 71 (2), 99–125.

Conger, J. A. (1989) *The charismatic leader: Beyond the mystique of exceptional leadership.* San Francisco: Jossey-Bass.

Conger, J. A. and Kanungo, R. N. (1988). The empowerment process integrating theory and practice. *Academy of Management Review*, 13, 471–482.

Deloitte. (2012). *Inclusive leadership: Will a hug do,* www2.deloitte.com/content/dam/Deloitte/au/Documents/human-capital/deloitte-au-hc-diversity-inclusive-leadership-hug-0312.pdf, accessed on 8 July 2015.

Department for Business Innovation and Skills. (2012). *A summary of the evidence for the value of investing in leadership and management development,* https://assets.publishing.service.gov.uk/government/uploads/system/uploads/attachment_data/file/32327/12-923-leadership-management-key-to-sustainable-growth-evidence.pdf, accessed on 31 May 2018.

Eagly, A. (2004). Few women at the top: How role incongruity produces prejudice and the glass ceiling. In van Knippenberg, D. and Hogg, M. A. (eds.), *Identity, leadership, and power.* London: Sage.

Eagly, A., Johannesen-Schmidt, M. and van Engen, M. (2003). Transformational, transactional, and laissez-faire leadership styles: A meta-analysis comparing women and men. *Psychological Bulletin*, 129 (4), 569–592.

Echols, S. (2009). Transformational/servant leadership: A potential synergism for an inclusive leadership style. *Journal of Religious Leadership*, 8 (2), 85–116, http://arl-jrl.org/Volumes/Echols09.pdf, accessed on 8 July 2015.

EEF and CIPD. (2003). *Maximising employee potential and business performance: The role of high performance working,* 28 November.

Ferrario, M. and Davidson, M. (1991). Gender and management style: A comparative study. Paper presented at the *British Academy of Management Conference,* University of Bath.

Fiedler, F. E. (1994). *Leadership experience and leadership performance.* Alexandria, VA: US Army Research Institute for the Behavioural and Social Sciences.

Fletcher, C. and Baldry, C. (1999). Multi-source feedback systems: A research perspective. In Cooper, C. L. and Robertson, I. T. (eds.), *International review of industrial and organisational psychology,* Vol. 14, pp. 149–193. New York, NY: John Wiley & Sons.

Forde, C., Mcmahon, M. and Dickson, B. (2011). Leadership development in Scotland: After Donaldson. *Sottish Educational Review*, 43 (2), 55–69.

Gill, C. and Meyer, D. R. (2008). High and low road approaches to the management of human resources: An examination of the relationship between business strategy, human resource management and high performance work practices. *International Journal of Employment Studies*, 16 (2), 67–112.

Gosling, J., Bolden, R. and Petrov, G. (2009). Distributed leadership in higher education: What does it accomplish? *Education*, 5 (3), 299–310.

Greenleaf, R. K. (1970). *The servant as leader,* www.leadershiparlington.org/pdf/TheServantasLeader.pdf

Greenleaf, R. K. (1977). *Servant leadership: A journey into the nature of legitimate power and greatness.* New York, NY: Paulist Press.

Hartog, D., House, R. J., Hanges, P. J., Ruiz-Quinantilla, S. A., Dorfman, P. W. and Associates. (1999). Culture specific and cross culturally generalizable implicit theories: Are attributes of charismatic/transformational leadership universally endorsed? *Leadership Quarterly*, 10, 219–256.

Hersey, P. and Blanchard, K. (1982). *Management of organizational behaviour: Utilizing human resources*. Upper Saddles River, NJ: Prentice-Hall.

Hofstede, G., Hofstede, G. J. and Minkov, M. (2010). *Cultures and organizations: Software of the mind*. 3rd edition. New York, NY: McGraw-Hill.

Hollander, E. P. (2008). *Inclusive leadership: The essential leader-follower relationship*. New York, NY: Routledge.

Hollander, E. P. (2012). *Inclusive leadership: The essential leader-follower relationship*. New York, NY: Routledge.

House, R. J. (1977). A 1976 theory of charismatic leadership. In Hunt, J. G. and Larson, L. L. (eds.), *Leadership: The cutting edge*, pp. 189–207. Carbondale, IL: Southern Illinois University Press.

House, R. J. and Dressler, G. (1974). The path-goal theory of leadership. *Journal of Contemporary Business*, 3, 81–97.

House, R. J., Hanges, P. J., Ruiz-Quintanilla, S. A., Dorfman, P. W., Javidan, M., Dickson, M., Gupta, V. and Associates. (1999). Cultural influences on leadership and organizations: Project globe. *Advances in Global Leadership*, 1, 171–233.

Howard, A. and Bray, D. W. (1988). *Management lives in transition: Advancing age and changing times*. New York, NY: Guilford Press.

Hunt, J. G. (1999). Transformation/charismatic leadership's transformation of the field: An historical essay. *Leadership Quarterly*, 10, 129–144.

ILO Supporting Workplace Learning for High Performance Working. (2002). http://www.ilo.org/skills/lang--en/index.htm, accessed on 2 September 2010.

Judge, T. A. and Bono, J. E. (2000). Personality and job satisfaction: The mediating role of job characteristics. *Journal of Applied Psychology*, 85, 237–249.

Judge, T. A. and Piccolo, R. (2004). Transformational and transactional leadership: A meta-analytic test of their relative reliability. *Journal of Applied Psychology*, 89 (5), 755–768.

Kanter, Rosabeth Moss. (1977). *Men and women of the corporation*. New York, NY: Basic Books.

Kelan, E. (2015). *Linchpin – men, middle managers and gender inclusive leadership*. Cranfield International Centre for Women leaders, www.som.cranfield.ac.uk/som/dinamic-content/research/Linchpin.pdf, accessed on 30 September 2015.

Kellerman, B. (2015). *Hard times: Leadership in America*. Stanford, CA: Stanford Business books.

Kotter, J. (2013). Management is (still) not leadership, January, https://hbr.org/2013/01/management-is-still-not-leadership

Kotter, J. P. (1990). What leaders really do. *Harvard Business Review*, 68, May–June, 103–111.

Leadership Foundation for Higher Education. (2018). *The impact of academic leadership behaviours on BME student attainment*, Insight Report, https://tinyurl.com/y836mly6

Linkage, www.diversityjournal.com/13313-moving-dial-measuring-inclusive-leadership/, uploaded in 2014.

Lowe, K. and Kroeck, K. (1996). Effectiveness correlates of transformational and transactional leadership: A meta analytic review of the MLQ literature. *Leadership Quarterly*, 7 (3), 385–426.

Lunenberg, F. (2011). Leadership versus management: A key distinction – at least in theory. *International Journal of Management, Business and Administration*, 14 (1), 1–4, https://cs.anu.edu.au/courses/comp3120/local_docs/readings/Lunenburg_LeadershipVersusManagement.pdf, accessed on 1 August 2018.

Luthar, H. (1996). Gender differences in evaluation of performance and leadership ability: Autocratic vs. democratic mangers. *Sex Roles*, 35 (5–6), 337–361.

Mann, R. D. (1959). A review of the relationships between personality and performance in small groups. *Psychological Bulletin*, 56 (4), 241–270, http://dx.doi.org/10.1037/h0044587

Martins, A., Martins, I., Pereira, P. and Brown, K. (2011). High performance working practices: The new framework for nurturing sustainability. *First World Sustainability Forum*, November, 1–30.

McClelland, D. C. (1973). Testing for competence rather than for "intelligence." *American Psychologist*, 28 (1), 1–14.

Miller, D. (1996). Equality management: Towards a materialist approach. *Gender Work and Organisation*, 3 (4), 202–214.

Mintzberg, H. (1982). If you're not serving Bill and Barbara, then you're not serving leadership. In Hunt, J. G. Sekaran, U. and Schriesheim, C. A. (eds.), *Leadership: Beyond establishment views*, pp. 239–259. Carbondale, IL: Southern Illinois University Press.

Moss, G. (2016). Inclusive leadership: Boosts engagement, productivity and organisational diversity. *Equal Opportunity Review*, 268, June, 5–8.

Moss, G. and Daunton, L. (2006). The discriminatory impact of deviations from selection criteria in Higher Education selection. *Career Development International*, 11 (6), 504–521.

Moss, G., Daunton, L. and Gasper, R. (2006). The impact of leadership selection on High Performance Working. *CIPD Professional Standards Conference*, 26–28 June, Keele University.

Moss, G., Sims, C., Dodds, I. and David, A. (2016). *Inclusive leadership . . . driving performance through diversity*. Employers' Network on Equality and Inclusion.

Moutafi, J., Furnham, A. and Crump, J. (2007). Is managerial level related to personality? *British Journal of Management*, 1, 272–280.

Nicola, M. P. and Thomas, M. (2004). Building an inclusive diversity culture: Principles, processes and practice. *Journal of Business Ethics*, 54 (2), 129–147.

Nitu, M. and Atewologun, D. (2015). Inclusive leadership: A systematic review of the evidence. *OP Matters*, British Psychological Society, 26, June.

Opportunity Now. (2014). *Inclusive leadership – from pioneer to mainstream maximising the potential of your people*, http://opportunitynow.bitc.org.uk/system/files/research/5815_executive_summary.pdf, accessed on 27 October 2015.

Oshagbemi, T. and Gill, R. (2004). Differences in leadership styles and behaviour across hierarchical levels in UK organisations. *Leadership & Organization Development Journal*, 25 (1), 93–106, doi.org/10.1108/01437730410512796

Pittinsky, T. L. (2010). A two-dimensional model of intergroup leadership: The case of national diversity. *American Psychologist*, 65 (3), 194–200, http://dx.doi.org/10.1037/a0017329

Rosener, J. (1990). Ways women lead. *Harvard Business Review*, November/December, 119–125.

Russell, R. and Stone, A. (2002). A review of servant leadership attributes: Developing a practical model. *Leadership and Organisation Development Journal*, 23 (3), 145–157.

Ryan, J. (2007). Inclusive leadership: A review. *EAF Journal*, 18 (1/2), 92–125.

Sarros, J., Gray, J. and Densten, I. (2002). Leadership and its impact on organisational culture. *International Journal of Business Studies*, 10 (2), 1–26.

Sashkin, M. (1988). The visionary leader. In Conger, J. A. and Kanungo, R. N. (eds.), *The Jossey-Bass management series: Charismatic leadership: The elusive factor in organizational effectiveness*, pp. 122–160. San Francisco, CA: Jossey-Bass.

Schein, E. (1996). *Organizational culture and leadership*. San Francisco, CA: Jossey-Bass.

Schein, E. (2010). *Organisational culture and leadership*. 5th edition. San Francisco, CA: John Wiley & Sons.

Silva, A. (2016). What is leadership? *Journal of Business Studies Quarterly*, 8 (1), 1–5, http://jbsq.org/wp-content/uploads/2016/09/September_2016_1.pdf, accessed on 26 December 2017.

Sparrow, J. and Rigg, C. (1993). Job analysis: Selecting for the masculine approach to management. *Selection and Development Review*, 9 (2), 5–8.

Spears, L. (1995). Introduction: Servant leadership and the Greenleaf legacy. In L. Spears (ed.), *Reflections on leadership: How Robert K. Greenleaf's theory of servant leadership influenced today's top management thinkers*, pp. 1–16. New York, NY: John Wiley & Sons.

Srivastava, S (2011). Assessing the relationship between personality variable and managerial effectiveness: An empirical study on private sector managers. *Management and Labour Studies*, 36 (4), 319–333.

Stevens, R. (2003). High performance workplaces. In *UK work organisation*, 1, 12–15, Nottingham: Nottingham Trent University.

Stogdill, R. M. (1948). Personal factors in leadership: A review of the literature. *The Journal of Psychology*, 1, 35–71.

Stogdill, R. M. (1974). *Handbook of leadership: A survey of theory and research*. New York, NY: The Free Press.

Trompenaars, A. and Hampden-Turner, C. (2015). *Riding the waves of culture: Understanding diversity in global business*. London: Nicholas Brealey Publishing.

Van Dierendonck D. and Nuijten I. (2011). The servant leadership survey: Development and validation of a multidimensional measure. *Journal of Business and Psychology*, 26, 249–267.

Van Dierendonck, D., Stam, D., Boersma, P., de Windt, N. and Alkema, J. (2014). Same difference? Exploring the differential mechanisms linking servant leadership and transformational leadership to follower outcomes. *The Leadership Quarterly*, 25 (3), 544–562, www.sciencedirect.com/science/article/pii/S1048984313001409

Verdict. (2017). *Gender diversity on boards actually decreased in 2017*, www.verdict.co.uk/gender-diversity-boards-actually-decreased-2017/, accessed on 22 December 2017.

Vinnicombe, S. and Singh, V. (2002). Developing tomorrow's women business leaders. In Burke, R. and Nelson, D. (eds.), *Advancing women's careers*. Wikipedia entry on Internet Marketing, http://en.wikipedia.org/wiki/Internet_marketing

Volckmann, R. (2012). Fresh perspective: Barbara Kellerman and the leadership industry. *Integral Leadership Review*, 6–8, http://integralleadershipreview.com/7064-barbara-kellerman-and-the-leadership-industry/ June, accessed on 9 May 2018.

Vroom, V. H. and Yetton, P. N. (1973). *Leadership and decision making*. Pittsburgh, PA: University of Pittsburgh Press.

White, J. (1995). Leading in their own ways: Women chief executives in local government. In Itzin, C. and Newman, J. (eds.), *Gender, culture and organizational change*. London: Routledge.

2

FACTORS PROMPTING INCLUSIVE LEADERSHIP

Factors prompting a shift to inclusive leadership

In March and April 2016, two reports appeared on inclusive leadership (IL). The first, coordinated by the Employers Network on Equality and Inclusion (enei), involving empirical work with eleven sponsoring organisations involved, was led by myself with a team consisting of psychologist, Dr Ceri Sims, strategist Alan David, and Diversity and Inclusion expert Dr Ian Dodds. The second report was produced by Juliet Bourke and Bernadette Dillon of Deloitte (2016).

Both reports dovetail nicely in terms of the factors that they suggest prioritise IL, and so the arguments advanced in these reports are summarised in some detail here. Do bear in mind while reading these that IL has – as will be apparent from Chapters 4–7 and 12 – the twin benefits of being a generic style of leadership that boosts employee outcomes (productivity, motivation and well-being) and customer outcomes (greater customer centricity) as well as a style that boosts the diversity mindset and diverse density of an organisation. Of course, cross-fertilisation between these two sets of benefits is, based on our findings, extremely likely to occur but these are separate benefits and IL is powerful as a style of leadership that values, respects and encourages the growth of empowered individuals while also being a style that can boos the diversity mindset in an organisation.

Turning to Deloitte's report (Bourke and Dillon, 2016), two of the four drivers that it offers for IL relate to the organisation's *external* environment and the need to achieve a better understanding of customers and markets while a further two relate to *internal* factors and the need for organisations to draw on diverse ideas and diverse personnel. In terms of the enei report (Moss *et al*, 2016), this identifies changing societal values as an important element in the movement towards IL, a factor that links to the evolving needs of a younger and more diverse employee base. So, there is variation but also overlap in the case made for inclusive leadership in these two reports.

We will now look in detail at the four drivers to inclusive leadership identified in these two reports.

Diversity of customers

The Deloitte report (Bourke and Dillon, 2016) creates a compelling case for IL by emphasising the increased choice available to consumers and their growing demand for personalisation. As the authors state, 'customer centricity is paramount' and they perceive that in order to adapt, organisations need to grow 'empathy' and 'connectedness' so as to develop customer-centric mindsets and capabilities.

One approach is to create a role such as 'chief customer officer', with the Australian mobile phone company, Telstra, leading the way with a 'director of customer advocacy'. Leadership style is viewed as central to the success of a connected customer strategy such as that at Telstra since it is thought to create the landscape within the organisation that can allow employees within an organisation to relate to the customer and their needs outside of it.

Interestingly, it was almost twenty years ago in 1995 that Michael Hammer, former Professor of Computing at the Massachusetts Institute of Technology (MIT), stated that business survival depends on shaping products and services around the "unique and particular needs" of their customer (Hammer, 1995), with business services re-configured around the needs of the customer. This launched the initiative known as 'Business Process Engineering' (BPR) and many consulting firms embarked on this process with their clients, developing BPR methods. The difference between Hammer's thinking back in the 1990s and the more recent thinking on customer centricity today is that solutions today are less likely to be regarded as lying in a systems approach to organisations than in one rooted in human factors.

According to this newer way of thinking, a greater emphasis on human factors could have a transformative effect on customer-centricity. Currently, 83% of consumer purchases are made by women (Moss, 2016), while the proportion of *executive* positions held by women on FTSE boards currently stands at under 10% (it is just the inclusion of the less significant *non-executive* female representation that boosts the board-level figure to over 31% (Kollewe and Hickey, 2015). An increase in female executive representation would ensure that women were part of the senior talent pipeline of organisations and not just occasional board members parachuted into organisations with otherwise staunchly masculine cultures. The figures in Table 2.1 show the slow pace of change in women's presence as executive board members on FTSE 100 boards in the UK.

The paucity of female input to decision-making, and design and marketing decision-making in particular, has been a recurring theme in my writing and research, and I have been beating the drum for decades on the need for an 'outside-in' perspective that allows organisations to configure themselves around the needs of the customer. Having an inclusive style of leadership may, as well as creating

TABLE 2.1 Figures showing the percentage of executive and non-executive females on the boards of FTSE 100 companies

%	2010/11	2012	2013	2014	Oct 2015
Female non-executive directors	15.6	22.4	21.8	25.5	31.4
Female executive directors	5.5	6.6	5.8	6.9	9.6

Source: Davies Review, cited in Kollewe and Hickey (2015)

a generic style of leadership that boosts productivity and motivation, create the organisational culture that facilitates a diversity mindset and the appointment of a greater proportion of women. More information on both the need and evidence for this can be found in Chapter 12.

Diversity of markets

The second factor identified by Bourke and Dillon (2016) as driving a need for IL is the increasing affluence and growth of the middle classes in Asia, South America and Africa. According to these authors, this growth is producing a new market that will grow from 1.8 billion in 2009 to 2.3 billion in 2025, with companies in the West only able to respond to this if they employ people with a global mind-set.

Bourke and Dillon (ibid) quote the global chief diversity officer of The Coca-Cola Company as saying that success in capturing the fastest growing markets in sub-Saharan Africa, India and China depends upon the company embedding itself in these cultures, a perception that leads him to pose the question, "Even if we get all the tactics and logistics right, can we win if we don't get the people part right?" (ibid). This is where IL comes into the frame in its ability to boost the Diversity Mindset within an organisation.

Diversity of ideas

The arguments for IL do not stop at customer centricity. Bourke and Dillon discuss an earlier Boston Consulting Group survey of 1,500 executives, three-quarters of whom describe innovation as being among their company's top three priorities (Boston Consulting Group, 2014). Despite this, 83% perceived their corporate innovation capabilities to be average (70%) or weak (13%) (ibid), with successful organisations succeeding only by virtue of casting their net widely for ideas. Failure to do this can sound the death knell for a company as a journalist writing in *Campaign* magazine explains (Agathou, 2017):

> more than 50% of Fortune 500 companies have gone bankrupt, been acquired or ceased to exist and it is projected that 40% of them will be gone in the next ten years. Little wonder that many Chief Executives have an "innovate or die" coffee mug on their table with the imperative of innovation well understood. (*ibid*)

It is clear that the writer assumes a lack of innovation to be a major problem in Fortune 500 companies, since discussion of the downfall of high proportions of these companies is linked to discussions of the way in which IL can enhance the pool of ideas from which organisations can draw.

More on the importance of innovation can be found in the later section on societal, organisational and individual values.

Diversity of talent

The final factor singled out by the Deloitte report (2016) concerns diversity of talent and the role that this plays in organisational success. Of course, mention of the contribution that diverse talent can make is nothing new, but what is new is the notion that shifting organisational demographics are favouring a move from command and control to inclusive leadership.

What demographic changes do the authors have in mind? The report refers to shifting profiles of age, gender and education, leading the authors to suggest that, "more than ever", future success will depend on a leader's ability to motivate a diverse talent pool. In the case of age, for example, they summarise their main concerns in stark terms:

> By 2030, China will have more graduates than the entire US workforce, and India will produce four times as many graduates as the United States by 2020. The Millennials, too, are coming of age. This generation will comprise 50 percent of the global workforce by 2020. With high expectations and different attitudes toward work, they will be integral in shaping organizational cultures into the future.

This leads the authors to argue that demographic factors will put greater pressure on leaders to create organisations with attitudes to people that match their concepts of positive working relationships. With millenials and others, this may mean offering a more inclusive and less transactional style of leadership than might have been acceptable in the past.

The impact of changing attitudes to workplace leadership also features in the enei report on inclusive leadership that the author of this book led in the same year as the Bourke and Dillon Deloitte report, and so it makes sense to look now at the arguments used there (Moss *et al*, 2016; Moss, 2016).

Three principle arguments are advanced there for inclusive leadership with employee diversity as the first; societal, organisational and individual values as the second and strategic factors as the third. We will begin by looking at employee diversity since it flows from the Deloitte discussion of diversity of talent and will then move on to looking at societal attitudes (section (d) below), following up on the points relating to age flagged up in the Deloitte report just discussed.

Employee diversity

In the enei report headed by myself and colleagues (Moss *et al*, 2016; Moss, 2016), it was suggested that leadership had an increasingly important role to play in bringing subgroups of people together into a collective. In speaking of subgroups, we were considering people with protected characteristics (age, disability, gender reassignment, ethnicity, marriage and civil partnership, pregnancy and maternity, race, religion and belief, sex and sexual orientation), cognitive diversity (diversity of thought) or a combination of both of these. However, increasing focus is being placed on the overlap or 'intersectionality' of these variables (Kelly and Smith, 2014), rather than simply on single strands, since people are thought to possess multiple identities and cultures. However, in many organisations, the emphasis is still on conformity and promotability (Yoshino and Smith, 2013) and this can encourage 'covering' identities, something that may lead to a lack of engagement and a desire to leave the organisation (Kelly and Smith, 2014).

In view of the complexity of intersectionality and the fact that research in this area is still in its infancy, reference in this book will continue to be to single-threaded strands of diversity. With this in mind and within the constraints of the current book, we explore the evidence on a selection of protected characteristics notably ethnicity/nationality, age and gender.

(a) Nationality

As world cultures become more interconnected, it is likely that national diversity in organisations will become ever more evident, something that may influence an organisation's tolerance for IL since, as we shall see in chapter 13, different national groups may have varying degrees of tolerance for IL.

High power distance cultures, for example, those with a high power gap between those yielding power and those at the receiving end of it, may struggle with IL (this would be the case with many Asian, South American or Mediterranean countries), while low power distance cultures (typically Scandinavian and to a slightly lesser extent Anglo-Saxon cultures) are likely to be considerably more at ease with this style. Where individualism/collectivism is concerned, one could imagine that the collectivist focus of many inclusive leadership attributes (for example those of empathy, listening, healing and growth) could make them easier to embed in collectivist than individualistic cultures unless organisations take steps to counter these tendencies.

For, as we will see towards the end of Chapter 13, the ideal context for inclusive leadership may be cultures with low power distance and low individualism. On this basis, and following survey findings by the renowned Dutch researcher, Hofstede (Hofstede *et al*, 2010), the most favoured countries would be Scandinavian, Dutch, Irish, Slovenian or Israeli. Anglo-Saxon countries (New Zealand, Canada, Great Britain, the US and Australia) with typically higher levels of individualism may have more difficulty in adopting IL although the four examples of IL presented in this book, all from Britain, show the extent to which the internal culture of an organisation can be fashioned (for example by fostering a collective approach to tasks) to create a strongly inclusive environment. In this way, it may be possible to create an organisational micro-climate that is distinct from the national environment in which the organisation is situated.

(b) Age

For the first time in history, we see five generations of employees working together under the same roof, each bringing a unique set of priorities and expectations (KPMG, 2017). The largest of the generations is that of the millennials (born 1980–1995), now 35% of the UK workforce (*ibid*), and predicted to represent an astounding 50% of the global workforce by 2020. The sheer size of this generation forces employers to understand their attitudes so that the workplace can be shaped to some extent around their needs and preferences.

Research on their millenial attitudes reveals the extent to which they are more likely than earlier generations to aspire to an inclusive culture that supports engagement, empowerment and authenticity (Smith, 2015). Moreover, they are said to value inclusion not merely as an abstract ideal but as a critical tool to facilitate business competitiveness and growth (*ibid*). It is perhaps the gap between their aspirations for an inclusive culture and the reality of many workplaces that may explain the lower levels of satisfaction experienced by this generation compared with older generations.

Millennial concerns for diversity may also be at the root of their intolerance for autocratic approaches to leadership (Deloitte millennial survey, 2015a) and the priority that they place on being valued for the multiplicity of their identities – their *whole self* – rather than conventional delineations based on group memberships (Geox, 2011). So, the millenial approach favours an approach to inclusion that is focused on intersectionality between diversity characteristics rather than a focus on single factors.

The generation behind the millennials is that of Generation Z (born 1996–2010) and research on this generation depicts attitudes that are strikingly similar to those of the millennial generation, not least in terms of a preference for inclusive rather than autocratic management. Further details of preliminary findings regarding this generation's views on leadership can be found in Chapter 6 later on in the book.

(c) Gender

The multiple benefits that inclusive leadership can bring to organisations – described in Chapters 4–7 and 12 as well as in the case studies in Chapters 8–11 – are such that few organisations can afford to ignore this style of leadership. The twin pillars on which IL rests are transformational and servant leadership, and there is a fair amount of research evidence concerning men and women's relative propensity for the transformational style of leadership, whether as one that they exercise themselves or one that is exercised over them.

The evidence shows in fact that women appear to be more drawn to exercising transformational style of leadership than men. As mentioned in Chapter 1, one study grouping the conclusions of several studies together, a so-called meta-analysis (Eagly *et al*, 2003), concluded that 'female leaders were more transformational than male leaders in their leadership style', a conclusion echoed by studies that not only documented divergences between male and female leadership constructs (Sparrow and Rigg, 1993; Alimo-Metcalfe, 1995; Moss and Daunton, 2006) but also revealed female managers as having more transformational aspects in their leadership style than men even when rated by direct male reports (Alimo-Metcalfe, 1995).

Conversely, male leaders are said to have more transactional aspects to their leadership, in particular more of the laissez-faire and management by exception (active and passive) components of transactional leadership, contributing to the observation from both Europe and the US that men and women 'manage differently' (White, 1995; Vinnicombe and Singh, 2002; Bird and Brush, 2002).

In terms of evaluations of the quality of the leadership exercised by men and women, one study (Luthar, 1996) showed a tendency for men to ascribe higher values to men's leadership skills than to women's, and for women to do the reverse (i.e. ascribe higher values to women's leadership skills than to men's). This evidence for people's preference for the leadership styles exercised by their own gender shows the inherent difficulty in producing impartial, objective evaluations of people's leadership skills. For, women's preference for transformational leadership in others, a reflection perhaps of their preference for exersising this style of leadership style of leadership as well perhaps of their preference for this style's sensitivity to gender-sensitive micro practices (Kelan, 2015, pp. 13 and 19), is in contrast to many men's alleged preference for the exercise of transactional leadership in others.

Of course, not all men and women will share leadership preferences but if the findings of the literature are broadly correct, then it is conceivable that men and women's propensity to be appointed to leadership positions will depend on the type of leader role envisaged. Were the requirements of a leadership role to be rooted in transformational leadership, for example, then this might be a role that a greater proportion of women than men felt comfortable exercising (Moss and Daunton, 2006; Moss et al, 2010; Moss, 2014, 2015) while a greater proportion of men than women might feel comfortable carrying out a transactional role. Could this be a factor perhaps in the fact that men, currently, constitute 70% of managers and leaders in organisations in 55% of 128 countries (ILO, 2015)? Could a shift to inclusive leadership, a style that has part of its roots in transformational leadership, bring greater gender parity to the exercise of leadership (Kelan, 2015)? Only time will tell but a shift to inclusive leadership could not only boost productivity, motivation, well-being and customer centricity but also facilitate a diversity mindset that might facilitate the employment of female managers. This, (following research on men and women's propensity to transformational leadership, a component of IL) might also boost the quality of the inclusive leadership within an organisation.

(d) Societal, organisational and individual values

The enei report on inclusive leadership in eleven organisations (Moss et al, 2016; Moss, 2016) highlighted the fact that shifts in societal, organisational and individual values could lead to the favouring of inclusive over top-down leadership.

In terms of *societal* values, it was predicted that by the early years of this century short-term capitalism would give way to long-term shared stakeholder value capitalism (Porter and Kramer, 2006) and that organisational environments would face greater volatility, uncertainty, complexity and ambiguity (VUCA) (Wolf, 2007). Were these shifts in societal values to occur, it is likely that they would favour the use of inclusive over command and control leadership on the basis that an empowering form of leadership like IL is more effective than directive leadership at increasing proactive behaviours (Martin et al, 2013).

A word on these two trends. It was Porter and Kramer who coined the phrase 'creating shared value' (CSV), a phrase denoting the way that corporate objectives could be repositioned to address the challenges and needs of society and thereby create value for it. Porter and Kramer suggested that CSV would help companies focus on profits that create social benefits rather than diminish them, thereby kickstarting a positive cycle of company and community prosperity that would reconnect business with society. This would also drive the next wave of innovation and productivity growth since, so they argued, markets would be defined not just by conventional economic needs but by societal needs. Finally, CSV was presented not as a redistribution approach but as an approach to expand the total pool of economic and social value.

In terms of the trend to greater VUCA, this notion emerged from the US Army War College in the early 1990s and referred to the multilateral, volatile and uncertain world that emerged at the end of the Cold War. Fast forward two decades and following the global financial crises of 2008 and 2009, the phrase was applied to the business environment. Here, the term 'volatility' was used to describe the type, speed, volume and scale of change faced by businesses; the term 'uncertainty' was used to describe the inaccuracies of forecasting; that of 'complexity' was used to describe the widespread confusion resulting from these two factors; while the term 'ambiguity' referred to the multiple meanings within the conditions surrounding people's lives.

How would a VUCA environment affect organisations? According to a specialist consultancy focusing on leadership coaching, the behaviours needed for a VUCA environment include asking different types of questions and taking on multiple perspectives (Oxford Leadership, 2016 www.oxfordleadership.com/leadership-challenges-v-u-c-world/). These skills appear to mirror those demanded of the 'adaptive firm' that can adjust and learn better, faster and more economically than their peers. According to the BCG, the ability to be do this provides an "adaptive advantage" that typifies firms such as Apple, Google, 3M, Target and Amazon.

The BCG concept of 'adaptive' leadership consists of three elements. The first of these, distributed leadership, is a feature of inclusive leadership since it is defined as "sharing leadership at the top and developing leaders at every level". The second element is 'clear charter' – clarity of purpose – while the third is 'mutual trust', defined as the ability of people to:

> express divergent views . . . let down their guard to acknowledge when they need help . . . to fully trust each other to critique ideas within the team; . . . [to] demonstrate a willingness to listen to opposing views and perspectives and [to give everyone] equal space to express their own opinions.

This is an interesting set of elements that draws on at least two of the eleven servant leadership attributes underpinning IL, namely 'listening' and 'unqualified acceptance'. So, IL would have an important role to play in operating successfully in a VUCA environment.

In terms of *organisational* values, the need for greater innovation, greater customer-centricity and greater employee engagement has prioritised a move away from command and control leadership to something more fluid and people-focused. The attractions of IL in this regard are great given its ability to enhance employee engagement (see Chapter 5 for evidence of this) employee innovation as well as customer-centricity. One factor that can assist the delivery of innovation and customer-centricity is a diversity mindset in organisation, something that IL can encourage. Be aware though that having a diversity mindset can take an organisation beyond simply embracing the protected characteristics to embracing cognitive and experiential diversity as well. Where customer-centricity is concerned, it can be particularly helpful when the diversity mindset inside the organisation matches that of the customer and where innovation is concerned, a diversity mindset can according to one commentor (Philips, 2014) have the near-miraculous effect of:

> ......encouraging the search for novel information and perspectives, leading to better decision-making and problem solving. Diversity can improve the bottom line of companies and lead to unfettered discoveries. Even simply being exposed to diversity can change the way you think.

Moreover, the fact that Il can boost employee engagement is all-important given the multiple benefits associated with it. At the organisational level, it is responsible for great financial success. As two commentators have written (Alban-Metcalfe and Alimo-Metcalfe, 2009):

> a US survey of 24 publicly listed traded companies with a total of over 250,000 employees conducted over the last 5 years, found that the stock prices of the 11 highest morale companies increased an average of 19.4%, whilst those of other companies in the same industries increased by an average of only 8% – a margin of 240% (Sirota Survey Intelligence, 2006). In addition, a Watson Wyatt study (2005) asserts that a company with highly engaged employees typically achieves a financial performance four times greater than a company with poor employee attitudes. High job and organisation commitment, which are affected significantly by levels of engagement, also leads to reduced absenteeism and turnover. In large public sector organisations, the costs of absenteeism and of training new staff are among the highest financial burdens.
>
> *(p. 16)*

At the employee level, a sense of engagement can bring increased well-being and health, higher self-efficacy, commitment, increased self-esteem, job satisfaction and fulfilment, and reduced work-related stress (Alimo-Metcalfe and Alimo-Metcalfe, 2007). One of the authors (Alimo-Metcalfe, 2010) even writes of an increasing awareness of the role that employee engagement can play in enhancing customer satisfaction. So important are these themes that the role that IL can play in increasing employee engagement and customer centricity will be taken up again in Chapters 5 and 13 respectively.

Meanwhile, the demands of developing the knowledge economy and creating an organisation that is able to respond in an agile way to emerging markets, digital-inspired cultural change and downturns in the economy have all prioritised a leadership style that is more adaptable than a transactional style (Opportunity Now, 2014, p. 5). (*ibid*, p. 5).

It is this wide range of values that has inspired discontent with transactional leadership and led to calls for a new style of leadership to meet these needs.

Until now, regrettably, there has been no consensus on the attributes that make up IL, but it is hoped that the more rigorous definition rooted in transformational and servant leadership, and now tested empirically (see Chapters 5–7) in eleven organisations and two universities, can now permit wider application and evaluation of this style.

(e) Contextual and strategic factors

There is an important literature discussing the extent to which particular leadership styles, including participative leadership styles (of which IL has elements) are dependent on the organisational context in which they operate. We will now look at the main contextual and strategic factors discussed in this literature.

(i) Favourability

As we saw earlier in chapter 1, a study from the late 1950s, still well regarded and also available in an updated publication (Fiedler, 1994), defined the contextual conditions for participative leadership, a type of leadership that has elements of IL. One of the conditions cited concerns the nature of the relations between leader and subordinate, another to the relative degree of task structure and a third and final condition to the relative power of the leader (itself a function of the extent to which a leader delegates). In this way, Fiedler predicted that conditions favouring participative leadership would include:

- Moderate relations between leader and subordinate
- Moderate task structure
- Moderate power (i.e. some delegation takes place)

When we look at the case study examples of IL in Chapters 8–11, we will see the extent to which these factors seem to be in place or not.

(ii) Strategic factors

The academic study of business strategy has attempted to define the leadership styles that work best in different strategic contexts and this work has produced ground-breaking findings. For example, one study found that a 10% improvement in the alignment of leadership behaviour to strategy produces a 20% improvement in the clarity of direction and consequent commitment of the workforce, producing a 40% overall improvement in performance (King and Glowinkowski, 2015).

So what strategies are favoured in competitive times when organisations face greater volatility, uncertainty, complexity and ambiguity (VUCA)? Moreover, what kind of leadership style will best suit such conditions?

In terms of optimum strategies for a VUCA environment, the literature speaks of the need for organisations, in both the profit and not for profit sectors to show greater 'strategic agility' in responding to faster moving and more turbulent environments (Sambamurthy *et al*, 2003). This strategic agility is said in fact (*ibid*) to manifest in three ways: the first is as *marketing agility* – the ability to read quickly and effectively signals from complex (global and multicultural) environments; the second is as *operational agility* – the ability to quickly reconfigure elements of the value chain to respond effectively to new customers or, in the case of the not-for-profit sector, beneficiaries; and the third is as *partnering agility*, the ability to work effectively in partnerships and strategic alliances and to be sensitive to cultures as well as organisational systems and procedures.

What leadership style will best support overall concept of strategic agility? One important Danish study (Håkonsson *et al*, 2012) sheds important light on this question by defining the leadership style that can best support two sets of strategies. The first is the *explore* versus *exploit* strategy (March, 1991), reflecting an emphasis on the new as against existing strategies; the second is the older, four-option strategy of *defender, prospector, analyser* or *reactor* modes (Miles and Snow, 1978).

A word on Håkonsson *et al*'s 2012 study. The results were based on data from 407 small and medium-sized (SME) Danish manufacturing firms, so this was a pretty substantial piece of research. The findings highlighted the fact that performance losses occurred where executive style was not aligned with strategy, with correct alignment thought to be especially critical in organisations pursuing 'explore' strategies focused on change and innovation. So, it is not surprising to learn that Håkonsson *et al*'s model is considered to be one of the most enduring of the last twenty-five years (Hambrick, 2007).

The all-important model can be found in Figure 2.1 below, but before looking at it, it is worth having a good understanding of the concepts contained within it. These include March's notions of 'explore' and 'exploit' strategies– outlined briefly in the preceding paragraph – as well as Miles and Snow's four strategic positions (1978). One of these four positions, the 'defender' strategy, is one in which secure and often premium niches are controlled, producing little engagement with product market development but plentiful engagement with issues relating to operational efficiencies, stability and reliability. The 'prospector' strategy, on the other hand, prioritises engagement with new opportunities and new product-market development, while the so-called 'analyser' strategy exhibits characteristics of both defender and prospector modes, prospering through greater product-market innovation than the 'defender' mode offers but exercising more caution than the 'prospector' mode allows. Finally, the 'reactor' strategy avoids innovation and in so doing is regarded as being dysfunctional.

Short descriptions of these four positions, and the way that they relate to March's 'explore' and 'exploit' concepts are shown in Table 2.2.

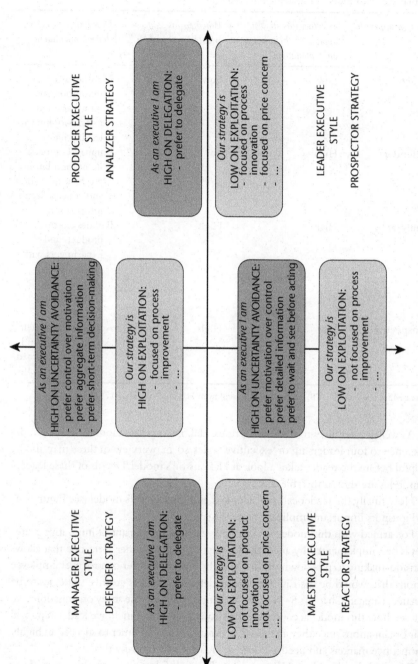

FIGURE 2.1 How leadership styles map to the strategic environment (Håkonsson *et al*, 2012)

The diagram contains the following labelled boxes:

PRODUCER EXECUTIVE STYLE / ANALYZER STRATEGY
- *As an executive I am* HIGH ON DELEGATION:
  - prefer to delegate
- *Our strategy is* LOW ON EXPLOITATION:
  - focused on process innovation
  - focused on price concern
  - ...

LEADER EXECUTIVE STYLE / PROSPECTOR STRATEGY

MANAGER EXECUTIVE STYLE / DEFENDER STRATEGY
- *As an executive I am* HIGH ON UNCERTAINTY AVOIDANCE:
  - prefer control over motivation
  - prefer aggregate information
  - prefer short-term decision-making
- *Our strategy is* HIGH ON EXPLOITATION:
  - focused on process improvement
  - ...

- *As an executive I am* HIGH ON UNCERTAINTY AVOIDANCE:
  - prefer motivation over control
  - prefer detailed information
  - prefer to wait and see before acting
- *Our strategy is* LOW ON EXPLOITATION:
  - not focused on process improvement
  - ...

- *As an executive I am* HIGH ON DELEGATION:
  - prefer to delegate
- *Our strategy is* LOW ON EXPLOITATION:
  - not focused on product innovation
  - not focused on price concern
  - ...

MAESTRO EXECUTIVE STYLE / REACTOR STRATEGY

TABLE 2.2 Four modes of strategic intervention

Strategic approach	Whether this strategic approach is high or low on exploitation	Whether this strategic orientation is high or low on exploration	Description of the strategic orientation
Reactor	Low	Low	No strategy of innovation and information; is inward-looking and lacking focus
Defender	High	Low	Emphasises process innovation but not product innovation and collects detailed information
Analyser	High	High	Refines existing products and experiments with new products, using complex information processing
Prospector	Low	High	Aggressive approach to innovation and dealing with broad information

Source: Miles and Snow (1978), adapted by A. David from Håkonsson *et al* (2012)

As well as references to strategic options, Håkonsson *et al*'s model (2012) includes reference to four leadership or 'executive' styles, so an overview of these may also be helpful before the reader takes a look at Håkonsson's model. Details of these leadership styles are shown in Table 2.3.

Now, finally, the reader can take a look at Håkonsson *et al*'s model (see Figure 2.1) and grasp its important implications for organisations:

For, armed with this model, we can now see how the pursuit of innovative strategies is best implemented by a leader adopting a so-called 'leader' style, one that allows decision-making to pass down the line, thereby ensuring looser control over employee actions than would be the case were more defensive and less creative strategies to be pursued. Later, in Chapters 8–11 when looking at the four case study organisations, we will see how this model accounts for the strong presence of inclusive leadership in all four organisations since they all follow an *explore* strategy in order to succeed in highly competitive markets and need a 'leader' approach to accompany this.

What this book adds to Håkonsson *et al*'s insightful work is a fleshing out of the leadership attributes demanded of the so-called 'leader' style that it is recommended accompany an *explore* or *prospector* strategy. This further fleshing out of the key elements in this leadership style is the subject of Chapter 5.

TABLE 2.3 Types of executive style aligning with strategic orientation

Leadership style	Whether this style is considered high or low on delegation	Whether this style is considered high or low on uncertainty avoidance	Description of the leadership style
Maestro	Low	Low	Involved closely in decision-making which can lead to bottlenecks
Manager	Low	High	Short-term, high-detail focused managers, emphasising tight control and focus
Producer	High	High	Long-term focus with much decision-making passed to subordinates but control retained by the manager
Leader	High	Low	Future, long-term focus with much decision-making and control passed to subordinates

Source: Håkonsson *et al* (2012)

References

Agathou, A. (2017). *Innovate or die*, 12 April, www.campaignlive.co.uk/article/innovate-die/1420446#IFTrEcPw8657qckm.99

Alban-Metcalfe, J. and Alimo-Metcalfe, B. (2009). Engaging leadership part one: Competencies are like Brighton pier, *The International Journal of Leadership in Public Services*, 5 (1), 10–18, https://www.realworld-group.com/files/engaging-leadership-part-1-competencies-are-like-brighton-pier-570f82cbf38fe.pdf, accessed on 14 January 2019.

Alimo-Metcalfe, B. (1995). An investigation of female and male constructs of leadership and empowerment. *Women in Management Review*, 10 (2), 3–8.

Alimo-Metcalfe, B. (2010). Developments in gender and leadership: Introducing a new inclusive model. *Gender in Management: An International Journal*, 25 (8), 630–639.

Alimo-Metcalfe, B., Alban-Metcalfe, J., Semele, C., Bradley, M. and Mariathasan, J. (2007). *The impact of leadership factors in implementing change in complex health and social care environments: NHS Plan clinical priority for mental health crises resolution teams*, www.netscc.ac.uk/hsdr/files/project/SDO_FR_08-1201-022_V01.pdf, accessed on 26 December 2017.

Alimo-Metcalfe, J. and Alimo-Metcalfe, B. (2007). The development of a private version of the (Engaging) Transformational Leadership Questionnaire (ELQ). *Leadership and Organisational Development Journal*, 28 (2), 104–121.

Alimo-Metcalfe, B. and Alban-Metcalfe, J. (2003). Leadership: A masculine past, but a feminine future? Paper presented at the *BPS Occupational Psychology Conference*, Bournemouth, 8–10 January.

Bird, B. and Brush, C. (2002). A gendered perspective on organization creation. *Entrepreneurship Theory and Practice*, 26, 41–65.

Boston Consulting Group (BCG). (2014). *Innovation in 2014*, 28 October, https://www.bcg.com/en-gb/publications/2014/innovation-in-2014.aspx, accessed on 10 January 2019

Boston Consulting Group (BCG). (2012). *Winning practices of adaptive leadership teams*, www.bcgperspectives.com/content/articles/leadership_people_management_human_resources_winning_practices_of_adaptive_leadership_teams/, accessed on 31 December 2017.

Bourke, J. and Dillon, J. (2016). *Thriving in a diverse new world*, Deloitte, April. www2.deloitte.com/insights/us/en/topics/talent/six-signature-traits-of-inclusive-leadership.html

Deloitte. (2014). *The Deloitte consumer review: The growing power of consumers*, www2.deloitte.com/uk/en/pages/consumer-business/articles/the-growing-power-of-consumers.html

Deloitte. (2015a). *Fourth millennial survey: Mind the gaps*, www2.deloitte.com/global/en/pages/about-deloitte/articles/millennialsurvey.html, accessed on 26 October 2015.

Deloitte. (2015b). *Telstra's ambition to connect everything to everyone: Transforming business through customer-centricity*, www2.deloitte.com/au/en/pages/human-capital/articles/telstras-ambition-connect-everything-everyone-transforming-business-through-customer-centricity.html

Eagly, A., Johannesen-Schmidt, M. and van Engen, M. (2003). Transformational, transactional, and Laissez-Faire leadership styles: A meta-analysis comparing women and men. *Psychological Bulletin*, 129 (4), 569–592.

Fiedler, F. E. (1994). *Leadership experience and leadership performance*. Alexandria, VA: US Army Research Institute for the Behavioural and Social Sciences.

Geox, D. (2011). *Millennials in the workplace*, Bentley University, Center for Women and Business, www.scribd.com/doc/158258672/CWB-Millennial-Report?secret_password=2191s8a7d6j7shshcctt, accessed on 4 May 2018.

Håkonsson, D., Burton, R., Obel, B. and Lauridsen, J. (2012). Strategy implementation requires the right executive style: Evidence from Danish SMEs. *Long Range Planning*, 45 (2–3), 182–208.

Hambrick, D. C. (2007). The field of management's devotion to theory: Too much of a good thing? *Academy of Management Journal*, 50 (6), 1346–1352.

Hammer, M. (1995). *Reengineering the corporation*. London: Nicholas Brealey Corporation.

Hofstede, G., Hofstede, G. J. and Minkov, M. (2010). *Cultures and organizations: Software of the mind*. 3rd edition. New York, NY: McGraw-Hill.

ILO. (2015). *Women in business and management: Gaining momentum*, www.ilo.org/global/publications/books/WCMS_316450/lang – en/index.htm, accessed on 18 August 2018.

Kelan, E. (2015). *Linchpin – men, middle managers and gender inclusive leadership*, Cranfield International Centre for Women Leaders, www.som.cranfield.ac.uk/som/dinamic-content/research/Linchpin.pdf, accessed on 30 September 2015.

Kelly, W. and Smith, C. (2014). *What if the road to inclusion were really an intersection?* Deloitte University Press, http://d27n205l7rookf.cloudfront.net/wp-content/uploads/2014/12/DUP_1003_Intersectionality_MASTER.pdf, accessed on 19 December.

King, R. and Glowinkowski, S. (2015). *The 10-20-40 opportunity – strategy, people, implementation – taking strategy to action through effective change leadership*. Panoma Press.

Kollewe, J. and Hickey, S. (2015). A third of boardroom positions should be held by women, UK firms told. *The Guardian*, www.theguardian.com/business/2015/oct/29/a-third-of-boardroom-positions-should-be-held-by-women-uk-firms-told, accessed on 31 December 2017.

KPMG. (2017). *Meet the millennials*, https://home.kpmg.com/content/dam/kpmg/uk/pdf/2017/04/Meet-the-Millennials-Secured.pdf, accessed on 31 December 2017.

Luthar, H. (1996). Gender differences in evaluation of performance and leadership ability: Autocratic vs. democratic mangers. *Sex Roles*, 35, 5–6, 337–361.

Martin, L. and Campbell, E. M. (2013). Directive versus empowering leadership: A field experiment comparing impacts on task proficiency and proactivity. *Academy of Management Journal*, 56 (5), 1372–1395.

Miles, R. and Snow, C. (1978). *Organizational strategy: Structure and process*. New York, NY: McGraw-Hill.

Moss, G. (2014). Unconscious bias as a mechanism for indirect discrimination. *Equal Opportunities Review*, 252, November, 11–12.

Moss, G. (2015). Nationality and gender-related structural and non-structural factors affecting promotion to partner in a Magic Circle Law firm. *Equal Opportunities Review*, 255, January, 17–22.

Moss, G. (2016). Inclusive leadership: Boosts engagement, productivity and organisational diversity. *Equal Opportunity Review*, 268, June, 5–8.

Moss, G. and Daunton, L. (2006). The discriminatory impact of deviations from selection criteria in Higher Education selection. *Career Development International*, 11 (6), 504–521.

Moss, G., Daunton, L. and Gasper, R. (2006). The impact of leadership selection on High Performance Working. *CIPD Professional Standards Conference*, 26–28 June, Keele University.

Moss, G., Farnham, D. and Cook, C. (2010). Women managers in Latvia: A universal footprint for the future. In Moss, G. (ed.), *Profiting from diversity*. Basingstoke: Palgrave Macmillan.

Moss, G., Sims, C., Dodds, I. and David, A. (2016). *Inclusive leadership . . . driving performance through diversity*. London: Employers Network on Equality and Inclusion.

Opportunity Now. (2014). *Inclusive leadership – from pioneer to mainstream maximising the potential of your people*, http://opportunitynow.bitc.org.uk/system/files/research/5815_executive_summary.pdf, accessed on 27 October 2015.

Oxford Leadership. (2016). www.oxfordleadership.com/leadership-challenges-v-u-c-world/, 14 September, accessed on 31 December 2017.

Philips, K. (2014). *How diversity makes us smarter*, 1 October, https://www.scientificamerican.com/article/how-diversity-makes-us-smarter/

Porter, M. and Kramer, M. (2006). Strategy and society: The link between competitive advantage and 1corporate social responsibility. *Harvard Business Review*, 84 (12), 78–92, December, https://sharedvalue.org/sites/default/files/resource-files/Strategy_and_Society.pdf, accessed on 31 December 2017.

Rosener, J. (1990). Ways women lead. *Harvard Business Review*, November/December, 119–125.

Sambamurthy, V., Bharadmaj, A. and Grover, V. (2003). Shaping agility through digital options: Reconceptualising the role of information technology in contemporary firms. *Management Information Systems Quarterly*, 27 (2).

Smith, C. (2015). *The radical transformation of diversity and inclusion: The millennial influence*, Deloitte University, https://www2.deloitte.com/content/dam/Deloitte/us/Documents/about-deloitte/us-inclus-millennial-influence-120215.pdf

Sparrow, J. and Rigg, C. (1993). Job analysis: Selecting for the masculine approach to management. *Selection and Development Review*, 9 (2), 5–8.

Vinnicombe, S. and Singh, V. (2002). Developing tomorrow's women business leaders. In Burke, R. and Nelson, D. (eds.), *Advancing women's careers*. Wikipedia entry on Internet Marketing, http://en.wikipedia.org/wiki/Internet_marketing

Watson-Wyatt Research Report. (2006). *Effective communication: A leading indicator of financial performance – 2005/2006 communication ROI study*. Ann Arbor, MI: University of Michigan.

White, J. (1995). Leading in their own ways: Women chief executives in local government. In Itzin, C. and Newman, J. (eds.), *Gender, culture and organizational change*. London: Routledge.

Yoshino, K. and Smith, C. (2013). Uncovering talent: A new model of inclusion. *Deloitte University Leadership Center for Inclusion*, December, 1–20.

Watson-Wyatt Worldwide. (2006). Effective communication: A leading indicator of financial performance – 2005/2006 communication ROI study™. London.

Wolf, D. (2007). *Prepared and resolved: The strategic agenda for growth, performance and change*. dsb Publishing.

3

TRANSACTIONAL LEADERSHIP AND ITS IMPACTS

As we saw in the first chapter, two well-known models of leadership have been in the forefront of thinking on leadership since the 1980s, namely transactional and transformational leadership. In this and the next chapter we put the spotlight on these two types of leadership, focusing on transactional leadership in this chapter and on transformational and inclusive leadership in the next. Why do we do this? Well, transactional leadership is still widespread and we need to understand what we may be jettisoning as well as gaining in moving to inclusive leadership.

So, here we look at the first of these two styles, transactional leadership, reviewing historical instances where leaders have adopted this style and then moving to the present day to hear people speak of their personal experiences of working under transactional leaders. In the next chapter, we will do the same in relation to transformational and inclusive leadership, enabling the reader to form their own views as to the merits and demerits of these two styles. First, we will hear from an unlikely source on differences between leaders' and bosses, with the concept of the 'boss' having much that is transactional about it.

Real' leaders' versus 'bosses'

The story of Harry Selfridge, the self-made American who made a great success of Selfridge's in London, is familiar to many. Spotting an opportunity to develop the western end of Oxford Street, he invested £400,000 in a new store which opened as Selfridge's in 1909. His retail genius shone through all he did, whether it was in allowing goods to be seen and touched, or using the word 'sale' to promote customer interest, or promoting the notion – then radical – of shopping as a leisure activity with encouragement offered to the customer to remain in the store by offering comfortable and attractive amenities. His wife's death in 1918 derailed Harry somewhat since it unleashed a period of womanising and gambling in which he squandered

TABLE 3.1 Transactional leadership and its attributes

Transactional attribute	What the attribute involves
Active management by exception	With the objective of monitoring the process, leaders monitor the lack of compliance with established rules and standards, and when required undertake corrective measures.
Passive management by exception	In order to manage the process, leaders intervene only in cases in which set objectives are not achieved.
Monitoring followers' performance and correcting mistakes	Little autonomy or scope for self-control is offered to followers.
Laissez-faire management	Leaders avoid making decisions, and those involved in the process relinquish all responsibilities.
Contingent reward	The recognition of achievement by rewarding efforts and good performance.

Source: Taken from Bass (1990)

much of his wealth and things eventually came to a head in 1941 when, following problems in the mid-1930s, he was asked to leave the Selfridge board.

Despite Harry's departure from the board, the Selfridge brand lived on as also his pithy thoughts on leadership where he contrasted the behaviour of 'bosses' - 'transactional' leaders *avant la lettre* - with that of 'leaders' - 'transformational and inclusive in today's terms. So, reading these aphorisms about the 'boss' will give you a sense of the transactional leadership that is the focus of this chapter.

> "The boss drives his men; the leader coaches them."
> "The boss depends upon authority; the leader on good will."
> "The boss says 'I'; the leader "we."
> "The boss fixes the blame for the breakdown; the leader fixes the breakdown."
> "The boss says 'Go'; the leader says 'Let's go'."

In more formal terms, the attributes that make up transactional leadership are shown in Table 3.1.

Did history prove Harry Selfridge right about the superiority of a leader with a coaching style to an autocratic 'boss' relying on transactional attributes? The following stories from history, followed by the opinions of present-day witnesses to transactional leadership, may help you decide. This evidence, of course, is qualitative rather than quantitative, but positivist, 'scientific' findings can be found in Chapters 5, 6 and 7 after we have looked at qualitative feedback on transformational and inclusive leadership in the next chapter.

Qualitative findings: stories from history and industry

Does a remote, non-personal style of leadership work? We present six historical examples of transactional leadership and leave the reader to decide for themselves.

Airship experiments

Our first story comes from the mid-1920s in Britain, when research into airship technology was at its height. The reward for success was tangible with the prospects of travel to India in five or six days; Egypt in two to three days; Canada in three days and Australia in ten days, cutting by half the duration of steamship travel and improving links with distant parts of the British Empire. In 1924, the British government announced a research and aviation project to establish the commercial and technical viability of giant rigid airships with work concentrated in two locations. One was in Howden, Yorkshire where the Airship Guarantee Company worked on building the R100 on a fixed-price contract with Vickers while the second was at the Royal Airship Works in Cardington, Bedfordshire with government subsidies permitting work on the R101 (Bedford Borough Council website).

Work on both projects began in 1927 and the first to complete was the R100, an orthodox airship built on known principles by an experienced team. By the time of its first flight on 17 December 1929, it was probably the fastest and finest rigid airship built in Britain, and its return flight to Montreal, Canada, on 29 July 1930 was a great success. There was now immense pressure on the Royal Airship Works in Cardington to surpass this achievement.

Trial flights of the R101 took place in 1929, early in 1930 and later on in the summer. It was already known that both the R100 and R101 were lacking in the disposable lift originally planned by the Imperial Airship Scheme in 1925 so to achieve this additional lift, R101 had a new central bay and gas bag installed. These alterations were completed by 26 September 1930 and the R101 could then be gassed up and floated in its shed. By 1 October, the first trial flight had taken place and, in the smooth flying conditions that prevailed, the only setback had been an engine cooler failure that limited the trial to 17 rather than 24 hours.

Heated debate followed as to whether a longer trial should take (something that would have been normal before a long voyage) or whether the airship should leave for Karachi without delay so as to be back in London by 20 October for the high-profile Colonial Conference. Conflicting messages emerged from the Air Ministry, with signed minutes agreeing to a "slow, cautious and progressive testing of the airship" and a note from the then Secretary of State for Air, Lord Thomson on 2 October advising that people were not to allow "my natural impatience or anxiety to start to influence you in any way. You must use your considered judgement" (Fuller, 1979). On the other hand, Lord Thomson had written a minute stating that, "I must insist on the programme of the India flight being adhered to as I have made my plans accordingly" (Wintringham, 1930).

Why the peremptory tone? Lord Thomson had plans of making a grand entrance to the Colonial Conference in London on the return leg of a successful trip by R101 to Karachi but, in the event, this was not to happen. On 4 October, the R101 crashed in gusting winds, close to Beauvais, with fifty-four men on board, forty-seven of whom, including Lord Thomson, never returned. Arguably, a different style of leadership on his part, more focused on listening to followers, might have produced a different outcome.

Hotel chain

Leona Helmsley's property portfolio was, on paper at least, the stuff of dreams. It included the Empire State Building, New York, the Park Lane Hotel, London, the Helmsley Palace Hotel and a 100-seat private jet with a bedroom attached. At its peak, Helmsley's fortune was estimated at over $5bn.

Unfortunately, dreams have a way of turning into nightmares. On one occasion, Leona refused to pay the $88,000 fees of a builder refurbishing her 27-room mansion, Dunnellen Hall, a $3m property purchased for private use with her husband in 1983. This prompted other contractors to send the *New York Post* innumerable invoices in which expensive refurbishments (a marble dance floor; a $130,000 stereo system) were charged to corporate accounts. This triggered a federal inquiry and an 18-month jail sentence.

Why did contractors betray her? The short answer is her unreasonableness. For example, after a waiter had delivered a cup of tea with a tiny amount of water on the saucer, Helmsley had got the poor man to get on his hands and knees to beg to keep his job. Another employee, a secretary who had worked at the company for eight years, had been summarily dismissed after using the Helmsley Palace dry cleaner following an accidental spillage. Not surprising then that Leona was dubbed the 'Queen of Mean' since she had demanded perfection of everyone on her payroll, whether regular employees or top managers and executives, and had treated them in an autocratic and high-handed manner. This approach, reflected in her view that "only the little people pay taxes", were intimately connected to her downfall.

Marks and Spencer

This British firm was created in 1884 when Michael Marks, a Polish refugee, opened a market stall in Leeds, with the slogan "don't ask the price, it's a penny" (Bevan, 2001). Ten years later, Marks went into partnership with Thomas Spencer, a former cashier from the wholesale company, Dewhirst, and a decade later, Marks and Spencer opened their first shop in a covered arcade in Leeds in 1904. Fast-forward to the 1920s, and the firm adopted the then revolutionary policy of buying directly from suppliers, being the first British retailer in 1934 to pioneer new fabrics in its own laboratory and, in 1948, launching a Food Technology department to work closely with suppliers, producers and farmers.

These landmarks in the firm's history are taken from the Marks and Spencer online archive 'Marks and Spencer, A short history' (Marks and Spencer website), and it is interesting to note the line drawn under events in the firm between those in the first half of the twentieth century and the appointment of Stuart Rose and Marc Bolland as CEOs in 2004 and 2009.

Why the silence? Could it be because some of Rose's predecessors had left somewhat tainted legacies? For example, Sir Richard Greenbury, appointed CEO in 1988, does not get a mention despite being a protégé of Marcus Sieff (grandson of Michael Marks) and despite being promoted to managing director in 1977 at the tender age of 41. Greenbury had come to the attention of an ageing Simon Marks when he (Greenbury) was manager of the Marble Arch store, a flagship store extending over 16,000 square metres (17,000 square feet) and the largest in the group's empire. Simon Marks was known for his aggressive style as was also Greenbury who is credited with punching a customer and having frequent tantrums when playing for the Middlesex tennis team.

Greenbury's redeeming features? He was strong on drive and crisis leadership and able to keep most external and internal stakeholders on board throughout a steady programme of change, for example when drastically reducing the number of suppliers. This resilience pushed M&S into the limelight in 1998 as the ninth largest company in Britain, and the second most profitable retailer in the world after Wal-Mart in the world. Moreover, for every year that Greenbury had been in charge, M&S held more than twice the clothing market of any other high street name, resulting in profits exceeding £1 billion by May 1997. This stratospheric performance was repeated in 1998 making M&S the first British retailer to achieve pre-tax profits in excess of £1 billion (*The Telegraph*, 1998). Reaching this target had been Greenbury's personal aim for some time, so why the silence in the M&S online archive regarding his leadership?

The reality is that Greenbury's leadership style had grown increasingly autocratic over the years, isolating him from other staff, producing risky decision-making and inhibiting the development of his executive team. His strong focus on results had had a number of unfortunate consequences such as directors unwilling to challenge him (one later admitted that he ruled by fear) and store managers feeling obliged to bury bad news. Moreover, one of the factors that had produced pre-tax profits of £1bn had been a reduction in staff headcount, through natural wastage, of 5,000 people, a loss that depleted the know-how and tacit knowledge in the firm. Moreover, suppliers had been asked to cut their margins in a drastic way and journalists were strongly rebuked by Greenbury not only for writing about M&S but also for getting anything wrong (the company had a policy of no communications with the press). What is more, Greenbury thought that his judgement was infallible, something that may explain the words embroidered on a cushion in his office: "I have many faults, but being wrong is not one of them".

In fact, Greenbury's intransigence and autocratic leadership style were to prove his undoing. According to one of his secretaries, he had no idea how he came across and if he lost an argument, would seek revenge, thriving as he did on combat. Moreover, his judgement may not have been as sharp as he thought since he failed to spot changes in clothing trends and expectations of a more exciting shopping experience, a problem compounded by a "monolithic" corporate culture (Mellahi *et al*, 2002, p. 25) that discouraged commercial flair, rewarding conformity and sycophancy instead. Other problems related to the lack of new blood, a tendency for existing managers to protect themselves, and retail policies that preserved the UK's monopoly on product sourcing (Mellahi, 2002).

All these problems came to a head between 1998 and 2001 when pre-tax profits declined from £1.15 billion to £0.14 billion. During this period, the firm's share of the UK clothing market collapsed from 13.9% in 1997 to 10.9% in 2000, and the share price fell from a high of £6.60 in October 1997 to a low of £1.70 in October 2000(Mellahi, 2002).

The moral of the story? More inclusive and less autocratic leadership would have allowed good ideas to filter up from employees and customers to the board-room, facilitating more informed and better decision-making. As it was, as one insider remarked, entering the boardroom was like entering another world since the board 'lived in a world of its own' (Mellahi, 2002, p. 24).

Sunbeam Corporation

Overlapping with Greenbury's reign at Marks and Spencer was that of Albert J. Dunlap at Sunbeam, a homeware products manufacturer in the US. Dunlap became chief executive officer in 1996 and wasted no time in stamping his autocratic style of leadership on the company. In his twenty-month stint, he was responsible for indiscriminate across-the-board firings resulting in the loss of 11,000 people, the equivalent of 40% of the workforce. While these draconian moves improved the bottom line – much as the loss of staff did temporarily at M&S during the reign of Greenbury – the loss of talent meant that the company faced erosion of value and long-term decline. So, after Dunlap was asked to leave in June 1998, the company filed for bankruptcy a few years later in 2001. The *sobriquets* of "Chainsaw Al" and "Rambo in pinstripes" would follow Dunlap right up to his death in January 2019 even though the Sunbeam Corporation no longer existed.

The lesson? Autocratic leadership and taking the knife to staff jobs can suck the very lifeblood from an organisation.

Royal Bank of Scotland

In 2007, the Royal Bank of Scotland (RBS) was a commercial colossus that pro-duced hourly profits of £1 million and an operating profit of £10.3 billion, mak-ing it the fifth largest bank in the world. Then, in 2008, the bank collapsed with a declared loss of £28 billion, the biggest loss in British corporate history. The British government bailed out the bank to the tune of £46 billion.

Just as we saw at M&S and Sunbeam, there was an autocrat at the helm. This was Fred Godwin, a man who micromanaged staff and even designed the company's Christmas card yet remained oblivious to the bank's excessive exposure to toxic loans. Not surprisingly perhaps since the top person shapes the culture of an organ-isation (Schein, 1996), his dictatorial style filtered right down to lower levels and, at the beginning of 2018, a memo came to light from 2009 (Burton, 2018), the year of the bail-out, in which a manager at the Global Restructuring Group (GRG) had provided directives on how customers should be treated. The manager responsible had written, "Rope: Sometimes you need to let customers hang themselves. You have gained their trust and they know what's coming if they fail to deliver".

At the time, thousands of small companies were struggling to survive the recession that followed the financial meltdown caused by RBS and its fellow banks, and those struggling to repay debts to the lender were directed to the GRG. Theoretically, the GRG was there to help them get back on their feet but the memo tells a very different story. For, it encourages RBS staff to lumber companies with sanctions and ratchet up monthly fees if the companies are unable to settle their bills. The language of the memo is unforgiving in its instruction to "deliver monthly fees or else" and to sign customers up for deals that "they cannot afford" so that penalty costs can be imposed. As if this is not bad enough, the memo encourages staff to pressure owners into signing documents since "if they sign, they can't complain". To add insult to injury, it adds that "missed opportunities will mean missed bonuses".

This note came to light in January 2018 under pressure from the UK Government's Select Committee Inquiry Chairman, Nick Morgan and RBS's current boss, Ross McEwan, defended the bank by stating that the memo had been written by a junior manager, now an ex-employee. Moreover, he stated that the note had only been circulated around three GRG offices and that it did not reflect bank policy or guidance. RBS then launched a £400m compensation scheme for mistreated GRG customers – a massive 92% of eligible businesses apparently – and since at its peak, the GRG was handling 16,000 companies, thousands of entrepreneurs and family owners will have been affected by the RBS's mistakes.

Just imagine how different this might all have been had the person at the top adopted an inclusive rather than transactional approach to leadership.

Vivendi

Of course, autocratic leaders are not the exclusive preserve of the Anglo-Saxon world. French utility company General des Eaux was controlled by Jean-Marie Messier, who turned it into a media empire through the acquisition in 2000 of Canal Plus and Seagram (then owner of Universal and Universal Studios). This string of deals carried a price tag of £100bn, and it was not long before the French multi-media giant Vivendi experienced massive losses. In 2002, Messier was ousted from the company and in 2014 received a suspended ten-month jail sentence for the multi-million pay-off that he received when forced to resign from the company. For, the 'golden parachute' that he received was said to have included 18.6m euro severance pay and a chauffeur for his wife.

Given the *penchant* for attributing soubriquets to Albert Dunlap at Sunbeam, it is not surprising that Jean-Marie was known as 'Jean-Marie Messier Moi-même, maître du monde', m*aster of the world*!

Looking back at autocratic leaders

How common is poor leadership? According to the US Center for Creative Leadership study, 50% of leaders and managers are estimated to be "ineffective, incompetent or a mis-hire" (Alasadi, n.d.). The same article reports on a survey by 14,000 HR professionals in the US in which only 26% of respondents rated the quality of leadership in their company as excellent or very good. Moreover, in the specific instance of the public sector, a US-wide poll conducted in 2012 (the National Leadership Index (NLI)) by the Center for Public Leadership at the Harvard Kennedy School and the Merriman River Group found that in only two sectors measured in the year's report – military and medical – did the leaders receive above-average confidence scores. Ratings for the remaining eleven sectors surveyed remained or fell into the below-average range (*ibid*).

Of course, the US does not have a monopoly on ineffective managers. On the other side of the pond, in the UK, a study by the Department for Business, Innovation and Skills (2012) showed that nearly three-quarters (72%) of organisations in England reported a deficit of management and leadership skills. The same survey noted that managers of nearly two-thirds (65%) of respondent organisations reported senior managers to be deficient in management and leadership skills.

Factors underlying autocratic leadership

Understanding the deficits in leadership in the UK and elsewhere has been a preoccupation of Christine Porath, a Business Professor at Georgetown University, who has documented a steady decline in civility in the US workplace. So, in a 1998 survey, just a quarter of those surveyed reported being treated rudely at least once week at work, a figure that rose to nearly half in 2005 and to over half in 2011 (2015). While Porath was documenting this increase in incivility in the US, researchers at INSEAD in France, Petriglieri and Petriglieri (2015), were mapping a shift from leadership as a cultural enterprise to one with a more intellectual or commercial basis, something that they term the "dehumanization of leadership". In fact, according to the INSEAD researchers, much modern leadership "distances aspiring leaders from their followers and institutions, resulting in a disconnect between their inner and outer worlds" (Petriglieri and Petriglieri, 2015).

Other signs of poor leadership have been documented by Robert Sutton, Professor of Management at Stanford University and author of *The No-Asshole Rule: Building a Civilized Workplace and Surviving One That Isn't* (2008). According to him, there are two tell-tale signs of toxic leadership:

- people feeling oppressed, humiliated or otherwise worse after meeting this leader than before
- people less powerful than the leader being targeted by that person

On reading this, you might ask whether there are specific personality features that predispose people to this more distant style of leadership? According to Dotlich and Cairo, authors of *Why CEOs Fail: The 11 Behaviors That Can Derail Your Climb to the Top and How To Manage Them* (2003), and Finkelstein, author of *Why Smart Executives Fail* (2013), underlying traits include *hubris, ego* and a lack of emotional intelligence. Meanwhile, according to research in the Netherlands (Nevicka *et al*, 2011), narcissism may also be a factor. For, despite the fact that narcissistic leaders appear to be effective – in large measure due to their displays of authority – the reality is that they inhibit information exchange and so can have a negative impact on group performance. Then, just a few years later, fresh research (Williams, 2017) identified a new set of the behaviours and attitudes that typified toxic leaders and these included management by exception behaviours (an element of transactional leadership), an absence of concern for employee well-being and an absence of empathy. He wrote a short essay in fact summarising his thoughts on modern "predatory plutocrats" (2016), and this is definitely worth a read.

Autocratic leaders and their impacts on people

We have looked at the behavioural characteristics of autocratic and transactional leaders and the $64,000 question relates to their likely impact on the organisations and environments in which they work.

In terms of impacts on health, research at the Stress Institute in Stockholm (Nyberg, 2009) involving more than 3,100 men in typical work settings over a ten-year period found that employees with managers who were incompetent, inconsiderate, secretive and uncommunicative were 60% more likely to suffer a life-threatening cardiac condition or heart attack than employees with 'good' leaders who were 40% less likely to suffer heart problems.

Where impact on the organisation as a whole is concerned, one study (Chaterjee and Hambrick, 2007) found that narcissistic leaders were most likely to produce either big wins or big losses, suggesting that employing autocratic leaders is something of a high-risk strategy. Charles A. O'Reilly and colleagues, in the US, moreover, found that narcissistic leaders tended to receive higher remuneration than less narcissistic CEOs, a reality that could reduce staff morale and cause talent to leave the organisation (2014). What is more, Sutton's research (2008) shows the extent to which abusive bosses can reduce productivity and long-term profitability, a factor that leads him to take issue with high-tech leaders and many in Silicon Valley who unreservedly extol the virtues of former CEO of Apple, Steve Jobs, a man whose behaviour often led to tears and difficult times for employees. In the words of former Apple PR Chief Laurence Clavere, for example, the experience of working with Steve Jobs was "incredibly challenging, incredibly interesting. It was also sometimes incredibly difficult" (Elkind, 2008). So, although some have described the combative side of Steve Jobs as necessary to building a successful company, Sutton challenges the notion that if you're a winner, it's okay to be "an asshole" (Sutton, 2008).

Of course, investigating the impact of autocratic leadership on individuals and organisations is methodologically challenging, not only because other variables may affect a situation but also because there is no easy way of knowing how things might have transpired had leaders managed in a less autocratic way. So, short of turning the clock back, we have to rely on the findings of academics as well as those who have been at the receiving end of autocratic leadership and can vouch for its effects in an objective way. Having now looked at the academic findings, it remains to look at the individual experiences of those who have personally experienced autocratic or 'transactional' leadership in the public or private sectors. Their thoughts were gathered in 2017 with the promise of anonymity in order to assure honesty of response, and each response is presented in full, in unabridged form, in order to preserve the unique richness of individual responses.

You will see that after each person's thoughts, a short discussion appears with all the points pulled together in a conclusion. In terms of sequence, we begin with the private sector and then move to the public, where you might expect more traditional, in other words more autocratic and transactional leadership.

Qualitative findings: interview feedback

The *verbatim* comments of twelve people follow, all expressing vividly what it feels like to work under leaders who are transactional in their style (Bass, 1985; Bass and Avolio, 1990). As the reader will know by now, this is a style in which leadership is exercised in a distant way with leaders interacting with followers largely only to follow up on objectives, and then intervening only when things go wrong. So, it is very much a style that is 'hands off', demonstrating what is known as 'management by exception'.

What is lacking in this type of leadership is any sense that management is there to get to know people as individuals and support them in achieving their tasks. On the contrary, individuals are known purely in relation to their ability to reach targets, with the whole thrust of management focused around this. By way of reminder, the main attributes associated with this style were previously shown in Table 3.1.

The main question put to respondents related to how it felt to work under a leader who operated with a transactional style of leadership. In terms of the selection of respondents, this was done through a process known as 'snowballing', where initial respondents can select others for interview. So, in this case, we started with respondents who had a background in Human Resources Management and they then suggested the names of other people who might be able to offer their views. Conveniently, this produced the names of people working in both the public and private sectors, and you can read the thoughts of those working in the private sector first. As you will see, all accounts are written in the first person with respondent's thoughts quoted *verbatim*, and brief comments following afterwards in order to highlight particular points of interest.

Respondents from the private sector

Diversity and inclusion consultant, formerly HR director within a large British international paints and chemicals company

"The manager with the transactional leadership style was the personnel manager for the Organics Division within the company where I worked and I reported directly to him. He took very little interest in what I was about and I found that very demotivating. My job title was organisation development manager for the division and I got no development support from him since I never received feedback from him except if I had done something wrong or perhaps said something that was out of place.

I was a young man, keen and ambitious and received no development support from him, ever. Basically, I just found him very demotivating. It didn't affect my work because I had a very good relationship with the chief executive who was a very inclusive leader and it is possible that the manager was jealous of the excellent relationship that I had with the CEO.

At one point, I had an inclusive leader and this was the works manager at one of the company's factories. He worked with me to develop a vision of success for the factory and he gave me enormous scope to contribute in delivering that. This felt terrific and so I was highly motivated, delivering great results. I worked above and beyond and far exceeded what I thought I was capable of and all because Bill developed a vision of success, took an interest in how I was delivering and also supported me in these endeavours."

Comment: these comments illustrate the demotivating impact of the hands-off, 'management by exception' approach to people management found in transactional leadership and the contrasting, more motivating impact of a more inclusive approach. From a strategic point of view, the personnel manager may have been using a leadership style that had a place in stable times when a 'defender' strategy and 'manager' approach to leadership will have had a greater role to play than in more modern, competitive times (see 'Strategic factors' in Chapter 2). Even if we discount the strategic context, however, it could be said that the 'defender' strategy (Miles and Snow, 1978) practised by the personnel manager would not have been as effective as the 'producer' approach practiced by the works manager, since the latter offered developmental opportunities through its emphasis on delegation (Håkonsson et al, 2012).

Diversity and inclusion manager in the transport sector

"In my working life, I have worked with more people who have demonstrated transactional than inclusive leadership. In my experience, the 'active management by exception' element encourages risk aversion because you know that corrective measures will be taken if you fail. Moreover, you sense that those who display 'passive management by exception' intervene only because of a weakness in their capability or because of a lack of confidence.

In a general sense, once you are aware of being monitored, you do not feel prepared to have a go, to innovate, to produce new ideas since the context is so restricting and you sense that you are not really growing. In a transactional culture, there is also an impression that leaders are avoiding decision-making, often producing a laissez-faire environment in which the stronger followers can take over. This can lead to a situation in which power is wielded in ways that are at odds with the formal authority and in ways that can lead to a bullying environment. One of the consequences is that in a team where the leader doesn't seem to care, strong characters can start to set the direction to their benefit and if you don't follow them, it can lead to bullying and harassment.

As far as 'contingent reward' is concerned, basing financial rewards on results can lead to unfairness. Some employees, for example, may tend to get rewarded more than others and some may get rewarded for things that are not necessarily appropriate. For example, I have known people who have given their all and not got recognised and some who have done little and been rewarded. Unless contingent reward is delivered appropriately, and it often is not, it can lead to a deficit in effort since people think 'why should I bother'. This can have a dramatic and negative effect on output.

So, the overall effect of transactional management? Employees can feel restrained and be less open than with inclusive managers. What is more, transactional leadership can impact on your personal life and well-being since you may feel less confident and less valued and sense that you are not able to grow and progress."

Comment: this manager's experience is that transactional leadership stunts individuals' growth both inside and outside of work. Although the industry in which he works currently had a 'defender' strategy, he works within a function that prioritises 'Best Practice human relations', so his comments reflect a tension between strategic best fit (see 'Strategic factors' in Chapter 2) and best fit from a human point of view.

Director of sales in one of the UK's largest internal sales organisations (recently privatised)

"What does it feel like to work under a transactional leader? In a way, it can be good for certain kinds of employee since you are being told what to do and you don't need to accept responsibility for your actions. This means that you can say 'I delivered what you wanted me to deliver but it hasn't worked' so it does have its good points if that is the kind of person that you are but if you are not, it's tremendously frustrating.

Industry used to be run in this way and one factor was that, in some big public sector organisations, generals and colonels were in positions of leadership with an ex-colonel being one of my former bosses for example. The legacy is seen in the language of 'leave' rather than 'holidays', and 'duties' rather than 'responsibilities', all dating back to before the Second World War. I joined this organisation in 1978 and it is difficult to try and change this transactional culture.

It can feel very frustrating to work under transactional leaders. It feels as if you are just a number, not empowered, and that your leader does not really care about you as a person, just someone who has met the metrics and then metrics that you have not agreed. I used to be like this as a leader and used to leave my brain at home since, because you were being told what to do, you didn't need to have it with you. I was just giving 25% of myself.

If your particular manager has this transactional style of leadership, then it is likely that most of the other leaders in the organisation will be working in a similar way. They are reinforcing a way of working in which you leave your brain at home and in which managers adopt a laissez-faire attitude. Under transactional leadership, you are not being inspired to bring the whole of you to the job and you are generally operating at a level below where you should. One reason is that transactional leaders like to work at a level that they feel comfortable with and this is often at your level, so they push you down to a lower level than you are capable of. If, by contrast, you stretch yourself into the next space then you have to be challenging and push the person who is in that space to move up. So it sometimes becomes more comfortable to go down a space."

Comment: the respondent's opinion and experience is that transactional leaders can greatly reduce the productivity, creativity and growth of individuals. This particular respondent works for an organisation that has shifted from an 'analyser' to a 'prospector' strategy, with norms of leadership moving from that of 'producer' to a that of a 'leader' as defined by Håkonsson et al, 2012. Both types of leadership place the emphasis on delegation, but as we saw in Chapter 2, a 'leader' style will work best within a context of an organisation that has an 'explore' rather than 'exploit' strategy, and a 'low uncertainty avoidance' rather than 'high uncertainty avoidance' context.

Senior sales leader in a recently privatised organisation working under the sales director whose views are shown above

"The monitoring and correcting element that is part of transactional leadership gives rise to micro-management and a blame culture as well. In this way, instead of being picked up for the positive things that you have done, you are picked up for the things that went wrong. An organisation with transactional leadership is very much a manager-led organisation in which managers tell employees what to do so the organisation loses a lot of employees' thought processes since they are merely acting on what they have been told to do.

At one point, I worked for a director that made people so scared of him that people did all that they could to please him. At one point, though nervous about doing this, I put an idea forward only to have it dismissed. I realised that what he says goes and that I just needed to fit around this person. Then I moved into a creative agency within the same organisation until I moved into the Sales area that I am in now. At that stage, Sales was run on a command and control basis and then things started to change."

Comment: according to this person's experience, transactional leadership can block the creative flow of ideas within an organisation. The respondent is working in the same organisation as the immediately preceding respondent, so working for an organisation that has moved from an 'analyser' to a 'producer' and then 'prospector' mode following privatisation of the organisation (see 'Strategic factors' in Chapter 2).

Railways manager in an engineering role

"I have worked in the railway industry for the last ten years and the department I work in functions under a system of transactional leadership. My role within the company is to renew and maintain the infrastructure that the train service relies upon every day with safety as a top priority, since the railway environment can be very dangerous both for the public and for employees. In order to keep everyone safe, strict rules and regulations need to be adhered to and each member within the department needs not only to know their roles and responsibilities but also to perform their job efficiently. The company cannot allow an employee to fail in their role since this could have catastrophic consequences and a transactional style of leadership is required in order to ensure that each individual undertakes their jobs in a safe and professional manner."

Comment: this railways manager highlights the positive role that transactional leadership can play in an environment in which rules and regulations need to be adhered to. The technical part of the railways industry has the characteristics of a 'defender' industry with a focus on secure and often premium niches and operational efficiencies, stability and reliability but little engagement with product market development (Miles and Snow, 1978). According to research (Håkonsson et al, 2005), the optimal leadership style in a sector with a 'defender' strategy is a 'manager' style (Håkonsson et al, 2012), with managers focused on the short-term detail – rather than the big picture – and tight control.

Senior consultant in diversity and inclusion

"The appropriateness of transactional leadership is dependent on the sector and type of work that people do.

In a production line and military context, the transactional style is probably more suitable than inclusive leadership. However, in a modern knowledge economy in which most of us now work as knowledge workers, the transactional model is problematic. Not only is it less relevant for structural reasons but also because it fails to understand the factors that motivate individuals in relation to their work. In this respect, Daniel Pink has marshalled academic findings to show that rewards, by their very nature, narrow people's focus, something that is helpful when there is a clear path to a solution but an obstacle when problems are complex. For, rewards narrow down people's thinking and stop them from seeing new ways of thinking. What people want, according to Pink's study of the academic literature on motivation, is a sense that managers value their opinions and this will not come from transactional leadership.

I say this having had experience of working with transactional leaders in the context of knowledge working, an environment that doesn't demand this kind of leadership. Why do I say this? Knowledge workers tend to be passionate about their job and the presence of transactional management, often more questioning than encouraging, can constrain their ideas. Being at the receiving end of transactional leadership can be disempowering with a negative effect on motivation, and this kind of leadership prompted me to leave various places of work. After a while, transactional leadership becomes the straw on the camel's back since transactional leaders are a constant drain on energy and, even if you are quite resilient, you can only cope with this for a while. Of course, you could argue that if you have lots of autonomy, the impact of transactional leadership is less severe but even if you have autonomy, there is still this constant sense of a manager who is not there but is there, not in a supportive way but in a 'why are we doing this' sort of way.

There is an idea that if the working environment offers you a lot of autonomy, this can free you up from the command and control structure and the worst effects of transactional management. However, if the manager doesn't support you, then this style of leadership can affect how you feel about your work. Even if you have lots of autonomy, you still want the sense that the manager is backing and supporting you and that you are on the same page. However, what you are getting with a transactional manager is pretty hit and miss.

Fundamentally, we are dealing with a clash between the character of transactional leaders and that of most knowledge workers. If transactional leaders are managing people who are of similar style to themselves it won't be a problem, but most knowledge workers will have a different style to transactional managers and then it will be a problem. Many transactional managers, of course, think that they are there to give direction to knowledge workers, but that doesn't work anymore since knowledge workers don't want to be dictated to – they want to share their ideas and take ownership of projects. If a transactional manager is not able to flex their style, it becomes problematic and you then get disengagement with people either leaving or, if they stay, mentally checking out. What knowledge workers want is to be treated as adults where in fact the transactional style of leadership has an adult–child element to it.

Most of the managers I have worked with have been transactional managers, although I did have a manager who was transformational and having a leader with this style had a very positive impact on people's psychology and motivation. In terms of actions, the manager was interested in involving people, asking for ideas, making people feel part of the team and involved, and having a manager who was encouraging and supportive of your ideas had a spiral effect and made you work harder. A lot of leaders don't have the human touch or a human mind-set and they actually don't value these things. In fact, they see inclusive leadership as soft and fluffy and criticise this style because it does not match theirs."

Comment: this expert on diversity and inclusion makes the point that there is likely to be a clash between transactional leaders who are looking to impose structure and control and knowledge workers who are looking to expand the boundaries and innovate. So, if we reframed this in the language of strategy, we see a knowledge worker seeking to work within a 'prospector' environment all the while being controlled by leaders who are working with a 'defender' or 'reactor' mind-set. The effect of this mismatch is to demotivate the knowledge worker who may 'mentally check out' or actually leave an organisation.

Vice-president of a well-being institute

"I have worked under several transactional leaders in the course of my career and you don't always see all five competencies identified by Bass (1990) manifesting at the same time. My feelings about individual attributes follow with my impressions not always being based on the same job."

Active management by exception (AMBE)

"When I have worked under leaders who used active management by exception, I tended to end up feeling somewhat lonely and stressed knowing that I was probably quite alone and that, if I strayed from my objectives, someone else would walk in and take over my job. It would have been preferable if I could have felt that someone was regularly by my side rather than someone there for a short span of time to undertake corrective measures.

The feeling of being looked over is not a great deal of fun to me. My own management style is far more consultative so that, if you fall over, I'll pick up the mess. For this reason, I tend to prefer the second transactional competence, that of *passive management by exception*, a style that might be particularly appreciated by new recruits although longer-term employees may find it stressful. For, I've personally always found the monitoring of followers to be stifling and have always felt that if one can't trust other people to perform, one should not recruit them in the first place.

In the last few years, I have understood through the work of Deci and Ryan (2000) how important autonomy is in fostering creativity and engagement in other people. According to my understanding of their work, Deci and Ryan are responsible for modern 'self-determination theory' according to which people respond to autonomy and self-determination in ways that are consistent with their internal interests. So, providing people with autonomy over time fosters creativity and allows people healthier interpersonal relations, since they will sense that they can act consistently with their personally held interests and values.

The positive attributes of autonomy discussed in Deci and Ryan resonate with Western philosophy and the thinking in Aristotle's *Nicomachean Ethics* (350 BC) where *eudaimonia* (meaning 'happiness' or 'flourishing') is said to be closely tied to a person's ability to make decisions and have autonomy. According to Aristotle, autonomy will lead someone to take actions that are consistent with self-fulfilment, satisfaction, purpose and meaning in life so, like Deci and Ryan, Aristotle thought that happiness was best attained through autonomy rather than constraint.

It should be said that passive management by exception, like active management by exception, can also feel lonely. However, when line management is not simply monitoring a person's success or failure to achieve objectives, it can feel less stressful since it is nice to have someone to bounce ideas off."

Laissez-faire management

"This type of management is just ghastly, isn't it? In a system of 'laissez-faire management', one doesn't necessarily have the authority to make decisions and if managers don't make decisions either then nothing gets done. This is very disengaging and people working within this system wonder what the point of it all is. Do the managers care? Is it my fault? Is it their fault? These questions lead to a vicious circle of doubt and uncertainty."

Contingent reward

"Contingent reward is there to reward effort and performance but one can make a great deal of effort and the performance may still not be good. The norm is to reward objective-based measures of performance that are a mixture of personal, team and organisational objectives. Contingent reward is part of the *quid pro quo* of organisational life and they can be people and/or behaviour-based as well as based on performance."

Comment: the respondent has a view of transactional leadership that is negative overall since he regards it as reducing creativity and well-being, making it unsuitable for 'explore', 'analyser' and 'prospector' organisations in which priority is placed on the development of new products and services. In the view of this respondent, transactional leadership is unlikely to have a positive impact in today's modern competitive environments.

Director in the property sector speaking of corporate experience in the real estate and banking sectors

"During my time in the 1980s at an international real estate advisory firm, the business was led by partners who were dominant and male and you were fundamentally an apprentice doing what you were told. It was a highly disciplinary approach in which you were led more by fear and in an atmosphere where it was acceptable for a partner to tell you to get a haircut. These bosses were driving around in Aston Martins, were all males and were perceived as 'gods' in the industry. There was a strong regimented all-male culture and plenty of 'work hard, play hard' attitude and very few women in executive positions.

There were positives and negatives about this leadership style. On the negative side, it was clearly dogmatic and you made little contribution at junior levels to the growth or aspirations of the company since that aspect of the business was controlled by the partners. On the positive side, you did very well so long as you did what you were told. The system was monitored through active management by exception and you did not need to apply any particular creativity in order to be judged as doing well.

In 1989, when I questioned the growth forecast in the business plan, a sense of disconnectedness with the prevailing thinking emerged and I felt that I needed to leave to join a more 'inclusive' business. My questioning distanced me from the prevailing 'group think' and I was no longer perceived to be a fully committed team member despite having been promoted to 'salaried' partner level.

I moved to the compliance-conscious world of investment banking and fund management. Up until 1987, there was a traditional approach to city investment which was more in the passive management by exception (MBE) category than in that of active MBE. The 'City' was a club, a gentleman's club, in which people forged long-term careers through rules of conduct and a certain reputation developed over time. Then, Big Bang and the globalisation of markets made it possible for people to behave in a different way to city 'gents', bringing opportunities for people to behave badly. The big global investment banks dictated the pace and their changing 'culture' created the environment in which 'bad behaviour' flourished, a factor that led ultimately to the collapse of Lehman's in 2007. The pendulum gradually swung to active MBE since there was a sense that people could not be trusted otherwise to perform.

The consequence? The compliance departments were dubbed the 'Business Prevention Units' and if you were driven by the desire to succeed, the culture was enormously frustrating. Every time you opened your mouth, you were seen as letting people as well as the system down. The parent bank realised that they needed to shift from passive MBE to active MBE and in the late 1980s took over and pursued the American post-1987 Big Bang dream of globalised, cross-border transactions. Then in 1995, after major internal disruption, the parent bank ran the private bank more actively. Suddenly, the customer became irrelevant and the focus shifted to trading the customer's money across borders in order to create a large bonus pool for the senior people in the parent bank. This was the 'contingent reward' aspect of transactional leadership, and the bigger you were in the organisation, the more clout you had.

In the mid to late 1990s, the parent bank destroyed a very capable team of people. So, in 2003, after working for the private bank for a period of 14 years, I decided to leave since working there had become massively dis-incentivising. I had experienced a period during which leadership changes happened frequently as a result of corporate acquisitions, mergers or a new leader jetted in. Typically, the new leaders would begin by trying to change everything that they felt would not help their bonus pot. So, they would question how things worked even if the reasons behind their questioning, and the changes that would follow this, would affect customers.

How to react? In a culture like this, you have limited time in which to make a case to these senior leaders since they are invariably flying long-distance in order to ensure that their Gold Card is restored! When eventually you get to see them, you are perceived as parochial and annoying since you are not there to discuss how to purchase a Japanese trading pot. Incidentally, bosses could be on £10m bonuses.

The more I reflected, the more I realised that big business is typically made up of small incentivised groups of senior people who need to achieve people's buy-in at the departmental level. So, mistrust developed between the two levels which in time turned to cynicism and battening down the hatches, with people essentially giving up on making any contribution to the organisation.

Looking back, I would say that transactional leadership has the following two characteristics:

- it facilitates the survival of people who are not interested in the business, but use their time there to implement personal objectives for growth
- it demands that many people are employed to monitor the performance of employees to ensure that they don't make mistakes, thereby preserving the bonus pots of senior personnel.

Over a period of 14 years at the bank, I had developed a business that delivered £5m in profit each year to the bank. In 2008, this business was given away for £1.00! By that point, I had left the bank but the experience left me feeling that 14 years had gone up in smoke and that a lot of good effort had been wasted. This all goes to show the way in which a business and a brand can destroy itself through its leadership system. It was also a reflection of the prevailing transactional style of leadership even though the bank had some sub-leaders for whom I had huge regard."

Comment: the bank appears to have been adopting a 'defender' strategy with a significant emphasis on exploitation and uncertainty avoidance, and minimal emphasis on delegation. So while the transactional leadership described here may be considered 'best fit' for a defender strategy, we can see the extent to which this style of leadership, even in a defender context, can stifle morale and initiative. The experience painted here of working life in the bank suggests that an overt move to a 'prospector' strategy could have provided a glue that held together the work of people at different levels.

Respondents from the public sector

Views were collected from four respondents, three from British universities and one from the British Civil Service, with senior leadership in universities appearing to be transactional and that in the Civil Service increasingly considerate of its impact on employees.

Pro-vice-chancellor in a Russell Group university

What type of leadership is exercised in universities?

"Over time, universities have shifted between inclusive and transactional leadership. When there were fewer external metrics and institutions were smaller, they were run on the basis of trust but as organisations became bigger, all sorts of inequalities emerged. The need to respond to issues such as workload, equality and diversity (including the Athena Swan initiative) as well as initiatives such as the Research Exercise Framework (REF, the system for comparing British universities' research output) and Teaching Excellent Framework (TEF, the system for comparing British universities' teaching quality) has made university leadership increasingly transactional. This move has been inevitable not only because of outside pressures but also because of inside pressures to ensure fairness and equality in relation to staff workloads for example.

A while ago, Hirschman (1970) detailed the options facing employees at failing institutions with these including 'exit' (leaving the organisation), 'voice' (speaking up about issues) and 'loyalty' (remaining with the organisation) with the relative priority accorded to the 'exit' and the 'loyalty' routes influenced by subject discipline. For example, academic staff in Business and Economics may view their publications as 'currency' and a bargaining tool in pay negotiations both in the course of employment and when seeking new employment. In terms of management response, this is often transactional rather than inclusive in character on account of the subject under discussion."

What does it feel like to work in an organisation with transactional leaders?

"Working under a transactional leader encourages people to think in terms of working-to-rule and not much more than that. There's an exchange with the employer providing the salary and the employee providing the work and this can be quite boring for an employee. You just do as you're told and that's that. On the plus side, you tend to get clarity about expectations and what you are supposed to be doing but on the negative side, you have a sense of being of less value than you might be in an inclusive environment since you perceive that your whole being has been reduced to key performance indicators (KPIs). With a less transactional leader, you might perceive yourself to be of greater value.

In my experience of work, I have often found transactional leadership to be common where the management of lower grade jobs is concerned and less commonly the case where higher level jobs are concerned. In this second case, people's work tends to operate as part of a team approach and decision-making tends to be more inclusive and, in terms of motivation, this inclusive environment often stops people from counting the hours."

Comment: this respondent describes the increasingly transactional style of leadership in British universities, something that he describes as having a de-motivating impact on colleagues. In fact, as we saw in Chapter 2, a transactional style is best suited to organisations operating under threat and adopting a 'defender' strategy, and it is strange that the university in question should be adopting this style of leadership since it is a member of the relatively privileged Russell Group of universities, so in a comfortable position and not under immediate threat. Moreover, Russell Group universities are research-intensive, and the literature on knowledge management emphasises the importance of teamwork and trust (Moss et al, 2007), thereby providing an additional reason for questioning the appropriateness of a transactional style in this context.

Humanities professor who has worked both in the private and higher education sectors for twenty years, working with home, international and mature students

What style of leadership is exercised in universities?

"I have not experienced transactional leadership directly from a departmental manager but have experienced it from more senior people in the next line up, at the level of head of school and then head of faculty. Faculties in universities tend to be large structures and management at the faculty level does not have a powerfully consultative role in working with the staff within schools. Where it occurs, consultation with staff tends to happen between staff and head of department (HOD), but the nature of the consultation is limited since procedures arrive from the faculty level and discussion is restricted to methods of implementation.

Unquestionably, higher levels of management practice transactional leadership, and being at the receiving end of this can feel very uncomfortable because:

- it feels as though your views are not being taken into account
- there isn't a channel through which your views can be expressed.

In reality, policies are produced at the top for use across the university and they may not be a particularly good fit for your section of the organisation. For example, a grading system could be drawn up for a large science area that is intended also to apply to a social science setting with fewer staff and a less clean fit. Other manifestations of transactional leadership? The setting of goals is pretty common and the effect can, again, be negative on the basis that:

- if you find it easy to hit the target, it can feel as though the target is not very fulfilling
- if you are unable to hit the target, you might feel uncomfortable

An example would be targets for student recruitment, a case where it is not always clear where the target comes from other than saying that we want a 10% increase in student numbers. In one year, the numbers can go up and in other years, they can go down, and the assumption on the part of leadership is invariably that the worker has it within their competence to hit the target. This is despite the fact that the measure can be heavily dependent on external circumstances beyond the employee's control."

The drivers to a transactional culture in UK higher education institutions (HEIs)

"The British government works in a transactional way by giving British universities targets/goals to meet related to financial rewards and penalties. These targets can change very rapidly, thereby offering universities little time for consultation within the organisation. In fact, government policy is handed to universities for implementation rather than consultation.

Subject discipline can also impact the style of leadership used in some parts of the university. For example, some of the science subjects are managed more transactionally than other disciplines because more money is at stake. In the same way, financial pressures can vary between disciplines with those relating to student recruitment greater in the arts and humanities than in the sciences where the corresponding pressures on research grant funding are greater, since more research money can be earned in the sciences than in the arts and humanities. By the same token, expectations of obtaining funding can be greater in the sciences than in the humanities not least because of the existence of a greater number of research councils in the sciences than in the arts and humanities where essentially the only two funding bodies are the (i) Arts and Humanities Research Council and (ii) the Leverhulme Trust."

Impacts of the transactional style

"A large proportion of the people in higher education (HE) went in, not because they were looking for a target-driven culture (the culture that prevails) but rather because they were looking for a culture that offered debate. This is different from a sector such as say finance where I imagine people enter the sector expecting it to be a target-driven. Consequently, in HE, there may be a mismatch between staff and career expectations and academics will feel disempowered if they think that there is no alternative to current ways of doing things.

Some of this mismatch between staff expectations and the reality of university life is linked to the fact that academic staff are trained in critical thinking and have a tendency to question things so, in my experience, and given the questioning nature of academic staff, the best way to get things done would be to ask academics questions and take part in a more inclusive process. Academics are experts in particular fields as well as in critical thinking, so having a system of inclusive leadership would work well in my view and would make a virtue of the critical faculties of academic staff. In other words, inclusive leadership would be a productive model for staff in higher education.

As it is, the incidence of inclusive leadership in HE is restricted largely to departmental level where it is expected that departmental staff will engage with and implement targets that arrive transactionally from on high. In monitoring these targets, the focus of transactional leadership is largely on measuring outcomes rather than the methods used in achieving these results."

Comment: this university professor, just like the previous senior academic whose views were reported, believes that the leadership style at senior levels in universities is largely transactional. As mentioned above, such a style might be appropriate were universities adopting a purely 'defender' strategy whereas, in fact, there is a strong emphasis in higher education in the UK on knowledge creation. Developing new knowledge is a task credited in the knowledge management literature as necessitating teamwork and trust in relationships and so the emphasis on transactional leadership is at odds with many of the conditions that favour knowledge creation (Moss et al, 2007).

Professor of education and head of a school of education in a Russell Group university

"The university where I work ran a big staff engagement survey in 2017 and had it measured the degree of inclusive leadership in the institution, it would not have achieved a high score since there is little evidence of listening to followers. In fact, the opposite is the case with managers not listening to followers and not being inclusive in their style of leadership. In fact, the leadership style here is probably quite transactional in nature. One factor in this may be what Professor Stephen Ball has identified as 'The terrors of Performativity' with Ball writing of 'Performativity' as:

> A technology, a culture and mode of regulation that employs judgements, comparisons and displays as means of incentive, control, attrition and change based on rewards and sanctions (both material and symbolic). The performances (of individual subjects or organisations) serve as measures of productivity or output, or displays of "quality", or "moments" of promotion or inspection. . . . The issue of who controls the field of judgement is crucial. . . [despite] the technology of performativity appear[ing]s as misleadingly objective and hyper-rational.
>
> *(2003, pp. 216–217)*

Professor Ball quotes Du Gay (1996) in referring not to 'the abandonment by the State of its controls, but to the establishment of a new form of control that Du Gay (1996) terms 'controlled de-control' (Ball, p. 217) and a system in which 'performance has no room for caring' (Ball, p. 224).

Of course, how leadership is perceived will vary and be dependent on the nature of the relationship that individuals have with individual leaders. For example, in my role as Head of School with over 100 employees, the perception that my direct reports have of my own leadership style may be different from the perception of those colleagues who do not report directly to me, that is unless the mass of people in the school can experience my leadership style vicariously."

Comment: this professor confirms the transactional nature of the senior leadership in his university and the difficulties that a leader has in diffusing their style across a number of people. The notion of 'performativity' is referred to as a factor that may set in train a transactional style of leadership, triggering what in effect can be seen as a 'defensive' strategy on the part of universities. This implied (not stated) positioning of educational institutions as 'defensive' would appear to prevent higher education institutions from adopting more of an 'explore' and 'prospector' strategy, something that might, a priori, be considered more appropriate for HEIs given their mission as knowledge creators.

In fact, if Kuhn's (1970) is accepted that HEIs are engaged predominantly in 'normal', non-paradigmatic shifting research, then HEIs might indeed be better served by an 'analyser' strategy with a 'producer' style of leadership in which control remains with management. Were there, however, to be a move away from a focus on so-called 'normal' science (Kuhn's term for research building on an existing paradigm (1996) and a move away from pressure to publish in the so-called 'top' publications that support this kind of non-paradigmatic changing work, then lesser control over staff and a more inclusive style of leadership might be appropriate. To kick-start this, a debate on the role of universities in society would be needed to establish whether a climate of greater freedom in research was desirable.

Civil servant in a British government department

"I have worked in the Civil Service for 34 years occupying eight different roles. In the first, the environment was extremely transactional with leadership efficiency judged in terms of the speed and accuracy with which papers could be moved around. In the course of a period of twelve years, I received three promotions and ended up as the local Training Officer.

What does it feel like to work under transactional leadership? In my first role, I saw leaders of teams who gave little attention to the well-being and health of team members and only considered how many inputs they could take to another part of the system. These inputs were, if you like, the widgets of the day and were written with carbon paper. It was only over the next years that the inputs could be processed using technology, but even then there was no attention to the human being.

The big change came about five years ago when the appraisal system was changed across the Civil Service and the system moved from an exclusive focus on 'what' the appraisee had done to an equal focus on 'what' and 'how' objectives had been achieved. Around 400,000 people are employed in the UK Civil Service and a number of managers found it difficult to consider the 'how' in relation to their own work as leaders of people, and so moved out of the Civil Service completely. Some managers have stayed and we refer to them as 'robust' managers.

Reasons behind the shift? One was a concern to reduce the volume of stress in the workplace, a problem that had risen from being the second most significant factor in long-term absence in the public sector (behind musculoskeletal disorders (HSE, 2009)) to the number one factor, along with mental health issues, in long-term absence (CIPD and CBI surveys, 2011).

The hierarchical system was ubiquitous in the Civil Service and when I first came across it, I simply embraced it, albeit uncomfortably, and just got on with it. As a team member, I felt that line managers were not there to take an interest in the lives that people led outside the workplace, and if you ask me what it was like, I felt imprisoned. We would often refer to our work as 'the factory' and we would speak of 'surviving'. At Christmas time, we would escape and just have a real blast to remind ourselves that we were human. In fact, our Christmas parties became infamous – we'd just let it hang out because it was our way of coping.

In my first job in the Civil Service, the mantra was 'leave yourself at home', the words of someone vey senior in the section I worked in then. One of the most insensitive managers in that section actually ended up taking his own life and one can't help wonder how much of this was about his own inability to express himself."

Comment: the Civil Service environment described here is one rooted in a 'defender' strategy and even though transactional leadership is theoretically suited to this, the comments – like those of the employee in the bank – show the mind-numbing and negative emotional impacts that this can have. The respondent, as we shall see in the next chapter, later refers to experiences of a different style in the Civil Service and the extent to which this afforded greater scope for job satisfaction and bringing the whole self to work, reducing the stress that working in the sector occasioned. This suggests that the continued reliance on transactional leadership in sectors with a defender strategy may be anachronistic and a source of unwanted stress and that even those organisations with a 'defender' strategy might wish to consider moving away from transactional leadership.

Summary: impacts of transactional leadership on individuals

According to the testimonies of twelve respondents from both the public and private sectors, leaders exercising a largely transactional style can have strongly negative impacts on those affected by their actions. With the single exception of the Railways Manager who commented on the importance of transactional leadership in the maintenance of track safety, other respondents refer to the detrimental effect of transactional leadership in stultifying creativity, initiative, human potential and individual identity. These negative impacts risk alienating employees, derailing a defender-led strategy and triggering long-term stress and absence from work.

The litany of negative impacts from transactional leadership identified by interview respondents include:

- demotivation
- lack of employee growth
- encouragement of risk-averse attitudes
- leaders avoiding decision-making
- unfairness of contingent reward
- followers guarded and closed with managers
- negative spill-over into private life and reduced confidence
- followers' views not taken into account
- followers told what to do, reducing the amount of ownership and responsibility passed to employees
- reduced creativity
- high levels of staff turnover and/or followers mentally checking out ('presenteeism')
- lack of support for followers which can influence their feelings about their work
- clash between transactional leaders and knowledge workers which can lead to disengagement and being forced into a parent–child relationship
- lonely when you know that corrective action can be taken in the event of failure
- stifling monitoring of work.

So overall, transactional leadership gets a bad press from respondents, and historical instances of transactional leadership reinforce this negative impression.

There may also be some possibly unexpected findings for readers. For those not familiar with the climate of higher education in Britain in the latter half of the second decade of the twenty-first century, it may come as a surprise to read that the leadership and culture at the top of universities is transactional in character. One of the surprises may be that transactional leadership, an appropriate element in a 'defender' strategy to exploit an existing vein of knowledge, is being used in a sector that many would assume exists to develop *new* sources of knowledge.

'Surely', you might say, 'universities are in the business of creating new knowledge?' That is a fair assumption except that, according to American academic Kuhn (1996), the majority of academics are engaged in what he terms 'normal science', in other words research that supports existing paradigms rather than calling these into question. In fact, you might say that the research climate in the UK and possibly in other parts of the world as well (at the point of going to press) is accentuating this conservative tendency, with increasing priority attached to publication in high-ranking journals that tend to be conservative rather than radical in their leanings. So, in the UK's Research Excellence Framework (REF) – an exercise in which the research outputs of universities across the UK are ranked and compared – published journal article outputs will only attract government funding if they are at the top 4★ level. As mentioned, given the somewhat conservative nature of many of these 'top' journals, this reinforces the sense that higher education in the UK is intended to consolidate existing knowledge and only expand it in limited ways.

Of course, were it to be the intention to create blue-sky thinking in universities, the prioritisation of publication in higher ranking journals would be relaxed as would also the style of leadership exercised. As it is, the incidence of transactional leadership in higher education in the UK and elsewhere may serve to control and limit thinking and initiative.

Toxic workplaces

The litany of problems associated with transactional leadership produces toxic workplaces where the organisation and often the individuals within it spiral down into negativity. The word 'toxic' comes from the Greek *toxicon* meaning 'arrow poison' and according to industrial psychologist Professor Theo Veldsman, a toxic organisation is one that "erodes, disables and destroys the physiological, psycho-social and spiritual well-being of the people who work in it in permanent and deliberate way" (Veldsman, 2016). Healthier organisations, on the other hand, have the opposite effects and can also produce lower levels of stress (CIPD, 2009). In fact, according to the Chartered Institute for Personnel and Development (CIPD), specific leadership behaviours are known to reduce workplace stress, and a quick scan of the behaviours recommended by the CIPD list reveals a significantly greater number of transformational than transactional leader behaviours:

- speaks to people personally
- provides regular opportunities to speak one to one
- returns my calls/emails promptly
- is available to talk to when needed
- is sociable
- socialises with the team

- is willing to have a laugh at work
- empathetic engagement
- encourages colleagues' input in discussions
- listens when asked for help
- makes an effort to find out what motivates colleagues
- tries to see things from their point of view
- takes an interest in colleagues' life outside work
- regularly asks colleagues how they are
- treats all colleagues equally.

Reading these behaviours after the litany of negative outcomes reported by respondents subject to transactional leadership is to be transported not just to a different planet but to a different universe. Remember how the British Civil Servant remarked on the lack of 'attention to the human being' and how the staff party at Christmas was a way of reminding people that they were human? One of the effects of the distant style of people management experienced in the Civil Service was to produce high levels of stress and absenteeism, and a change in appraisals from an exclusive focus on the 'what' to the 'what' *and* the 'how' was an attempt to stem these negative side effects.

The link between stress and absenteeism had become clear, since stress had been revealed as the number one factor in long-term absenteeism (CIPD and CBI surveys, 2011) with leadership behaviour as one of the top three factors causing employee stress (CIPD, 2009). A further factor related to the lack of control that many employees have over job demands (Karasek, 1979), a problem highlighted in comments from respondents in UK higher education.

Of course, stress can manifest not only in absenteeism but also in presenteeism, a phenomenon in which 'employees are physically present but mentally absent' (Gilbreath *et al*, 2012). If stress then mutates into depression, something that arguably it can (Khan and Khan, 2017), the loss to organisations can be roughly three times greater than the depression-related productivity loss attributed to absence from work (Hemp, 2004).

Stress is of course just one side-effect of transactional leadership. The element that sees managers interacting with subordinates only when things go wrong – the 'management by exception' aspect of transactional leadership – can lead to feelings of isolation on the part of staff. As we heard from the vice-president of a well-being institute:

> I tended to end up feeling somewhat lonely and stressed knowing that I was probably quite alone and that, if I strayed from my objectives, someone else would walk in and take over my job. It would have been preferable if I could have felt that someone was regularly by my side rather than someone there for a short span of time to undertake corrective measures.

Sentiments of loneliness and exclusion can have numerous negative consequences, according to Professor Mary Rowe of MIT (2008), including a poor psychological contract. Her discussion is principally focused on what she terms 'micro-inequalities' – the small acts that can make individuals feel overlooked – but the sentiment of loneliness evoked by 'management by exception' appear to have much in common with the feelings provoked by micro-inequalities. These effects are summarised in Table 3.2.

In fact, many of the exclusionary effects noted by Rowe chime with respondents' reactions to a regime of transactional leadership. For example, demotivation and disengagement were noted by the Diversity and Inclusion Consultant who spoke of his experience in the Chemicals industry, noting that the manager:

> took very little interest in what I was about and I found that very demotivating. . . . I got no development support from him since I never received feedback except if I had done something wrong or perhaps said something that was out of place. . . . I was a young man, keen and ambitious. . . [but] basically, I just found him very demotivating.

By analogy, a very experienced Diversity and Inclusion consultant took the view that:

> [b]eing at the receiving end of transactional leadership [could] be disempowering with a negative effect on motivation, and this kind of leadership prompted me to leave various places of work. After a while, transactional leadership becomes the straw on the camel's back since transactional leaders are a constant drain on energy and, even if you are quite resilient, you can only cope with this for a while.

The withholding of ideas and opinions is another recurring theme in terms of impacts of transactional leadership. For example, a Diversity and Inclusion Manager in the Transport industry expressed the view that 'once you are aware of being monitored, you do not feel prepared to have a go, to innovate, to produce new ideas since the context is so restricting'. In a similar way, the Sales Director of an extremely large Sales operation states that transactional leadership "reinforc[es] a way of working in which you leave your brain at home". Not surprisingly perhaps, a Senior Sales Leader in the same organisation described transactional leadership as creating "manager-led organisation[s] in which managers tell employees what to do

TABLE 3.2 Effects of exclusion

Area in which micro-inequality may be experienced	*Effect of the micro-inequality*
Performance	Disengagement
Morale	Withholding of ideas and opinions
Absenteeism	Absenteeism
Leave	Turnover

Source: Rowe (2008)

leading to the loss of 'employees' thought processes since they are merely acting on what they have been told to do". The Senior Consultant in Diversity and Inclusion was of the same view in suggesting that "If a transactional manager is not able to flex their style . . . you . . . get disengagement with people either leaving or, if they stay, mentally checking out".

This links to absenteeism with a respondent from the Civil Service describing the introduction of an appraisal system monitoring the 'what' as well as the 'how' as a strategy to reduce stress and absenteeism, something perceived perhaps to be related to the previously ubiquitous transactional leadership in the system. So, it seems that the exclusionary effect of transactional leadership mirrors the exclusionary effects of micro-inequalities so eloquently described by Professor Mary Rowe.

Conclusion

A study of the academic literature, historical accounts of transactional leaders and the opinions of twelve people show the extent to which transactional leadership can create working environments that undermine performance, motivation, creativity and well-being. We move on now, in the next chapter, to consider the impact of a rather different style, that of transformational and servant leadership, twin elements that combine to produce the subject of this book, inclusive leadership.

References

Alasadi, T. (n.d.). *Why hypocrites succeed in winning the general public*, www.researchgate.net/post/Why_hypocrites_succeed_in_winning_the_general_public, accessed on 29 May 2018.

Ball, S. (2003). The teacher's soul and the terrors of performativity. *Journal of Education Policy*, 18 (2), 215–228.

Bass, B. M. (1990). From transactional to transformational leadership: Learning to share the vision. *Organizational Dynamics*, 18 (3), 19–31.

Bass, B. M. and Avolio, B. (1990). Developing trans-formational leadership: 1992 and beyond. *Journal of European Industrial Training*, 14, 21–27, www.scirp.org/(S(351jmbntvns jt1aadkposzje))/reference/ReferencesPapers.aspx?ReferenceID=1269334, accessed on 9 May 2018.

Bass, B. M. (1985). *Leadership and performance beyond expectation*. New York, NY: The Free Press.

Bedford Borough Council, www.bedford.gov.uk/leisure_and_culture/local_history_and_heritage/airship_r100_and_r101.aspx, accessed on 2 May 2018.

Bevan, J. (2001). *The rise and fall of Marks and Spencer*. London: Profile books.

Burton, J. (2018). Banker told staff let customers 'hang themselves. *Daily Mail*, www.dailymail.co.uk/news/article-5284609/RBS-banker-told-staff-let-customers-hang-themselves.html#ixzz54r4h3vSh

CBI. (2011). *Healthy returns? Absence and workplace health survey*. London: CBI.

Chaterjee, A. and Hambrick, D. (2007). It's all about me: Narcissistic chief executive officers and their effects on company strategy and performance. *Administrative Science Quarterly*, 52 (3), 351–386.

CIPD. (2009). *Preventing stress, promoting positive management behaviour*, www.cipd.co.uk/ Images/preventing-stress_2009-promoting-positive-manager-behaviour_tcm18-16794. pdf, accessed on 6 June 2018.

CIPD. (2011). *Absence management.* Annual Survey Report 2011. In partnership with Simply Health.

Department for Business Innovation and Skills. (2012). *Leadership and management in the UK – the key to sustainable growth: Summary of the evidence for the value of investing in leadership and management development*, www.gov.uk/government/uploads/system/uploads/ attachment_data/file/32327/12-923-leadership-management-key-to-sustainable-growth-evidence.pdf, accessed on 24 January 2018.

Dotlich, D. and Cairo, P. (2003). *Why CEOs fail: The 11 behaviors that can derail your climb to the top and how to manage them.* San Francisco, CA: Jossey-Bass.

Du Gay, P. (1996). *Consumption and identity at work.* London: Sage.

Elkind, P. (2008). The trouble with Steve Jobs. *Fortune*, http://fortune.com/2008/03/05/ the-trouble-with-steve-jobs/

Finkelstein, S. (2013). *Why smart executives fail: And what you can learn from their mistakes.* New York, NY: Penguin.

Fuller, J. G. (1979). *The airmen who would not die.* New York, NY: G. P. Putnam's Sons.

Gilbreath, B. and Karimi, L. (2012). Supervisor behaviour and employee presenteeism. *International Journal of Leadership Studies*, 7 (1), 114–131.

Håkonsson, D., Burton, R., Obel, B. and Lauridsen, J. (2012). Strategy implementation requires the right executive style: Evidence from Danish SMEs. *Long Range Planning*, 45 (2–3), 182–208.

Hemp, P. (2004). Presenteeism: At work but out of it. *Harvard Business Review*, https://hbr. org/2004/10/presenteeism-at-work-but-out-of-it

Hirschman, A. (1970). *Exit, voice and loyalty: Responses to decline in firms, organisations and states.* Cambridge, MA: Harvard University Press.

HSE Information Services. (2009). *Self-reported work-related illness and workplace injuries 2008/09: Results from the Labour Force Survey.* London: HSE Information Services.

Karasek, R. A. (1979). Job demands, job decision latitude, and mental strain: Implications for job redesign. *Administrative Science Quarterly*, 285–308.

Khan, S. and Khan, R. (2017). Chronic stress leads to anxiety and depression. *Annals of Psychiatry and Mental Health*, 5 (1), 1091, www.jscimedcentral.com/Psychiatry/psychiatry-5-1091.pdf

Kuhn, T. (1996). *The structure of scientific revolutions.* 3rd edition, Chicago: University of Chicago Press.

Marks and Spencer. (n.d.). *A short history of Marks and Spencer*, https://marksintime.marksandspencer.com/download?id=996, accessed on 13 January 2018.

Mellahi, K., Jackson, P. and Sparks, L. (2002). An exploratory study into failure in successful organisations: The case of Marks and Spencer. *British Journal of Management*, 13, 15–29.

Miles, R. and Snow, C. (1978). *Organizational strategy: Structure and process.* New York, NY: McGraw-Hill.

Moss, G., Kubacki, K., Hersh, M. and Gunn, R. (2007). Knowledge management in higher education: A comparison between individualistic and collectivist cultures. *European Journal of Education*, 43 (3), 377–394.

Nevicka, B., Ten Velden, F., De Hoogh, A. and Van Vianen, A. (2011). Reality at odds with perceptions: Narcissistic leaders and group performance, *Psychological Science*, 22 (10), 1295–11264.

Nyberg, A. (2009). Managerial leadership and ischaemic heart disease among employees: The Swedish WOLF study. *Journal of Occupational and Environmental Medicine*, 66 (1), 51–55.

O'Reilly, C., Doerr, B., Caldwell, D. and Chatman, J. (2014). Narcissistic CEOs and executive compensation. *Leadership Quarterly*, 25, 218–231.

Petriglieri, G. and Petriglieri, J. (2015). Can business schools humanize leadership. *Academy of Management, Education and Learning*, 14 (4), 625–647, https://journals.aom.org/doi/abs/10.5465/amle.2014.0201

Porath, C. (2015). No time to be nice at work. *New York Times*, 19 June, www.nytimes.com/2015/06/21/opinion/sunday/is-your-boss-mean.html

Rowe, M. (2008). *PhD. Micro-Affirmations & Micro-Inequities*. Cambridge, MA: MIT Press.

Ryan, R. M. & Deci, E. L. (2000). Self-determination theory and the facilitation of intrinsic motivation, social development, and well-being. *American Psychologist*, 55, 68–78.

Schein, E. (1996). *Organizational culture and leadership*. San Francisco, CA: Jossey-Bass.

Sutton, R. (2008). *The no-asshole rule: Building a civilized workplace and surviving one that isn't.* London: Robert Sutton.

The Telegraph. (1998). Marks and Spencer: A recent history, 2 July, https://www.telegraph.co.uk/finance/newsbysector/retailandconsumer/2792584/Marks-and-Spencer-A-recent-history.html, accessed on 15 January 2019.

Veldsman, T. (2016). *Toxic leadership and its effects*, www.uj.ac.za/newandevents/Pages/UJ%E2%80%99s-Prof-Theo-Veldsman-on-toxic-leadership-and-its-effects.aspx, 19.1.2016, accessed on 5 June 2018.

Williams, R. (2016). *Why it's time to humanize leadership*, https://raywilliams.ca/why-its-time-to-humanize-leadership/

Williams, R. (2017). *Eye of the storm: How mindful leaders can transform chaotic workplaces.* Vancouver, BC: Ray Williams Associates.

Wintringham, T. H. (1930). *Labour monthly*, www.marxistsfr.org/archive/wintringham/1930/12/x01.htm

4

TRANSFORMATIONAL AND INCLUSIVE LEADERSHIP AND THEIR IMPACTS

In the last chapter, we looked at the instance of transactional leadership and its lamentable effects on employee productivity, creativity, motivation and well-being. With this litany of negative impacts, one wonders why organisations in competitive times continue to support leaders with this style. Why moreover should leaders persist in using this style when its negative effects are so apparent?

In this chapter, we will ring the changes and look at the impacts of transformational and servant leadership, the twin elements of inclusive leadership as defined in this book. Once again, we will seek the views of people who have been at the receiving end of this style, hearing from all those who bore witness to transactional leadership in the previous chapter. This time, the question relates to what it feels like to be managed by a leader with a repertoire of skills that includes transformational and servant leadership. In the next chapter, we will build on this by reporting on an extended industry study into the impacts of inclusive leadership, and then, in the following two chapters (Chapters 6 and 7) describe similar studies conducted in universities in the UK and in Norway. After that, in Chapters 8–11, we offer in-depth case studies of four organisations in a range of sectors – sales, real estate, recruitment and school education – where inclusive leadership is practised and celebrated (in order to jog the reader's memory, the twin pillars of this style of leadership are shown in Table 4.1). As we shall see, the four case study organisations are all working in highly competitive markets and responding to this with an inclusive culture style that boosts creativity and staff engagement. In the words of a manager at Royal Mail Sales, one of the case study organisations:

> Inclusive leadership, of the type that we have here, creates a culture of positivity, of empowerment. It creates an entrepreneurial culture within Sales in which people feel valued and in which they sense that what they do is valued. People will do the best that they can for their organisation so there are huge positives. It also ensures that you have a broader range of ideas than

TABLE 4.1 Attributes in inclusive leadership

Inclusive leadership attributes	Description	Whether the attribute derives from Transformational (Tf) or Servant Leadership (SL)
Individualised consideration	Showing individual interest and offering one-to-one support for followers	Tf
Idealised influence	Having admirable qualities that followers want to identify with	Tf
Inspirational motivation	Providing an appealing vision that inspires followers	Tf
Intellectual stimulation	Encouraging followers to develop their ideas and to be challenged	Tf
Unqualified acceptance	Being inclusive in considering followers	SL
Empathy	Putting oneself mentally and emotionally into the follower's place	SL
Listening	Actively listening to followers	SL
Persuasion	Being able to influence followers	SL
Confidence building	Providing followers with opportunities and recognition	SL
Growth	Encouraging followers to reach their full potential	SL
Foresight	Having the ability to anticipate events and where they might lead	SL
Conceptualisation	Having a vision about possibilities and articulating that vision to followers	SL
Awareness	Being fully open and aware of environmental cues	SL
Stewardship	Articulating the belief that the organisation's legacy is to contribute to society	SL
Healing	Helping followers cope with any burdens	SL

Source: Moss *et al* (2016)

you would have under a command and control system in which people are much less likely to share their ideas. Under a system of command and control leadership organisations will be missing out on something vital and this will stunt their ability to grow and progress.

As we shall see later, the four case study organisations featured all operate inclusive leadership in a context that has many of the so-called 'analyser' and 'prospector' elements described by Danish academic Håkonsson and her co-authors (2012). According to their study of Danish small and medium-sized enterprises (SMEs), organisations with these strategic elements are best supported by a leadership style with strong elements of delegation, of which inclusive leadership is an example. This is interesting since in the competitive world of the twenty-first century, many organisations will be adopting an 'analyser' or 'prospector' strategy even if they are unaware of these terms An 'analyser' strategy turns on feeding new products into an existing product-mix, and a 'prospector' strategy is a more aggressive approach to innovation. According to Håkonsson's study, only a 'defender' strategy will justify the use of non-inclusive leadership and so the case study organisations demonstrate Best Practice in proactively using IL to maintain a place in a competitive market.

Before stepping into the four case study organisations in a few chapters' time, we have a glimpse at two sectors, the macho worlds of the British army and of Premier League football where you might expect command and control but where in fact you find pioneering steps into the world of inclusive leadership.

Army

It is not rocket science to realise that if military leaders make mistakes, it is not just money that is wasted, but lives too. So good leadership is vital in the army and, for this reason, it is interesting to read the advice of General Sir Nigel Bagnall, chief of general staff and head of the professional army from 1985 to 1988. His view is that military people should 'always remember that what your subordinates think is far more important than concerning yourself with the views of your superiors' and, surprisingly, perhaps, his views are reflected in two recent army leadership strategies, both of which contain strong elements of inclusive leadership.

The first is the 2014 British army guide to developing leaders and the second is the Army Leadership Code with its seven principles (2015). Incidentally, some of the factors that triggered the introduction of the Army Leadership Code are explained by the current professional head of the British army and chief of general staff, General Sir Nick Carter, and include the new expectations of the younger cohorts in the army. As he explains in a video introducing the Army Leadership Code:

> We're leading a slightly different generation to the one that I grew up in. They have slightly different expectations. They also have significant expectations of their leadership which might not have been the case twenty or thirty years ago. I think that they also wish to see empowerment in the way that I didn't necessarily when I was an eighteen year old. What we have to do is move with the times, recognise that the people we are leading today have these sets of expectations and meet those expectations in a positive way.

He adds, significantly, that 'we have to recruit from a wider recruiting base than we might have in the traditional past'.

So, his drive for an appropriate leadership style leads him to take account of the needs of modern-day followers, many bringing a diversity of backgrounds. The army's solution is the so-called Army Leadership Code, consisting of seven guiding principles, namely:

Lead by example
Encourage thinking
Apply reward and discipline
Demand high performance
Encourage confidence in the team
Recognise individual strengths and weaknesses
Strive for team goals

If now we map the leadership attributes advocated in the British army guide to developing leaders (2014) and the British army code (2015) and compare them against those of inclusive leadership (IL), we find that the army leadership attributes all map closely to IL with the single exception of the part relating rewards to achievement, a competence derived from the transactional model of leadership and described there in the somewhat technical language of 'contingent reward'. Readers may remember this term from the first chapter where we discussed research associating 'contingent reward' and transformational leadership with 'high performance working', so while you might have been understandably surprised to see this element appear in an army context, you might equally justifiably be surprised to learn that the principles of good army leadership map so closely to IL. However, a glance at Table 4.2 shows the valid basis on which this conclusion is reached.

Why inclusive competencies for the British army? One of the drivers to the British Army Leadership Code (2015) was a 2014 survey into the prevailing culture

TABLE 4.2 Comparison of army leadership competences and those in (i) inclusive and (ii) transactional leadership (source of army attributes are 'Developing Leaders: A British Army Guide' (2014), and in the British Army Leadership Code (2015))

British army leadership attributes and whether from the Army guide to developing managers (GDM) or from the Army Leadership Code (ALC)	Inclusive leadership attributes (Tf = transformational; SL = servant leadership)	Transactional leadership attributes
Core values of moral and physical courage (GDM)	Idealised influence (Tf)	
Demand high performance (ALC)	Inspirational motivation (Tf)	

(Continued)

Table 4.2 (Continued)

British army leadership attributes and whether from the Army guide to developing managers (GDM) or from the Army Leadership Code (ALC)	Inclusive leadership attributes (Tf = transformational; SL = servant leadership)	Transactional leadership attributes
Humanity and compassion (to the dead, wounded, detainees, interpreters, local nationals, indigenous forces and others) ... importance of 'empathy' (GDM)	Empathy (SL)	
Persuasion and example – leadership achieves ends by "persuasion, compulsion and example" (GDM)	Persuasion (SL)	
Lead by example (ALC)		
Discipline-subordination of personal considerations to the collective (GDM)		
Respect for others – treating others as we would wish to be treated ourselves (GDM)	Unqualified acceptance (SL)	
Recognise individual strengths and weaknesses (ALC)		
Building organisations where team members feel valued and motivated (GDM)	Individualised consideration (Tf)	
Encourage confidence in the team (ALC)	Confidence building (SL)	
Treating all fairly and not being influenced by discrimination or bias Differences between people should be lauded and encouraged (GDM)	Unqualified acceptance (SL)	
Leadership should ... create individual and team growth by establishing an open environment that challenges the status quo (GDM)	Growth (SL)	
Importance of listening to others (GDM)	Listening (SL)	
Integrity in leadership leading to trust ... Leaders should encourage those they lead to think by giving them problems that stretch them and by encouraging them to find innovative solutions to established problems (GDM)	Intellectual stimulation (Tf)	
Encourage thinking (ALC)		
Good knowledge of the processes of problem solving enables the selection of the best strategy for the problem at hand (GDM)	Foresight (SL)	

British army leadership attributes and whether from the Army guide to developing managers (GDM) or from the Army Leadership Code (ALC)	Inclusive leadership attributes (Tf = transformational; SL = servant leadership)	Transactional leadership attributes
Reviewing and reflecting upon decisions (GDM)	Awareness (SL)	
Providing a vision of shared goals so that individuals and the team are inspired, have a shared sense of direction and pull together to achieve results (GDM)	Conceptualisation (SL)	
"Soldiers . . . need to know that their labours serve a higher purpose: one that is just and worthy of their sacrifice. Effective leaders use their judgement to communicate this at the right time and place, in an appropriate way." (GDM)	Stewardship (SL)	
"Danger, complexity, ambiguity, pressure and stress, particularly when suddenly introduced, can prevent clarity of thought, resulting in an inability to perform. Typically this is exhibited either as inaction, or as an incoherent flurry of activity with no clear purpose. Individuals can become accustomed to, and learn to overcome, these reactions through exposure and experience." (GDM)	Awareness (SL)	
"It is a leader's responsibility to gauge how particular circumstances are likely to affect each individual, and to develop a sincere knowledge of their lives outside the working environment – their families, aspirations and concerns – in order to establish a strong working relationship. The leader who can empathise is well placed to shape their leadership style in response to circumstances and personalities and so best motivate." (GDM)	Healing (SL); Empathy (SL)	
Leaders must accept responsibility for themselves and for their teams (GDM)		

(Continued)

Table 4.2 (Continued)

British army leadership attributes and whether from the Army guide to developing managers (GDM) or from the Army Leadership Code (ALC)	Inclusive leadership attributes (Tf = transformational; SL = servant leadership)	Transactional leadership attributes
Reward: appropriate use of contingent rewards incentivises individuals and reinforces what 'right' looks like. It builds self-esteem and self-confidence. Rewards can range from the 'everyday' to the exceptional: from a long weekend, to national recognition. (GDM) Apply reward and discipline (ALC)		Contingent reward

of the UK military, with one finding being that 90% of respondents thought the culture to be "overly sexualised or sexualised", with 39% having experienced sexual harassment or conduct short of sexual harassment. The plan is that implementation of these competencies will:

- change behaviours and attitudes, bringing about long-term cultural change
- challenge the status quo through a tool kit that leaders at all levels can use

Of course, there may be a long way to go before this new leadership style and new culture takes root, and in fact the head of personal services in the British army, John Donnelly, told the 2014 inquest into the death of teenage army recruit, Cheryl James, that culture change in the army was "not going to happen overnight" and that the army was not "anywhere near" where it needed to be (Davies, 2016).

Importantly though, reaction to the need for culture change, the army has taken the important step of determining the leadership it needs for the future. How good a fit is inclusive leadership in the army? A single comment from a commander of a battalion in the British army shows the potential that IL can bring:

> I have attempted to inculcate an inclusive approach in all that I do within my Battalion – to encourage my leaders to approach people and deal with them as individuals, and to empower them to be open and honest. The bureaucratic rank structure of the Army poses barriers to this so it is absolutely key for our leaders to import their personality to get around this barrier.
>
> *(Business in the Community website)*

It remains to be seen how quickly the Army guide to developing managers (2014) and the Army Leadership Code (2015) will effect a change in mind-set across the army so that the inclusive thinking of the battalion commander becomes the norm in the British army.

Premier League football

The Premier League is the most watched sports league in the world, broadcast in 229 territories to 900 million homes and is spending the rewards of new £8 billion-plus deals in broadcast revenue (Burt, 2016).

Two legendary coaches of the Premier League are Alex Ferguson (AF) and Jose Mourinho (JM) despite Mourinho having had a tricky stint at Manchester United at the time this book went to press. Here, we look at the leadership styles that they exercised as coaches, mapping what we know of them as leaders against transactional and inclusive attributes.

Why these two managers? Before retiring in 2013, Alex Ferguson spent twenty-six seasons as the manager at Manchester United, winning during that time thirteen English League titles and twenty-five other domestic and international trophies. The overall haul was almost double that of the next-most-successful English football team manager and, as acknowledgement of his greatness, a nine-foot statue of him looms outside Old Trafford in Manchester.

In terms of Jose Mourinho, Paul Merson, ex-Arsenal player turned pundit, described him as the "best in the business" (Winter, 2017) and Manchester United midfielder Nemanja Matic described him as "the best coach I have ever worked with" (Independent, 2017). Interesting assessments given that JM regarded football as "a human science" and one "about man, above everything else", comments that JM made on BBC Radio 4 in December 2011 (Haugstad, website). He went on to say that "A coach must be everything: a tactician, motivator, leader, methodologist, psychologist" and, with this last point in mind, quoted a teacher at university who told him [that] 'a coach that knows only about football is not a top one. Every coach knows about football, the difference is made in the other areas. He was a teacher of philosophy. I got the message'.

So, if JM is regarded as a manager with unique qualities (Independent, 2017), it is perhaps not by chance, since he subjected the job of football manager to intense scrutiny, taking the view that managing men with different cultures, brains and qualities is the most important thing. Every day, in fact, is an opportunity, in his words, "to analyse [him]self as a manager, as a leader" (Independent, 2016).

Speaking of analysis, the following table sets out the behaviours and attitudes of these two legendary coaches, with a note to the right indicating whether they correspond with transactional (Tc) or inclusive leadership (IL) attributes (in the latter case, these would further subdivide into transformational or servant leader attributes). In selecting these behaviours, the author simply noted down behaviours and attitudes ascribed to Alex Ferguson and Jose Mourinho, neither selecting nor deselecting behaviours that would sway the record in favour of Tc or IL. In fact, the underlying leadership style quickly becomes obvious.

TABLE 4.3 Comparison of football manager competences and those in (i) inclusive and (ii) transactional leadership

Football manager leadership attributes	Inclusive leadership attributes (Tf = transformational; SL = servant leadership)	Transactional leadership attributes
JM – "I never liked the kind of analysis of leadership where the boys say: He's my leader, I have to respect him. I prefer them to say: I respect him and he's my leader" (Live and Learn consultancy blog).	Idealised influence (Tf)	
Having a motivating vision. AF – spoke of the importance of having a vision and pinpointing expectations and standards. He also spoke of raising standards: "I had to lift players' expectations. They should never give in. I said to them all the time: 'If you give in once, you'll give in twice'. And the work ethic and energy I had seemed to spread throughout the club" (Elberse, 2013).	Inspirational motivation (Tf)	
JM – At Porto FC, JM's first major management job, most managers would have been happy with a domestic double. However, JM had an obsessive vision to conquer Europe's most elite competition, the UEFA Champions League (Live and Learn consultancy blog).	Foresight SL Conceptualisation (SL)	
JM – Former Chelsea captain John Terry described JM as a *master motivator* who unites players and makes them feel superior to the competition (Live and Learn consultancy blog).	Inspirational motivation (SL)	
	Intellectual stimulation (Tf)	
AF – After he stepped back from coaching, leaving that to his assistant coaches, he would notice changes in players' habits or a dip in their enthusiasm. He would then have a conversation with them, asking if there was a family problem, whether the player was struggling financially,	Individualised consideration (Tf)	

Football manager leadership attributes	Inclusive leadership attributes (Tf = transformational; SL = servant leadership)	Transactional leadership attributes
whether he was tired, what kind of a mood he was in. Sometimes he could tell that a player was injured even if he (the player) thought that he was fine (Elberse, 2013).		
JM – a cornerstone in Mourinho's 'methodology' (his favourite expression) is the tailoring of communication to each individual (Haugstad, 2012).	Individualised consideration (Tf)	
At Inter, JM noticed Wesley Sneijder was exhausted and encouraged a holiday. "All the other coaches [in my career] only spoke about training", said Sneijder. "He sent me to the beach. So I went to Ibiza for three days. When I got back, I was prepared to kill and die for him" (Haugstad, 2012).	Individualised consideration (Tf)	
JM – At União de Leiria, Mourinho asked David Barreirinhas, a member of the backroom staff, to become a spiritual and religious counsellor to the first team. Barreirinhas said: "I discovered a José Mourinho who was concerned with the fact that players were human beings as well as sports men and that they could have good and bad days" (Haugstad, 2012).	Empathy (SL) Unqualified acceptance (SL)	
JM – kept Luke Shaw in the Manchester United team despite his sustaining several injuries.	Unqualified acceptance (SL)	
• JM – according to former Chelsea captain, John Terry, JM individually praises players and in so doing, builds their self-confidence (Rindani, 2015).	Confidence building (SL)	
• AF – "I try to instil confidence in my staff and players through providing selective praise and recognising their worth. However, it's important my team are not over confident as this can lead to poor performances and	Confidence building (SL)	

(Continued)

TABLE 4.3 (Continued)

Football manager leadership attributes	Inclusive leadership attributes (Tf = transformational; SL = servant leadership)	Transactional leadership attributes
complacency. If I need to drop them for a game, I tell them it is only tactical, and that there are bigger games coming up in the future where they are needed more" (Elberse, 2013).		
During training sessions in the run-up to games, AF and the assistant coaches emphasised the positive (*ibid*).	Confidence building (SL)	
AF – "for a player – for any human being – there is nothing better than hearing 'well done'. These are the two best words ever invented. You don't need to use superlatives" (*ibid*, p. 3).	Confidence building (SL)	
JM brought in the stellar Armenian player Henrikh Mkhitaryan in 2016 following an excellent season at Dortmund. He had trouble adapting to the English game so JM made him train for an extensive period and dropped him from games to make allowance for his ongoing work. Henrikh was rewarded with chances in the Europa League and has since been involved in many goals.	Unqualified acceptance (SL) Growth (SL)	
AF – on his arrival at Manchester United in 1986, he set about creating a structure for the long-term by modernising Man U's youth programme. He established two 'centres of excellence' for players as young as nine. Signings from this included David Beckham and Ryan Giggs who AF identified as a skinny 13 year old in 1986 and went on to become the most decorated footballer of all time. With Paul Scholes and Gary Neville, the four formed the core of the Man U team of late 1990s and early 2000s (Elberse, 2013).	Growth (SL)	
When AF arrived at Man U, only one player in the first team was aged under 24. AF said, "the job of a		

Football manager leadership attributes	Inclusive leadership attributes *(Tf = transformational; SL = servant leadership)*	Transactional leadership attributes
manager, like that of a teacher, is to inspire people to be better" (Elberse, 2013). AF said that in developing young people, you are fostering a sense of family (*ibid*).	Growth (SL)	
JM – Mesut Ozil (MO) was given a dressing down following a languid game for Real Madrid. "You think that two beautiful passes enough – you think you're so good that 50% is enough? What do you want? To creep under the beautiful warm shower? Shampoo your hair? Be alone? Or do you want to prove to your fellow players, the fans out there and me, what you can do?" (Davis, 2017).	Inspirational motivation; (SL)	
MO admits to having felt hatred for JM but he played the best football of his career in Real Madrid's 2010–11 season when the club won La Liga with a record number of points and goals. MO later invited JM to write the foreword for his autobiography released in 2017!		
AF was chatting with an assistant manager who was complaining that he (the assistant manager) was only working with the youth team and that he (the assistant manager) should be helping AF with picking the team and training them. On hearing this, AF first said "no" and then, after thinking about it for a few days, delegated the training to the assistant manager while he, Ferguson, took on the role of observing the coaching (Elberse, 2013).	Listening (SL)	
AF – Player Ryan Griggs said of AF, "He's never really looking at this moment, he's always looking into the future". He believed that the cycle of a successful team lasts four years, so he was always visualising the team three or four years ahead (Elberse, 2013, p. 3).	Foresight (SL)	

(Continued)

TABLE 4.3 (Continued)

Football manager leadership attributes	Inclusive leadership attributes (Tf = transformational; SL = servant leadership)	Transactional leadership attributes
JM – While fans were booing the Belgian player, Marouane Fellaini, JM kept him in the squad, and the confidence that JM placed in him paid off since he became one of the most important players in the team, renewing his contract with Manchester United in June 2018. At that point, receiving a contract worth £100,000 per week, he said a special "thank for Jose and the faith that he has always shown in me" (Archer, 2018).	Conceptualisation (SL)	
AF – "Being positive and adventurous and taking risks – that was our style" (Elberse, 2013).	Foresight (SL)	
JM – is known to want to obtain a meticulous understanding of the competition, building training around that understanding.	Conceptualisation (SL)	
AF – "Employees need to know who you are, what your principles are and trust that you are right when you impose rules". He believed in making decisions quickly and then moving on (Elberse, 2013).	Stewardship (SL)	
• AF – believed that to motivate your team for greater performance levels, you need to take into account who you are disciplining, what level of assertion you apply and how the person reacts. Rio Ferdinand said that AF was successful in his people-management skills since he did not treat everyone in the same way.	Awareness (SL)	
o JM – "The more you understand your team the more you can lead them" (Rindani, 2015).	Individualised consideration (SL)	
o	Healing (SL)	
AF – believed that a manger has to achieve a position of "comprehensive control" (Elberse, 2013).		Active management by exception

Football manager leadership attributes	Inclusive leadership attributes (Tf = transformational; SL = servant leadership)	Transactional leadership attributes
		Passive management by exception
AF – responded forcefully when players violated standards, in which case they could be fined or let go. He took the view that a manager needed to point out mistakes when players did not meet expectations (Elberse, 2013). On the other hand, AF said, "you have to trust that [staff] are doing their jobs. If you micromanage and tell people what to do, there is no point in hiring them" (ibid).		
JM – was not wholly happy with the work rate of Luke Shaw and ultimately criticised him publicly, adding reference to his potential at the same time.		Monitoring followers' performance and correcting mistakes
JM – he often made selection for a match contingent upon behaving in a certain way. In this way, after Manchester United player Anthony Martial started working hard (after a period in which JM had to flag up issues relating to his work rate), JM rewarded him with 'starts'.		Contingent reward

So, an analysis of the attitudes and behaviours of two world-renowned football coaches has highlighted the tendency for their behaviours to map more closely to inclusive than to transactional leadership. This may perhaps come as a surprise given football managers' reputation for being blunt and severe. However, if this analysis is a fair reflection of the leadership styles of the two managers, based as it is on comprehensive accounts of their attitudes and behaviours, then the success of these world-renowned managers may owe a great deal to their inclusive style of leadership.

In the next section, we move away from the army and football to return to the respondents that offered their views on leadership in the last chapter. This time, however, their comments relate to the value and effects of inclusive leadership.

A view from the inside: in-depth interviews

What does it feel like to work under a leader with the inclusive attributes used as the defining features of inclusive leadership in this book and shown again in Table 4.1? All had contributed their thoughts on the effects of transactional leadership – all largely negative in flavour – and here they offer their thoughts on the effects of a rather different style, that of inclusive leadership.

Respondents from the private sector

Diversity and inclusion consultant, formerly HR director within a large British international paints and chemicals company

"I had an inclusive leader, the works manager at ICI. He worked with me to develop a vision of success for the factory and he gave me enormous scope to contribute in delivering that. This felt terrific and I was so highly motivated and I delivered great results. I worked above and beyond and far exceeded what I thought I was capable of. How was that possible? The works manager had developed a vision of success and not only took an interest in how I was delivering on that but also supported me in the work I did."

Comment: as noted in the previous chapter, the manager was working in a fast-changing industry sector with a 'producer' strategy (Miles and Snow, 1978) and so an accompanying emphasis on delegation (Håkonsson et al, 2012) would seem to have been highly appropriate.

Diversity and inclusion manager in the transport sector

"Inclusive leadership is the ideal environment to work under. It produces more motivation, productivity and less absence from work than transactional leadership and also produces a more competent life – if you feel valued at work there is a spillover into your personal life and you feel more confident about the future. In terms of your relationships outside, you are less fractious and less stressed.

In terms of the specific attributes grouped under the inclusive leadership umbrella, each has important strengths and I will run through these attributes here."

Individualised consideration

"What does it feel like to have a manger show you individualised consideration? Well, when I experienced it, I felt valued, supported and more than motivated, I felt enthused."

Idealised influence

"This refers to someone that you saw as a role model that you might emulate. Certainly, as a younger person, an encounter with someone who had influence on me guided me in a way to go, showing me a style that would be more accepted and that would see me, as an individual, succeed."

Inspirational motivation

"It is important to know what your leader is trying to achieve and once you know this, your manger can motivate and inspire you. I remember working with a manager that had a vision that I had an affinity with and this made me willing to put in discretionary effort."

Intellectual stimulation

"According to my way of thinking, intellectual stimulation is about creating an environment where people are prepared to 'have a go' with no consequences. This is very similar to the environment created by individualised consideration where you feel supported as an individual and intellectual stimulation can leave you enthused, motivated, supported and not worried about failing."

Unqualified acceptance

"The person who is led with unqualified acceptance becomes someone who feels they can 100% of themselves at work and who is prepared to do more. This new environment is created in these circumstances."

Empathy

"The same as unqualified acceptance but where the leader understands the need to create an environment where things are not hidden."

Listening

"This is key because the environments we have described where people feel supported are those where you will be listened to and not shunned."

Persuasion

"If done in a subtle way, you can persuade people in a way that will not make them aware that you are persuading them. There is a fine line between autocracy and persuasion and you need to be subtle but in the transformational environment, people don't notice the persuasion."

Confidence building

"This is very similar to 'intellectual stimulation' and 'unqualified acceptance' since the leader needs to be prepared to let people have a go and then people are able to thrive."

Growth

"If you are in an environment where you are being allowed to grow and explore, you are aware that the leader has an idea of your potential and what you might need to fulfil it. The leader needs to have individualised consideration to be able to help you grow."

Foresight

"If you're in an environment where leaders demonstrate this competence you would feel safe. You will feel because these people are second-guessing situations."

Conceptualisation

"This probably works in a similar way to 'inspirational motivation'."

Awareness of environmental cues

"This probably works in a similar way to 'empathy'."

Stewardship

"This probably works in a similar way to 'conceptualisation' and 'vision', with vision aligned to the organisation's vision."

Healing

"This probably works in a similar way to 'empathy'."

Comment: this manager is tasked with expanding diversity and inclusion within a transportation organisation, which moved fairly recently from the public to the private sector. Whereas many parts of the organisation would need to prioritise safety factors, creating a 'defender' strategy, this person's role appears to envisage a shift from a defender to an 'analyser' strategy and a move from low to high delegation. He is strongly of the view that an inclusive style of leadership will create higher levels of staff motivation which, presumably, in the context of transport, would allow the importance of safety considerations to be internalised.

Director of sales in one of the UK's largest internal sales organisations (recently privatised)

"There's now a new relationship between leaders and followers. In this, the leader operates in their space and the follower operates in theirs. Over the last year, since introducing inclusive leadership, the four senior sales leaders in the department just want to do more and this is within a context in which they have 'freedom within a framework'. You see, when you work in a big organisation, there have to be some rules/processes but even within those processes and rules there has to be an element of fun.

How do you put this into effect? It can start very narrowly with your 'freedom box' relatively small in more junior jobs but as you move up the hierarchy, your freedom box becomes bigger. Having said that, even in more junior jobs, it is important to have a 'freedom box' since unless people can operate differently, you'll never see innovation from people and they will leave their brains at home.

When you offer a 'freedom box' to manager grades, it is amazing how much more the people under them can contribute. You, as the manager, might imagine that certain people are capable of more than they have been doing but if you have the freedom to delegate and develop your staff, these people can actually end up doing much more than they themselves thought they were capable of. As a result, they will end up saying 'This has been the best year possible and I really didn't know that I could do this'."

How we got there from a transactional culture

"To move to inclusive leadership from transactional management you need to be very visionary and you need to involve your people in that process. If you don't, no one will believe that it will ever work against the backdrop of an organisation where the prevailing style still emphasises rules and processes. So, you have to help people believe that the 350 people in Sales can change. You have to create a microclimate using a vision, and once the vision is real then the microclimate can act as a change agent across the organisation. At that point, you can just get on with it and become a catalyst of change."

Consequences of a shift to inclusive leadership

"Since embedding inclusive leadership, engagement and involvement scores are second to none. Moreover, if you want strong followers, you need to be 'firm but fair' and need to invest in people. So, all Sales Managers in Sales are professionally trained coaches, having followed a coaching course lasting eight to twelve months and on which a considerable investment in training was made by the company. People also understood more about themselves through psychometric testing, and overall these initiatives have given managers the tools with which to engage their people. At the end of the journey, we asked managers to write a dissertation on their leadership journey and some submissions were truly inspirational – for example, one of the pieces of work included the notion that leaders should not be perceived as being a particular type of leader but as just being themselves.

What is more, some of the managers now coach outside of Sales. For example, some coach kids from disadvantaged backgrounds, helping them into work; some coach colleagues in operations where they are spreading the word and being evangelists.

Here in Sales, we have a philosophy of treating people with respect and dignity. Some people outside sales and in other organisations think that you can treat people in a less respectful way because those people are 'working' for you, but here in Sales, we engage with people and listen to them since, in the twenty-first century workforce, we're all volunteers. It is true that I work for this organisation but it is my choice to do this and one would not expect millennials to want to work for this organisation for years since nothing is a job for life any more.

In fact, we have low turnover, and organisations that have high turnover are not treating people as if they were volunteers. Employers need to understand that employees *choose* to work for them and that, if it is a good employer, employees will stay. The moment that the employer stops treating people as volunteers, the people who can leave will do so and work for someone else.

"You really need to care and not just say that you care. We had someone working with us in the organisation who had terminal cancer and in the course of his work moved from four to three to one day per week and we paid him the full time rate all of this time. His colleagues were helping him and we named an award after him."

Comment: this organisation's sales strategy appears to have elements of both an 'analyser' and a 'prospector' strategy necessitating a management style that is high on delegation as well as exploration. Inclusive leadership is a style that will release the creativity that people need in order to meet these strategic objectives whilst conveying the respect for people that will help people feel valued and so want to stay with the organisation. The Director of Sales speaks of the importance of giving people and managers a 'freedom box' within which they can grow and develop, with managers adopting a coaching style in helping and supporting their followers. Involving people in creating the organisation's vision is an important first step.

Senior sales leader in a recently privatised organisation working under the sales director whose views are shown above

"I am in the leadership team which, in this go-ahead sales organisation, is encouraged to be listening, to be thought leaders, to understand what is going on in academic research. That, coupled with the coaching training programme (all managers undergo an eight-month coaching training programme) encourages us as leaders. So, a lot of the time, we're helping our reports expand their way of thinking relative to business decisions but also relative to personal decisions, for example relating to their career.

"When we 'listen', we do more than that since we encourage our followers to revisit what they have been saying and we then provide feedback on the actions that they have taken. Even if we can't action something, we explain the reasons – the 'because' is such an important word in this whole process of active listening."

Communications

"We have a number of communications channels:

> Monday: every morning, there is an online listening and learning programme for Sales Managers with short input from a different speaker every week. This is an opportunity to coach on information/requesting information/

price changes. Pre-reading is sent out, and this is an opportunity for the sales leaders and managers to engage with the speaker.

Then the Sales Managers cascade this out to their teams directly and coach their teams in the topics.

Wednesday – professionally written bulletin goes out dealing with international issues, successes/failures/wins/sharing Best Practice

Friday – 'It's our Business' – this newsletter contains everything that's not prod-uct specific. It always starts with a view from the Sales Director, the co-called 'View from the Bridge' which will cover topics such as maintaining our focus in difficult times; or a new topic – people like that – for example, can be a 'getting to know you' for new members of the team.

There are also Sales Directors road shows. Every month, the Sales Director visits a different sales site (seven–eight sites across the year) and originally he gave a pres-entation. Then he just showed two or three pictures and now there are no slides at all – just an open conversation! The Sales Director shares confidences that he might not otherwise.

There's also an annual Sales engagement survey annually and feedback shows that people really see the value of these road shows. What is more, the Sales Director has picked up ideas from there since it really is a two-way exchange of information and people really appreciate this. The Sales Director is always seeking to hear the voice and tone of the people and this is replicated by his sales leadership team who also go out and do road shows in a similar way.

"Apart from self-empowerment initiatives coming from coaching and the road shows, there is also a Sales Diversity Board looking at how we empower people. Already, we're organising sessions fronted by millennial apprentices who are giving their thoughts on how to use social media."

Challenges to transformation from a transactional to an inclusive style

"You can't change immediately from a 'tell', 'this is how to do it' style, to a 'what do you think?' style. A coaching element has to come in between that will allow people to move away from a directive style and encourage them to think for themselves. You need to let out the leash very slowly since you can knock people's confidence in the process and you need to lead people through this process of moving from a 'tell' approach to a 'what is the best way?' all the way through to autonomy. We are all, to a great extent, responsible for our own destiny.

The Sales Director advises people to 'Fail quickly, take some measured risks but if it doesn't work, be quick to try something else'. There's probably a lot of sense in this!"

Comment: coming from the same organisation as the immediately preceding set of com-ments, it is not surprising to read of the objective of creating staff autonomy so that people can exercise more freedom and responsibility.

Senior consultant in diversity and inclusion

"I had a manager once who was transformational and who was very much about involvement, asking for ideas, supporting your ideas, making you feel part of the team and making you feel involved. Being treated like this has a great impact on your psychology and motivation since you feel that it has a spiral effect, definitely making you work harder.

Unfortunately, a lot of leaders don't have the human touch or a human mind-set and they actually don't value the capacity for this. They see inclusive leadership as soft and fluffy and criticise this style because it doesn't match theirs."

Comment: validation of the notion that inclusive leadership inspires followers to work harder comes from the views of this senior consultant in diversity and inclusion. As we saw from his earlier input in Chapter 3, most of his experiences of senior leadership have been transactional and despite extensive work in consultancy, it is disappointing to hear that his main experience of leadership has been transactional, particularly since he speaks of inclusive leadership as having such a strong impact and positive impact on motivation and productivity.

Vice-president of a well-being institute in the private sector

"My thoughts on what it feels like to experience inclusive leadership are many and varied, and it is simplest to take each factor in turn."

Individualised consideration

"In my experience, when I am shown individualised consideration, my tendency is to appropriate, reciprocate and emulate this behaviour."

Idealised influence

"To my mind, an instance of this is 'leading by example' and this is something that I think leaders should do. There is nothing worse than people who 'Do as I say not as I do' – that is pretty reprehensible."

Inspirational motivation

"A vision can inspire."

Intellectual inspiration

"I can be encouraged by leaders to develop my ideas, and it is wonderful to be given licence to do something new. It should be said, however, that this can come with the risk that one may be more or less creatively challenged and that others may not feel as enthusiastic about the new ideas as one is oneself! Having intellectual inspiration is very important, and the key is how one challenges others. There is an element of challenge in motivating people, but it is important also to think carefully about the amount of challenge offered since stress needs to be minimised. Having said that, if you don't develop people in a service setting, you might as well pack up business!"

Unqualified acceptance

"Being inclusive in considering followers is essential and if not, what is the point in having people in the workforce? When leaders are inclusive, it is hugely motivating, empowering and engaging for followers. The importance of being inclusive is clear, for example, from a study in the US of hospital cleaners and the factors that they perceived to be positive and as negative. The factor that caused the greatest negative reactions was being ignored whereas not being ignored evoked positive reactions (Dutton *et al*, 2014). Here are the concluding remarks of this study:

> In general, the valuing interactions recounted by the cleaners were marked by a sense of appreciation, gratitude, and happiness expressed in the telling of the stories. At their core, each valuing interaction conveyed to cleaners that they were recognized as human beings by others at the hospital. Valuing interactions in which cleaners were included, helped, or communicated with by others took this recognition several steps further to suggest that they were respected and deserving members of the organization. (*ibid*, p. 33)

Of course, I recognise that there are special cases, for example emergencies, where leaders need to make decisions and carry the can themselves since they can't include everyone, and in these cases followers will need to follow the direction of the leader.

"There are lots of ways of being inclusive with followers, including taking care with the type of questions that you use. There are two main types in fact:

- What do you think . . .?
- I am minded to think x, what do you think?

"One needs to know followers very well in order to make a judgement as to which kind of question would work best. It is fair to say that you are more likely in an Anglo-Saxon setting to find a leader using the first form of question ('What do you think?') and in France to use the second form of question ('I am minded to think x, what do you think?'), expecting also in France that the follower will follow the leader's point of view. Having said that, in the international organisation that I am in, I can see progress in the styles that leaders adopt, and this has come about through inter-cultural awareness training and exposure to new ideas/ways of doing things. In my view, we can learn pretty much anything so long as we are open to it. Of course, in all of this, there will be horses that won't ever drink."

Listening

"One of the precepts of mindfulness is the importance of listening (not necessarily to respond but certainly to hear since sometimes people speak just to be heard). We don't always have the discipline to listen, hear and think at the same time."

Empathy

"From the perspective of a follower, empathy certainly has its virtues. However, it can be frustrating coming from leaders who 'hear' but who don't act on what they hear since employees generally want to know that you don't just feel their pain but that you are also going to do something about it. That is not to say that there are not cases where an employee likes to be heard without any expectations of follow-up, but that will not always be the case."

Persuasion

"I remember going to the Royal Society of Arts (RSA) a few years ago and hearing a talk by a German professor on the differences between 'power' and 'authority'. He said that the quality of superiority is a given in the first case but something earned in the second case through the ability to influence rather than force followers. Having 'authority' is very important as part of the ability to persuade."

Confidence building

"When people have recognition, they feel good and really appreciate it."

Growth

"I've very often said to followers that I hope that they will develop to be better than I am."

Foresight

"When leaders have this quality of 'foresight', it is comforting and reassuring to followers and it underlines one of the key qualities of leadership which is to zoom in and out from the macro to the micro levels with ease. It's not the easiest thing to do but seeing it done well, apart from its positive impact on the organisation, helps me learn how better to do it myself and also helps me understand the good questions to ask. Some of leadership is not necessarily about knowing, this being the unwritten model in Anglo-Saxon countries according to cross-cultural research, but rather about asking the right questions."

Awareness

"This is defined as being 'fully open', something that leaders may not always be able to be for the good of followers, both because having lots of detail can be unsettling and because sometimes leaders need to withhold things. Having said that, awareness of environmental cues is vital because it's through this that people adapt and only through doing this that they can thrive. This is true both at the level of evolution and also as it relates to people in organisations."

Stewardship

"I prefer it when leaders articulate how the organisation contributes to society. I would sign up to the issue of a societally purposeful organisation and the most important part of this is to articulate *how* the organisation contributes to society, with Friedman's profit motive being an insufficient contribution on its own."

Healing

"This is change within the organisation that supports the people within it."

Comment: these views come from the head of a well-being institute in a service organisation in which the main asset is people. He shows how IL can galvanise people's energies and growth with individualised consideration and leading by example as key principles.

Director in the property sector speaking of corporate experience in the real estate and banking sectors

"In 2006–2009, I worked for an Asset Management business where the leadership was by inclusive committee management. There was a meeting and long debate about everything at every level.

I genuinely believe that the business was trying to manage the business better than would have been the case under transactional leadership which would have been the case twenty or thirty years earlier. However, when the inclusiveness becomes cultural to the point that everyone has an opinion, often very little gets done because you have a diverse range of views to consider. It often becomes a far more cautious environment and a far more debated and delegated environment and as a result, things can become very slow moving and almost embedded in procrastination. Organisations can often end up, in this situation, diluting true leadership. They will have moved away from transactional leadership and could end up with virtually no leadership.

In the Asset Management Business, difficult decisions needed to be made as the 2007 financial crisis unfolded. Some people battened down the hatches and hoped that the storm would 'blow over' and they could return to their normal roles. No matter how much individuals tried to emphasise the need for more decisive and defensive action it was seen as 'rattling the cage', the culture was very inclusive and protective and you couldn't do anything. When you have inclusive leadership there is a tendency to become part of a club and senior employees can get complacent. Everyone tends to protect everyone else.

The way forward for leaders? Ideally, you need something that merges the best of transactional and inclusive leadership. I'm a massive believer in mixing characters and cultures within an organisation since in doing that and creating a diverse organisation (in terms of age, gender, personality and culture), you create an eclectic mixture and a balance of views. The best leaders get the best results from 'creative conflict' and to achieve this, you need to bring in people at every level who will have diverse views and questions embedded in processes and culture. The balance between extracting the best from 'creative conflict' and the organisation becoming divided is a fine one. Great leaders tread this fine line skilfully, constantly adjusting their own views to align with the views that create change. Great leaders embrace change. Weak leaders resist anything that might threaten or question their position."

Comment: this organisation's strategy appears to be like that of the sales organisation looked at earlier, to have elements of both an 'analyser' and a 'prospector' strategy. This appears to draw on a management style that is high on delegation as well as exploration. Inclusive leadership is a style that will release the creativity that people need in order to meet these strategic objectives, but this respondent highlights the importance of management keeping control of the rudder so that the organisation is not lost in a mire of indecision.

Respondents from the public sector

There were three respondents from the public sector, of whom two were from British universities and one from the British Civil Service. As can be seen from the responses received (below) from senior people in universities, inclusive leadership tends to be in evidence mainly at junior levels of leadership. In contrast to this, the Civil Servant describes a shift in the British Civil Service from transactional leadership to a style of leadership that is more considerate of its impact on employees.

Pro-vice-chancellor in a Russell Group university

"It feels better working with inclusive leaders than those with a transactional style. Inclusive leadership makes you feel a follower and a contributor and not only makes one feel valued but also provides a sense of one's part in a bigger picture, thereby providing more clarity of purpose. You feel more motivated to engage and, following Hirschman's (1970) options of 'exit' (leaving the organisation), 'voice' (speaking up about problematic issues) and 'loyalty' (remaining with the organisation), encourages people to be loyal and remain with the organisation.

In a regime of inclusive leadership, colleagues tend to be on board with the organisation's vision and are likely to exhibit the same behaviours as those displayed by others around them. This is because inclusive leadership at the top of an organisation tends to cascade down to other levels in the organisation. If inclusive leadership is absent from the top, then this kind of consistency in behaviour may be absent and just visible in pockets of the organisation."

Comment: this respondent commented earlier on the increasingly transactional style of leadership in British universities, something described as having a de-motivating effect on colleagues. Since he is in fact working at a 'Russell Group' university, one whose existence is not under threat, his previous reference to the widespread use of transactional leadership in his university is interesting, leading one to question the appropriateness of this style. Here, he speaks of the motivational impact of inclusive leadership in a university setting, suggesting that perhaps there may be a case for more widespread use of this in the sector.

Humanities professor who has worked both in the private and higher education sectors for twenty years, working with home, international and mature students

"My experience of inclusive leadership has generally been at the intermediate line manager level, equivalent to Head of Department (HOD) in universities. In the UK higher education system, this position may typically be held for a maximum of circa three years, and there is a sense from staff that this person is your colleague rather than boss (which is often technically true). At that level, the HOD may have little or often no control over budgets since HODs are basically implementing objectives determined from above. It is understood as HOD that you have not made the decisions and that you are simply working out how people need to engage in order to work within the wider transactional environment. There is an ideology of equality within the body of teaching staff which means that, despite the status differences between teaching staff, the staff expect to team-work together (although they tend to behave individualistically since teamwork is rarely an aspect of humanities research, although this is different in the sciences). This inhibits a hierarchical environment at the department level.

An inclusive environment brings its own challenges with four main concerns:

(i)   *Time needed:* it takes a lot of time to fully listen to and engage with people who want a lot of debate on issues
(ii) *Reaching conclusions:* it can be challenging to get collective agreement.
(iii) *Enhanced expectations:* opening up discussions can raise expectations of what can be achieved.
(iv) *Adding complexity:* opening up discussions can elaborate problems unless the process is effectively managed and this can put pressure on the individual manager."

Comment: this university professor, like the previous senior academic, believes that the leadership style at senior levels is largely transactional. Here he vouches for the fact that inclusive leadership (IL) is likely to exist only at the lower departmental level in universities. As noted in respect of the previous respondent, it is far from clear why such a limited use of IL is present in British universities, an employer of knowledge workers, even though this respondent produces arguments against its use. Research could usefully explore this resistance to modernising leadership in the sector.

Civil servant in a British government department

"It was after several years in one section that a wonderful manager changed things. He insisted that, every Monday morning, before you took your writing implements out of the desk, you shared with team members how your weekend was. Everyone got to know each other this way since he was getting us to talk less about the work and more about ourselves.

The first time that I got temporary promotion and the chance to lead a team, I stole the idea since this manager (Barrie) had made me feel so special. He made me feel human and valued and that it was OK to make a mistake because the work was not the most important thing. He believed that if you felt valued and knew where your work fitted in, you would be better at your work, come up with better ideas and do the work more efficiently.

In fact, the appraisal system has been changed now throughout the British Civil Service so that instead of an exclusive emphasis on 'what' people have done, there is now an equal emphasis on 'how' people have achieved their objectives. This is encouraging a lot of Managers to consider how they treat their staff, which can only be positive.

I love my current job since I can be my whole self at work. It was not always like this."

> Comment: the Civil Service environment described here is one at odds with the transactional culture described in the previous chapter as flourishing until recently. The work demanded now may demand greater proactivity, but the principle reason offered for the change in approach is a concern to reduce the costs to the Civil Service of unwanted stress, the largest single factor underpinning absence from work in the UK.
>
> Such is the scale of the problem that in 2016/17, the Health and Safety Executive reported 12.5 million working days lost due to work-related stress, depression or anxiety in that year (www.hse.gov.uk/statistics/causdis/stress/). They also reported that work-related stress, depression or anxiety accounted for 40% of work-related ill health and 49% of working days lost, in 2016/17. The occupations and industries reporting the highest rates of work-related stress, depression or anxiety remained consistently in the health and public sectors of the economy (HSE, 2018).
>
> Noting the importance placed in the Civil Service of making leadership more inclusive in order, inter alia, to reduce levels of stress, it could be that the continued reliance on transactional leadership in sectors with a 'defender' strategy may be anachronistic and a source of unwanted stress. If this is the case, a 'defender' strategy may no longer be sufficient justification for the continued practice of transactional rather than inclusive leadership.

Summary: impacts of inclusive leadership on individuals

According to the testimonies of ten respondents, inclusive leadership can have extremely positive effect on organisations boosting creativity, initiative, human potential and a sense of individual identity. These positive effects can boost productivity, motivation and well-being, creating a virtuous circle that should feed into both organisational effectiveness and, ultimately, a country's GDP.

Specific positive effects mentioned include:

- clarity that comes from having a vision and being able to direct energies towards that
- enhanced motivation that helps people to exceed their normal abilities
- enhanced productivity
- reduced workplace absenteeism
- positive spill-over into private life
- feeling of being valued
- feeling supported
- facilitation of individual growth
- improved staff retention
- improved staff engagement
- enhanced opportunities for creativity and initiative
- enhanced empowerment.

In terms of frequency of responses, those elements highlighted most frequently include a sense of motivation/engagement, being valued, a sense of loyalty as well as enhancements in growth, creativity and productivity. Many of these bi-products of IL correspond with the three cornerstones of 'self-determination theory' namely competence, autonomy and relatedness (Ryan and Deci, 2000) and so IL appears to be one way of satisfying people's innate psychological needs for these three elements. In fact, it is easily apparent that the benefits attributed to inclusive leadership are the complete reverse to the long list of problems associated with transactional leadership. The only possible negative arguments advanced related the danger that inclusive initiatives could slow down or, in some cases, paralyse processes.

Conclusion

A cross-section of respondents have had extremely positive experiences of inclusive leadership, something that contrasts with their negative experiences of transactional leadership. These positive experiences are supported by the evidence that two of history's top football managers have used inclusive leadership to achieve what can only be described as outstanding results.

Of course, the views in this chapter and the last are based on the experiences of a relatively small number of people. In the next chapter, we look at the survey responses of just under 1,000 employees in over ten large UK organisations and see to what extent this validates or contradicts these conclusions.

References

Archer, B. (2018). Man Utd news: Marouane Fellaini sends Jose Mourinho a 'special' message after announcement. *Express*, 29 June, www.express.co.uk/sport/football/981626/Man-Utd-news-Marouane-Fellaini-Jose-Mourinho

British Army Leadership Code an Introductory Guide. (2015). www.army.mod.uk/media/2698/ac72021_the_army_leadership_code_an_introductory_guide.pdf, accessed on 1 August 2018.

British Army Guide. (2014). January, www.scribd.com/document/339058833/Developing-Leaders-A-British-Army-Guide

Burt, J. (2016). Richard Scudamore: Few things can influence a community quite like football – that's why the future excites me. *The Telegraph*, 12 August, www.telegraph.co.uk/football/2016/08/12/premier-league-broadcast-revenues-top-8-billion-and-yet-chief-ex/, accessed on 15 February 2018.

Business in the Community website, https://gender.bitc.org.uk/all-resources/case-studies/army-inclusive-leadership-imperative

Davies, C. (2016). 'Overly sexualised' army culture will not change overnight, inquest told. *The Guardian*, 13 April, www.theguardian.com/uk-news/2016/apr/13/cheryl-james-overly-sexualised-army-culture-inquest-deepcut, accessed on 1 July 2018.

Davis, C. (2017). Arsenal midfielder Mesut Ozil reveals furious dressing room row with Jose Mourinho. *The Telegraph*, 2 March, www.telegraph.co.uk/football/2017/03/02/mesut-ozil-reveals-furious-dressing-room-row-jose-mourinho/

Dutton, J., Workman, K. and Hardin, A. (2014). Compassion at work. *Annual Review of Organizational Psychology and Organizational Behavior*, 1 (1), 277–304.

Elberse, A. (2013). Ferguson's formula. *Harvard Business Review*, October, https://hbr.org/2013/10/fergusons-formula, accessed on 26 December 2017.

Håkonsson, D., Burton, R., Obel, B. and Lauridsen, J. (2012). Strategy implementation requires the right executive style: Evidence from Danish SMEs. *Long Range Planning*, 45 (2–3), 182–208.

Haugstad, T. (2012). *The psychology behind Jose Mourinho*, 5 June, www.haugstadfootball.net/2012/06/05/the-psychology-behind-jose-mourinho/, accessed on 19 February 2018.

Hirschman, A. (1970). *Exit, voice and loyalty: Responses to decline in firms, organizations and states*. Cambridge, MA: Harvard University Press.

HSE. (2018). Work related stress, depression or anxiety statistics in Great Britain 2018, http://www.hse.gov.uk/statistics/causdis/stress.pdf, accessed on 15 January 2019.

Independent. (2016). *Jose Mourinho press conference: The full transcript*, 10 June, www.independent.co.uk/sport/football/premier-league/jose-mourinho-press-conference-the-full-transcript-8652655.html, accessed on 1 July 2018.

Independent. (2017). *Jose Mourinho is the best manager in the world, says Manchester United midfielder Nemanja Matic*, 19 October, www.independent.co.uk/sport/football/european/manchester-united-news-jose-mourinho-best-manager-in-world-nemanja-matic-a8009261.html

Live and Learn consultancy blog. *Jose Mourinho's leadership qualities, coaching skills & philosophy*, www.liveandlearnconsultancy.co.uk/top-5-leadership-tips-from-jose-mourinho/

Miles, R. E. and Snow, C. C. (1978). *Organizational strategy, structure, and process*. New York, NY: McGraw-Hill.

Moss, G., Kubacki, K., Hersh, M. and Gunn, R. (2010). Knowledge management: The benefits of collectivism, in *Profiting from diversity*. Basingstoke: Palgrave Macmillan.

Rindani, M. (2015). *6 top leadership lessons from Jose Mourinho*, 13 December, www.linkedin.com/pulse/6-top-leadership-lessons-from-jose-mourinho-manan-rindani, accessed on 31 August 2018.

Ryan, R. M. & Deci, E. L. (2000). Self-determination theory and the facilitation of intrinsic motivation, social development, and well-being. *American Psychologist*, 55, 68–78.

Winter, L. (2017). Jose Mourinho is world's best manager: He's done this so well at Man United – Paul Merson. *Daily Express*, www.express.co.uk/sport/football/798197/Man-United-News-Jose-Mourinho-Paul-Merson

5

INCLUSIVE LEADERSHIP

Boosting engagement, productivity, motivation, mental well-being and organisational diversity

As we have seen from the last two chapters, we live in a world where transactional and inclusive leadership co-exist. Many organisations still rely on transactional styles of leadership while a brave few have responded to the winds of change, embarking on the exciting journey to inclusive leadership. There, they will meet unimagined riches beyond the reach of transactional organisations, or so the interview evidence in the last two chapters would lead us to believe.

Robust, quantitative evidence for the benefits of inclusive leadership was, regrettably, lacking until 2016 when the UK-based Employers Network on Equality and Inclusion (enei) commissioned a rigorous study on the topic. So, the study was to produce a reliable definition of inclusive leadership (IL) and examine, through rigorous qualitative and quantitative evidence, its effects on employee productivity, motivation and well-being. At the same time, the research would determine the extent to which IL strongly correlated with the *explore* strategies discussed at the end of Chapter 2, so this was important new research.

The research team behind this consisted of myself as project leader, Dr Ceri Sims (chartered psychologist and responsible for all the statistical work on the project and helping also with survey development), Dr Ian Dodds (diversity and inclusion expert responsible for conducting a large proportion of the interviews and collating interview data) and Alan David (strategy expert with all the strategy input into the project). Respondent organisations embraced the public and private sectors and included the four sponsoring organisations (the CIPD, EY, Santander and Affinity Sutton, all members of the project steering committee) as well as Network Rail, the National Health Service, PageGroup recruitment and Sodexo. As the reader can imagine, the research team took up the challenge with enthusiasm and, after a detailed examination of the leadership literature made a decision to anchor the concept in transformational and servant leadership. From this, a new definition of inclusive leader emerged as someone who:

- is aware of their own biases and preferences and capable of empathy and confidence building
- actively seeks out and considers different views and perspectives, listening to and accepting people in an unqualified way
- sees diverse talent as something that can be grown to produce competitive advantage
- inspires diverse people to drive organisational and individual performance towards a shared vision, showing interest in and unqualified acceptance of individuals

A survey was then created in which the questions on the leadership style perceived by employees in respondent organisations were rooted in transformational and servant leadership, with the second half of the survey seeking employee perceptions of their own productivity, motivation and well-being. The big unknown related to whether there would be an association between answers to the questions on leadership style and those relating to self-perceptions of productivity, motivation and well-being, something that interviews with just under sixty people at all levels would seek to independently review.

This chapter presents the findings of the world's first rigorous empirical study on inclusive leadership but first a word first about the factors that prioritised a study on IL.

The shift to inclusive leadership

Earlier, in Chapter 2, we reviewed some of the powerful drivers that are nudging organisations away from transactional leadership. These include the importance of satisfying people's psychological needs for autonomy, relatedness and competence (Ryan and Deci, 2000) as well as the needs of an increasingly diverse customer base and workforce. The millennial generation for example (born 1980–1995), now 35% of the UK workforce, is one that is more likely than earlier generations to view cognitive diversity as essential for an organisational culture (Smith, 2015). Then, in terms of shifting societal values, we saw how the growing 'volatility, uncertainty, complexity and ambiguity' in organisational contexts (Wolf, 2007) necessitate a form of leadership that can ride sudden changes, particularly since command and control is widely acknowledged to be too rigid a style to steer the boat in choppy waters. This is where inclusive leadership comes into view.

Spotlight on inclusive leadership

Inclusive leadership had been the object of much discussion but, as we saw earlier, there had been no widely adopted definition of the term. In fact, research conducted just a year before the new research reported in this chapter (Nitu and Atewologun, 2015) had found that just 12% of academic articles on inclusive leadership refer to a theoretically established form of leadership, with leader-member exchange and transformational leadership being the most frequently cited theories in this tiny subset of papers. Moreover, as we have seen in chapter 1, the non-academic, grey literature, produced a large number of definitions with no internal consistency and precious little justification for their use. This of course reduces the reliability and validity of the empirical work conducted in these particular studies.

So what definition was used in this new enei research? As mentioned in Chapter 1, a decision was made to use the combined attributes of transformational (Tf) and servant leadership (SL), since jointly these appeared to map the IL concepts present in the academic and practitioner literatures (for details, see Table 1.5 in Chapter 1). In particular, one academic discussion of IL suggested that the concept of IL was reflected in a combination of these models (Echols, 2009), and retrospective justification for the use of these two models was provided, moreover, by the interviews and survey conducted as part of this new research.

For, in terms of the *interview* findings, 75% of the attributes that thirty-eight managers (in eleven organisations) volunteered as constituting inclusive leadership corresponded with SL while the remaining 25% of the attributes advanced corresponded with Tf leadership. Where the *survey* was concerned, two findings justified defining inclusive leadership in terms of Tf and SL conjointly, and the reader will excuse the slightly technical nature of these somewhat important points put forward by Dr Ceri Sims, the psychologist on the project:

(i) A Principal Component Analysis of the IL survey results demonstrated statistically high correlations between the transactional (Tf) and servant leadership (SL) constructs used. This is interesting since earlier research had suggested that they worked in divergent rather than similar ways, with SL working through follower need satisfaction and Tf working through perceived leader effectiveness (van Dierendonck *et al*, 2014).

(ii) A Multiple Regression Analysis using (a) the IL ratings in the first part of the survey (based on the Tf and SL constructs in the questions) and (b) the self-perceived productivity ratings produced by respondents, demonstrated that servant leadership (SL) and transformational (Tf) leadership together accounted for 80% of the variance in performance, engagement and well-being outputs, with SL accounting for 6% of that variance and Tf accounting for under 1% of that variance. This means that 73% of the variance in the model is accounted for by SL and Tf working *conjointly*, a result that corroborates an earlier finding of a positive interactive impact of Tf and SL on engagement (van Dierendonck *et al*, 2014). Note also that the positive impact of Tf and SL on employee engagement is supplemented in this study by a finding of enhancements in the areas of productivity and well-being as well.

So, in summary, the firm foundations of this new research supported by enei were rooted in:

• a valid definition of IL, rooted in Tf and SL
• survey questions on employee perceptions of leadership style that map closely to Tf and SL attributes

- survey questions on employee perceptions of personal outcomes taken from earlier research findings
- large number of interviews on IL in eleven organisations with senior and middle managers (thirty-eight in total) as well as with those without management responsibilities (twenty-one in total). Questions spanned respondents' understanding of inclusive leadership; their perceptions of the presence and if so, impacts, of IL; their peerceptions of the influence of the top person; and the type of organisational strategies in evidence in order to establish whether certain strategies map against inclusive leadership.

With the methodology behind us, it is time to unveil the findings from this groundbreaking research.

Survey results: benefits of inclusive leadership

The survey sought perceptions of the general leadership style within the organisation and also self-perceptions by respondents of their personal productivity, motivation and well-being. It was completed by those with either no management responsibility or first line management responsibility, with 966 responses obtained across eleven organisations. The results? A correlation of 0.87 appeared between employee perceptions of leaders as inclusive and their self-perceptions of themselves as highly productive, motivated and with positive mental well-being.

For those of us drawn to optimising leadership, this is an extremely exciting finding. For those interested in the rigour of the survey instrument and the internal consistency of the attributes, there were important findings, teased out by the psychologist on the team, Dr Ceri Sims. For example, the responses to the scale used in the first part of the survey to measure the perceived strength of IL in organisations (consisting of thirty-eight questions) yielded an excellent level of internal reliability with all thirty-eight items correlating to a high degree with the total scale.

Another striking finding, as we have seen, was the extent to which ratings of the fifteen competences underpinning the IL construct − four from transformational and eleven from servant leadership − strongly inter-correlated. For, the Principal Component Analysis in the responses to the thirty-eight questions on IL detected a single rather than multiple clusters of responses, showing that the IL construct is a unidimensional rather than a multidimensional construct. In fact, as Dr Sims concluded, "the underlying construct at the heart of employees' understanding of IL appears to be one in which the leader inspires and motivates all employees to achieve" (Moss *et al*, 2016, p. 21).

Dr Sims, offered two possible explanations. One is that the broad range of behaviours and skills required for IL are interrelated and tend to co-exist within the same leaders, a view held in fact by Greenleaf, the creator of the 'servant leader' concept. Following this logic, the apparently separate elements of IL are, in fact, multiple expressions of a single desire to form strong interpersonal relations with followers. In fact, as Dr Sims concluded, "the underlying construct at the heart of employees' understanding of IL appears to be one in which the leader inspires and motivates all employees to achieve" (Moss *et al*, 2016, p. 21).

In terms of an alternative explanation, the high level correlations between scores on a variety of attributes could be a manifestation of bias in followers' perceptions of their leaders, with followers more likely to view their leaders in an overall positive light when they are perceived as displaying just some of the IL characteristics.

TABLE 5.1 Summary of the survey findings showing variations according to demographics

SURVEY FINDINGS
Demographic factors

1. Eleven large organisations participated in the questionnaire with 966 complete set of answers both on the inclusive leadership scale (thirty-eight questions) and on the twelve questions that are part of the self-performance rating scale. Responses were elicited from those without management responsibilities as well as from those with first line management responsibilities.
2. Of those providing demographic information, 58% of participants were women. Their responses indicated a greater involvement in childcare than the men's responses.
3. Although the largest overall length of time in job was over ten years, more men than women reported being in their job for over ten years. Women were more likely to have no management responsibilities compared to men (F = 61.4%, M = 56.2%) and men were more likely to manage more than twenty staff compared to women (F = 7.9%, M = 11.1%).
4. Although the questionnaire was targeted to reach all demographic groups, there were clear differences in percentage responses between different groups: groups with strong responses included those from the 35–53 years age group, those without caring (or childcare) responsibilities outside of work, those with a white ethnic origin, a heterosexual orientation, being Christian (or no religious affiliation), not having a disability, having an undergraduate degree, having worked for the organisation for over ten years and having either none at all or little in the way of management responsibilities.

Survey reliability and IL attributes

5. The inclusive leadership scale showed a very high level of internal reliability. The fifteen characteristics measured on the IL scale were inter-correlated, and the scale is shown to measure a single underlying construct.

Correlations between IL and self-ratings of productivity, satisfaction and engagement

6. IL ratings were strongly related to self-ratings of productivity, motivation and mental well-being.
7. The youngest age group (Gen Y) gave higher ratings of IL and self-performance compared with other age groups. Younger employees whose educational level was at diploma or undergraduate levels accounted for these higher ratings. Younger employees whose educational level was at postgraduate or professional levels provided comparably lower ratings similar to that of the other age groups.
8. New employees (working in their organisation for less than a year) gave higher IL and self-performance ratings compared with employees who had been in their jobs for longer periods.

(Continued)

TABLE 5.1 (Continued)

9. Small group differences were shown for ethnicity, religion, disability and caring responsibilities. White, non-Christian and non-disabled employees without caring responsibilities indicated higher levels of IL and self-performance than other groups. Further research is needed with larger group sizes to explore these effects in more detail.
10. There were no effects for gender, sexual orientation and managerial responsibility and no clear effects of educational level for age groups other than the youngest group.

Organisations

11. Three clusters of organisations emerged, with three organisations producing high ratings for both IL and leader-influenced self-performance, two organisations producing moderate levels of ratings and five organisations showing lower levels of IL and leader-influenced self-performance. It can be seen that those organisations in which employees perceived high levels of IL were more likely to report positive levels of productivity, mental well-being and engagement amongst employees than organisations in which high levels of IL were not perceived. These results indicate that developing an inclusive leadership style can have a strong influence on levels of employee motivation, productivity and metnal well-being.

This is a process of thinking that reflects the well-known 'halo' effect that we know can influence people's thinking.

It should also be noted that whilst the survey data reveals apparently strong uniform responses across the sample, it also reveals patterns of response by individual variables. The most significant of these occur in comparisons across organisations and across demographic variables (age, length of service, ethnicity, education level and disability) with differences summarised in Table 5.1. A further important finding was that three groups of respondents – BME employees, those with over five years' service and disabled persons – reported lower ratings of overall inclusive leadership. It was however interesting to note that there were no differences in the survey ratings of leadership style based on the gender, sexuality, religion, childcare responsibilities or educational achievement of the respondents.

Interview results: benefits of inclusive leadership

A key finding from the fifty nine interviews conducted across the eleven organisations was that inclusive leadership must be role-modelled from the person at the apex of an organisation in order to have the greatest impact, since the behaviours and attitudes of the top person have a massive impact on the attitudes and behaviours of other people in the organisation. A further important lesson was that organisations adopting an 'explore' rather than 'exploit' strategy were more likely to be perceived as manifesting an inclusive style of leadership (see summary of interview findings in Table 5.2).

TABLE 5.2 Summary of interview findings

Qualitative comments

Much of the richness of the research emerges from the comments made by interview respondents in in-depth telephone interviews. Respondents were either senior or middle managers or those without management responsibilities. Below is a sample of responses to questions.

What does inclusive leadership mean for you?

Both managers and non-managers perceive the elements and priorities of inclusive leadership similarly, with 75% of the prioritised attributes corresponding with servant leadership and 25% with transformational leadership attributes. Overall, all groups perceive the priorities of inclusive leadership as being within eight areas, the differences being only in the prioritisation of five of the eight areas these five relating to the: importance of openness and transparency; development of diverse talent; importance of leading by example; importance of willingness to learn about and understand individuals' differences; and being fair. A definition of IL that appeared to reflect the views of a large proportion of respondents was therefore the following:

"*It is about taking people along with you and exercising leadership through engaging people and not through authority and making sure that ideas are explored within the team* (NHS, senior manager).

Outcomes

When offered a definition of IL, respondents proposed a number of benefits including, in descending order of frequency of response:

- improved performance and productivity
- enhanced loyalty
- the advance of underrepresented groups
- enhanced creativity
- better services to clients, customers and service users
- better teamwork
- improved motivation to go the extra mile
- higher retention
- Diverse talent pool

The first of these mirrors the survey findings of a strong correlation between perceived inclusive leadership and self-performance ratings of enhanced performance and productivity, with a typical respondent comment being:

"*People work more efficiently and effectively when they are happy, validated and listened to*" (NHS, senior manager).

"*Since you are taking people's views into account, you build up trust between people. This is a massive benefit in a large company since everyone feels that everyone is on the same page. Everyone trusts what everyone is doing*" (PageGroup, non-management).

There were some responses that highlighted possible negative outcomes with almost one-third of respondents suggesting that inclusive leadership could be time-consuming, and that a focus on enhancing diversity could cause offence.

Influence of the behaviour and attitudes of the top person on other people in the organisation

Some 80% of managers agreed that the behaviour and attitudes of the top person influences those of others throughout the organisation with the following being a typical view:

(Continued)

TABLE 5.2 (Continued)

"The influence of the top person is great because they share a vision and we all participate in activities to align us with the vision. This means that the top person's behaviours influence other people's behaviours to a great extent" (Sodexo, non-management).

Contextual and strategic factors

No more than one-third of respondents consider that a great deal of emphasis is placed on delegating power within their organisation. This is a relatively low figure, and increasing rates of delegation may set the conditions for enhanced inclusive leadership. In terms of the impact of an 'explore' as against an 'exploit' strategy, organisations registering the highest levels of inclusive leadership appear to have a greater emphasis on 'explore' strategies than organisations with lower levels of such an approach. Moreover, one-third of the manager responses indicate that the organisation is perceived as careful and reluctant, with only a small minority of respondents registering the organisation as keen to develop new ideas.

Whether change is needed

The research findings show a sense in some organisations that change is needed in leadership style, with a small majority of respondents indicating that change in organisational culture is also needed, with leaders needing to be more engaging and better models of inclusivity. For example, one respondent commented that their organisation's leadership style was hierarchical and "top down". Others indicated that change had been initiated and was still underway with the following view typical of this category of response:

"You can start to see that the people being recruited are inclusive and less of the 'Tell do' approach. The organisation is looking at being more inclusive – there is a drive on inclusivity" (Santander, senior manager).

Overall findings

The survey and interview results combined show that people at all levels believe that inclusive leadership brings many positive benefits to the organisation and the individuals within it. The benefits of IL, moreover, prioritised in the interviews consisted of enhancements to a range of elements including performance and productivity, creativity, loyalty, services to clients, customers and service users, teamwork, employee motivation and retention and a diverse talent pool.

Conclusions

Informed by a robust definition, the research findings reveal the power of inclusive leadership to enhance productivity, satisfaction and employee engagement and foster greater diversity in the organisation. It is to be hoped that these powerful findings will motivate organisations to embark on the important journey to a more inclusive style of leadership.

References

Echols, S. (2009). Transformational/servant leadership: A potential synergism for an inclusive leadership style. *Journal of Religious Leadership*, 8 (2), 85–116, http://arl-jrl.org/Volumes/Echols09.pdf

Moss, G., Sims, C., Dodds, I. and David, A. (2016). *Inclusive leadership . . . driving performance through diversity*. London: Employers Network on Equality and Inclusion (enei) *executive summary*, www.enei.org.uk/publications.php/769/inclusive-leadership . . . -driving-performance-throughdiversity-executive-summary?id=769

Nitu, M. and Atewologun, D. (2015). Inclusive leadership: A systematic review of the evidence. In *OP Matters*. British Psychological Society, 26, June.

Ryan, R. M. & Deci, E. L. (2000). Self-determination theory and the facilitation of intrinsic motivation, social development, and well-being. *American Psychologist*, 55, 68–78.

Smith, C. (2015). *The radical transformation of diversity and inclusion: The millennial influence*, Deloitte University, https://www2.deloitte.com/content/dam/Deloitte/us/Documents/about-deloitte/us-inclus-millennial-influence-120215.pdf, accessed on 25 August 2015.

Van Dierendonck, D., Stam, D., Boersma, P., de Windt, N. and Alkema, J. (2014). Same difference? Exploring the differential mechanisms linking servant leadership and transformational leadership to follower outcomes. *The Leadership Quarterly*, 25 (3), 544–562, www.sciencedirect.com/science/article/pii/S1048984313001409

Wolf, D. (2007). *Prepared and resolved: The strategic agenda for growth, performance and change*. dsb Publishing.

6

THE IMPACT OF ACADEMIC LEADERSHIP BEHAVIOURS ON BME STUDENT ATTAINMENT, MOTIVATION AND WELL-BEING IN THE UK

Introduction

The empirical research detailed in the previous chapter was the first on inclusive leadership to be rooted in a rigorous definition of IL and so its finding that the perceived presence of IL can boost employee productivity, motivation and well-being are all the more important. Could a similar effect be observed in relation to students and their views of multi-level leadership?

In order to put this question to the test, the Leadership Foundation for Higher Education in the UK, a body with a watching brief over the quality of leadership in higher education, commissioned a research project looking at the impact of academic leadership style on student attainment. This was in 2016, and we publish here the full and final report of the research undertaken by the research team consisting of Gloria Moss (project leader), Dr Ceri Sims, John Tatam and Nona McDuff. A summary of the research appeared on the Leadership Foundation website (now named 'Advance HE', a new umbrella body for the sector) and you can find it at this link – https://tinyurl.com/y836mly6. Do note that the immediate focus in this research was the attainment of black minority ethnic (BME) students and the effect of leadership style on this – an issue probed in the interviews. However, the survey was completed by BME as well as white undergraduate students, so the survey conclusions speak for the whole student body.

The results, as the reader will see, reveal a very strong link between inclusive multi-level academic leadership and student productivity, motivation and well-being. This finding is potentially important not just for higher education but for the education sector as a whole – including further, secondary and primary levels – since there may be many areas there that remain as yet untouched by inclusive leadership.

We do hope that the reader will bear with the slightly academic style of this report, since the importance of the topic and the finding of a potential link with academic leadership style warrants a detailed rather than popularised summary. Corroboration of the findings are provided in the next chapter comparing the survey results reported here for the students in the UK university with similar findings from a Norwegian university.

Report: the BME attainment gap

UK higher education (HE) can claim some success in widening the participation of UK-domiciled BME students with the proportion of UK-domiciled BME students in HE up from 14.9% in 2003/4 to 21.8% in 2015/16 and a higher proportion of BME school leavers now attending British universities than their white counterparts (ECU, 2017; Tatlow, 2015). Regrettably however, BME students are less likely than white students to achieve a degree, to gain a first or upper second, to move on to graduate employment or study, or to obtain employment (HEFCE, 2013). So, of all UK-domiciled students graduating in 2016 across the UK, 78.4% of white students achieved a first or 2:1, compared to only 63.4% of BME students – a gap of fifteen percentage points (ECU, 2017). Or, to put it another way, 24% more of the white student cohort received a 1st or 2:1 than the BME student cohort. This is in contrast to schools where Indian, Bangladeshi, Pakistani and black African children all achieve better GCSE results on average than do white children (DfE, 2015). Unfortunately, no similar ethnicity-based data is reliably available in respect of 'A' level results.

Causes of the BME attainment gap

There is growing awareness that the causes of the BME attainment gap are multicausal. Initial explanations tended to focus on the 'deficiency' of the student in relation to factors such as entry qualifications, socio-economic status, work and family commitments or cultural differences. However, some large and well-controlled studies, for example Broecke and Nicholls (2007) and more recently the Higher Education Funding Council for England (HEFCE) (2015), have convincingly challenged this view. The 2015 HEFCE report, for example, compared results of over 280,000 students graduating from English universities in 2013/14, showing that the attainment gap of sixteen percentage points in those obtaining a first- or upper-second-class degree (76% white vs 60% BME) was only reduced to fifteen percentage points when controlling for entry qualifications, age, disability, a participation of local areas measure, gender, subject studied, previous school type and institution attended.

In contrast to the deficiency model, there is evidence that institutional context and culture may play a role in BME students' poorer results. It has, for instance, been suggested that an institutional culture traditionally geared for young, white students and the middle classes (Stuart *et al*, 2009a; Jabbar and Mirza, 2017) may have a negative effect on the identity and feelings of belonging of students from BME backgrounds. By way of example, the strong culture of drinking alcohol may serve as an exclusionary practice for Muslim students (Stuart *et al*, 2009b), and bias may be perceived in the reporting of racism on campus (Cousin and Cuerton, 2012; Tate and Bagguly, 2017).

Bringing these factors together, a major review of the literature, funded by HEFCE, identified four principal factors in the BME attainment gap, some institutional and some non-institutional (Mountford-Zimdars *et al*, 2015):

- *curricula and learning*, including teaching and assessment practices
- *relationships between staff and students* as well as between students themselves. A sense of 'belonging' emerged as a key determinant of student outcomes
- *social, cultural and economic capital factors*: differences in how students experience HE (sometimes a function of financial situations), network and draw on external support were noted
- *psychosocial and identity factors*: whether students felt supported and encouraged in their daily interactions within their institutions and with staff members was noted as an important factor

Despite the reference to staff/student relationships, the possible impact of institutional leadership on BME attainment was overlooked here and elsewhere. This is a major oversight given the importance given to leadership in the literatures on management and on schools. So, this small-scale study was the first to explore the possible impact of leadership behaviours, specifically inclusive leadership, on BME and white student attainment.

Leadership

The compendious research on leadership has produced no fewer than 1,400 definitions according to Kellerman (2012), who has advocated a move from focusing on traits to one emphasising the three interlinking factors of the leader, followers and context (Kellerman, 2015). This approach has analogies with distributed leadership (Bennett *et al*, 2003; Bolden *et al*, 2015) and its emphasis on a network of interacting individuals, open boundaries to leadership and expertise distributed across the many and not the few. Relatedly, leadership is described by education and industry commentators (Forde *et al*, 2011; Canwell *et al*, 2014 respectively) as a multilevel activity with the consistency (Oshagbemi and Gill, 2004) and 'connectedness' (Forde *et al*, 2011, p. 57) of leadership across the hierarchy creating the defining culture of organisations (Schein, 2010; Moss *et al*, 2016).

In the literature on school pupil attainment and school leadership, most studies estimate a direct effect of leadership on student attainment (Levačić *et al*, 2003) with the pupils' assessment of 'headteacher leadership' and the adults' rating of 'warm teacher–pupil relationships' having positive and significant effects in six out of the seven attainment measures. Unfortunately, there have been no studies relating leadership behaviours in Higher Education to student outcomes and this study fills the gap by considering the impact of multi-level academic leadership behaviours on student attainment as well as their motivation and well-being.

Higher education and leadership behaviours

Why a focus on leadership in HE? The sector is characterised by "rapid and extensive [sectoral] change" (Peters and Ryan, 2014), a lack of certainties (Bolden *et al*, 2015), increasing market pressures on UK HE (Dopson *et al*, 2016), the need to keep academics productive and happy (*ibid*) and a sense that HE institutions (HEIs) whose survival is not at risk should operate distributive and inclusive leadership (*ibid*).

What is the prevailing style of leadership in UK HEIs? Unfortunately, there appears to have been just one study in the last fifteen years addressing this question directly (Davies, 2002). Based on a study of fifteen HEIs, the study found an emphasis on management by exception, a feature as we know of 'transactional' leadership, and also found an absence of inspirational motivation and individual consideration, elements as we know of a 'transformational' style of leadership.

While this is the only study documenting the nature of leadership behaviours in UK HEIs, there have been several discussing ideal leadership behaviours. One study quoting the preferences of academic staff (Peters and Ryan, 2014) for example, identified a preference for an inclusive style of leadership with attributes such as 'warmth and morality' (*ibid*, p. 41). A second study (Tysome, 2014) called for a new style of leadership with leaders employing a 'light-touch' approach using good communication, persuasive argument and interpersonal skills to achieve clearly articulated outcomes.

A third and more recent study (Dopson *et al*, 2016) called for 'distributed, plural, or collective and relational leadership' (*ibid*, p. 56,) with the detail of this modelled on five dimensions identified in earlier studies as applicable to an HE context (Bolden *et al*, 2003, 2008). These dimensions are the *personal* (for example emotional intelligence, authenticity, openness, interpersonal and persuasion skills), the *social* (for example the leader's ability to develop trust, teamwork and delegation), the *structural* and the *developmental* (anticipating outcomes beyond the term of duty of the leader who thereby acts in an organisational stewardship role).

Inclusive leadership

Bolden *et al*'s dimensions map closely, as we have seen earlier in the book, to inclusive leadership (IL) and for those of you coming to this chapter fresh, you may wish to look at Table 6.1 showing the underpinning concepts of IL developed in earlier research by the author and Dr Ceri Sims (Moss *et al*, 2016; Sims *et al*, 2016). For those arriving here from previous chapters, you may wish to resume your reading from the paragraphs that follow Table 6.2.

TABLE 6.1 Attributes underpinning the concept of inclusive leadership

Competence	Description	Whether from Transformational (Tf) or Servant Leadership (SL) models
Individualised consideration	Showing individual interest and offering one-to-one support for followers	Tf
Idealised influence	Having admirable qualities that followers want to identify with	Tf
Inspirational motivation	Providing an appealing vision that inspires followers	Tf
Intellectual stimulation	Encouraging followers to develop their ideas and to be challenged	Tf
Unqualified acceptance	Being inclusive in considering followers	SL
Empathy	Putting oneself mentally and emotionally into the follower's place	SL
Listening	Actively listening to followers	SL
Persuasion	Being able to influence followers	SL
Confidence building	Providing followers with opportunities and recognition	SL
Growth	Encouraging followers to reach their full potential	SL
Foresight	Having the ability to anticipate events and where they might lead	SL
Conceptualisation	Having a vision about possibilities and articulating that vision to followers	SL
Awareness	Being fully open and aware of environmental cues	SL
Stewardship	Articulating the belief that the organisation's legacy is to contribute to society	SL
Healing	Helping followers cope with any burdens	SL

The manner in which these fifteen attributes mirror Bolden's recommended categories for HE are furthermore shown in Table 6.2, demonstrating the applicability (following Bolden *et al*) of inclusive leadership to an HE context.

Some readers might imagine servant leadership to be more leader-centric than distributed leadership given the number of SL constructs that reference the leader's

TABLE 6.2 The way that Bolden *et al*'s (2008 and 2009) concepts of distributive leadership in HE map against transformational and servant leadership concepts

Bolden et al (2008 and 2009) categories	Way that the 15 Transformational (Tf) and Servant Leadership (SL) attributes map against these
Personal (vision, values, ethics, emotional intelligence, openness, authenticity, interpersonal and persuasive skills)	Conceptualisation (SL); individualised consideration (Tf); empathy (SL); listening (SL); confidence building (SL); persuasion (SL)
Social (ability to navigate social groups, network and develop trust, mentoring, teambuilding)	Idealised influence (Tf); inspirational motivation (Tf); intellectual stimulation (Tf); unqualified acceptance (SL); empathy (SL); listening (SL); confidence building (SL); healing (SL)
Structural (devolution of responsibility)	Growth (SL)
Contextual (outer social and inner organisational contexts)	Foresight (SL); awareness (SL); healing (SL); conceptualisation (SL); stewardship (SL)
Developmental (having an impact over time and being organisational stewards)	Stewardship (SL); growth (SL)

rather than the follower's perspective but a recent study has described the *practice* of servant leadership as supporting 'academic freedoms' (Allen *et al*, 2016):

> The servant leader's commitment to individual growth cultivates an environment of academic Freedom and provides tools for effective scholarship . . . Servant leadership makes shared governance feasible . . . In a turbulent organisational landscape employers utilize shared governance as they rely on employees to be creative, autonomous problem solvers.
>
> *(ibid)*

Note that the reference to "shared governance" has echoes of distributed leadership, something that Bennis (2002) proposes should be present alongside trust, vision and meaning in a regime of servant leadership. In this way, the practice of servant and transformational leadership are both compatible with the delivery of distributed leadership, a style of leadership favoured, as we have seen, in recent reports on academic leadership in the UK (Bolden *et al*, 2008, 2009; Dopson *et al*, 2016). Note also that the authors go on to discuss the positive impact of servant leadership on student learning (Allen *et al*, 2015).

Leadership and BME attainment

The research described in this chapter then is the first to empirically investigate associations between IL and student academic outcomes in HE. It should be noted that the additional focus in this work on motivation and well-being provides an important context to students' learning (Mazzucchelli and Purcell, 2015) as well as to the leadership within the organisation (Kellerman, 2015). Note also that the inclusion of the concept of motivation was also driven by the BME interview respondents' rating of this as the most important factor in attainment. Note also that the concept of 'well-being' used in the survey, relates to health, stress and satisfaction with the course.

Methodology

General approach

This was a single-institution study involving a two-step process. In the first stage, a set of in-depth interviews were conducted and in a second stage, survey data was collected to test existing and emerging theory. Note that in the interview phase, most of the questions followed a deductive approach in testing reactions to the institutional and non-institutional factors already identified in the BME attainment gap literature with just a few questions following a grounded theory approach in testing reactions to the new factor of multi-level leadership. So most of the interview research was rooted in a deductive approach (Snieder and Larner, 2009), with just the questions on multi-level leadership rooted in an inductive, grounded-theory approach (Glaser and Strauss, 1999).

In terms of the selection of student interview respondents, key factors related to ease of access as well as the presence of equal numbers of men and women and undergraduates from across each of the degree years. Ethics approval was gained from the Ethics Committee of Buckinghamshire New University, employer of two of the project team members, and permission was gained in two stages, the first for the interviews and the second for the survey. The somewhat interesting results of the two phases follow.

Interviews

In a first stage, semi-structured interviews with a sample of BME students were held in order to obtain their views on the personal and institutional (including leadership) factors that they considered might affect their academic attainment. Homogeneous purposive sampling was used with BME respondents spanning the three years of degree study and a range of faculties and disciplines. Ten was the final number of BME student respondents accepted for interview based on two considerations:

(i) *Theoretical*: while it is commonly acknowledged that quantitative sampling is driven by the imperative of *representativeness*, qualitative sampling is concerned with the richness of data. So, the potential richness of qualitative data can place a lesser priority on representativeness than on the achievement of quality data (Gummesson, 1991) making non-probability homogeneous sampling an appropriate tool (Lincoln and Guba, 1986; Glaser and Strauss, 1999). A key issue then becomes identifying and gaining access to key informants (Crimp and Wright, 1995) and since the incidence of six respondents has occurred in peer-reviewed research in education (Barton and Tan, 2009) and since the use of small and appropriate samples is cited as a legitimate way of providing data on people's behaviour and especially attitudes (Smith and Fletcher, 2001), it was appropriate to conduct in-depth, semi-structured interviews with ten undergraduates. These were in-depth interviews with the average interview duration being one hour.

(ii) *Practical*: a short time span was available for recruiting students, since the host university placed a moratorium on interviews and surveys beyond a particular date, with all empirical work needing to be completed within the first semester of the academic year.

In terms of personnel, two interviewers undertook the interviews, one male and one female, both following a detailed schedule of questions (see below). Interviewees, for their part, self-selected in response to an email invitation to participate in the research and due to email spam rules, this was sent out in batches until the time limit for interviews had expired and ten students had responded. The students were then selected using a quote sampling approach to ensure representation from different faculties, with two from the first, seven from the second and a final respondent from the third year.

In terms of logistics, interviews were conducted by telephone in order to facilitate their scheduling, with ethical procedures read to the students and agreed orally by the interviewer and oral agreement offered by the student.

The intention was to understand issues from the student perspective, with a schedule of questions relating to the previous factors highlighted in the literature (see Tables 6.3 and 6.4) as well as to the new factor of multi-level leadership. Given the fact that all of the interview questions, bar those on the new factor of leadership, were picking up on factors discussed in the earlier BME literature, thematic analysis of the interview data was used on the basis that this is a 'powerful' and 'flexible tool' (Braun and Clarke, 2006, p. 78) suitable for data analysis in deductive, theory-based research searching for "repeated patterns of meaning" (*ibid*, p. 86) and unpicking or unraveling "the surface of 'reality'" (*ibid*, p. 81). Respondents' answers

TABLE 6.3 Factors discussed in student deficiency accounts of the BME attainment deficit

Factor	Study
Difficulty understanding academic language; secondary education has left ethnic minority students with poorer entry qualifications, and less effective forms of study behaviour; writing skills were viewed as being more problematic for BME overseas and male students.	Leathwood and O'Connell (2003); Dhanda, 2009; Richardson, 2008; Cotton *et al*, 2013

(Continued)

TABLE 6.3 (Continued)

Factor	Study
BME students, particularly males, more motivated by extrinsic factors (e.g. job prospects) than by intrinsic factors (interest in the subject) leading to greater surface learning. Parental influence can be relatively great in influencing course choice.	Cotton *et al*, 2013
BME male students more likely to miss lectures than female BME students. Female BME students meanwhile, especially home students, more likely to have childcare responsibilities.	Cotton *et al*, 2013
BME students develop mental health issues that impact academic attainment as a result of being a racial minority.	Bristol University, Students Union, 2016

to the new question on leadership, on the other hand, could be analysed in relation to the general literature on leadership.

For every question posed, BME respondents were asked to (i) comment on the issue (ii) offer a priority rating for that factor in terms of its impact on their academic attainment by providing a mark out of 10 (with 10 denoting the highest priority) and (iii) compare their impressions of the incidence of this factor at school with that at university. They were also, finally, asked to comment (iv) on the level(s) and type of leadership behaviours most likely to influence their attainment.

Survey

An analysis of the interviews highlighted the extent to which BME students perceived inclusive academic leadership behaviours as impacting their motivation to study and their academic success and this finding informed the development of a survey that would allow correlations to be perceived between students' perceptions of (i) the incidence of inclusive leadership in multi-level academic leadership in the university and (ii) their own academic productivity, motivation and well-being. At the same time, in order to compare BME and white students' responses, the questionnaire was distributed to BME as well as white students in order to establish whether or not there were unique features in the BME responses.

The survey was modelled on the inclusive leadership survey developed as part of the project for the Employers Network on Equality and Inclusion (enei) and described in Chapter 5 (Moss, 2016; Moss *et al*, 2016), with the language and concepts of the employee survey amended to suit an educational context and an audience of university students.

Some other points regarding the survey are worth drawing to the reader's attention:

TABLE 6.4 Factors, beyond the student deficiency model, advanced to account for the BME attainment deficit

Factor	Study
Cultural disconnects; discrimination addressed to BME overseas students	Gonzalez, 2003; Cotton *et al*, 2013
Social exclusion; lack of inter-ethnic integration; lack of sense of belonging and connection with the university culture	Gonzalez, 2003; Leathwood and O'Connell, 2003; Davies and Garret, 2012; Harper, 2013; Meeuwisse *et al*, 2014; Mountford-Zimdars *et al*, 2015)
Unconscious bias by academics; conscious bias	Milkman *et al*, 2014; Harper, 2013; NUS, 2011
Academics can place the blame for the attainment gap on BME students	Stevenson and Whelan, 2013; Stevenson, 2012
Unfair assessment and insufficient transparency in assessment systems	NUS, 2011
Reduced expectations of BME students by academics; BME students have a weak perception of their own intellectual abilities leading to low expectations and low confidence, although some evidence of over-estimation of abilities, particularly in BME males	Cockley, 2003; Leathwood and O'Connell, 2003; Dhanda, 2009; Cowden and Singh, 2012; Cotton *et al*, 2013
Under-representation of BME academics in elite UK universities; sense of being 'other' even before arriving at the university	Rathi and Ware, 2014
Non-inclusive curriculum	Patton, *et al*, 2007; NUS, 2011
BME students reluctant to ask questions in class	Cotton *et al*, 2010
Lecturers not being approachable before or after the lecture; a significant majority of students believe that more contact with lecturers outside formal lectures or classes would improve their performance	Dhanda, 2009

(a) Likely accuracy of student ratings of leadership behaviours of leaders

There are good reasons for supposing that follower ratings are more accurate than self-ratings of leaders, since leniency biases can interfere with the latter and bring overestimates of performance (Podsakoff and Organ, 1986).

(b) Amendments to the employee survey on inclusive leadership

The decision to amend the earlier employee survey on inclusive leadership behaviours was made after it became clear from the interview responses that students were seeking an inclusive style from the multi-level leadership in the university. As mentioned, the process then involved members of the team considering how each of the statements could be adapted for student use whilst keeping the meaning of statements intact.

(c) Format of the survey

As in the survey used in the industry study reported in the previous chapter, the modified survey instrument consisted of fifty questions, thirty-eight of which sought perceptions as to the academic leadership behaviours exercised by multi-level academic leaders within the university, with a further twelve questions focused on students' self-perceptions of their own academic productivity, motivation and well-being. Negatively worded items were reverse scored so that a rating of 5 indicated a high level of academic IL or self-ratings for each of the items on both of the scales. For example, a 'strongly agree' rating to the statement "I have little trust in leaders' abilities to create a university where all students are valued and respected" would indicate a low IL rating and would need reverse scoring so that high total scores on the questionnaire reflect high overall ratings of IL.

(d) Dissemination of survey

Methods of disseminating the survey included (i) social media, (ii) the university student webpage and (iii) email. Unfortunately, time constraints meant that the invitation to students to participate in the survey was live for only seven days and then only during the winter holiday period.

(e) Statistical analyses

Methods used included Pearson correlations and regression statistics to examine associations between IL and outcome ratings, and t-tests to examine differences, if any, between BME and white groups on each of the measures. Further analyses were conducted to explore any potential nuanced patterns within the BME sample, although analyses here were limited due to small group sizes.

Results

Semi-structured interviews

Responses relating to factors identified in the earlier BME attainment gap literature

Interview questions included elements, both individual and institutional, that had been identified in earlier literature as factors in the BME attainment gap. In terms of responses to the questions posed in relation to individual ('ind') and institutional ('inst') factors, these are shown in Table 6.5 below.

TABLE 6.5 Overview of interview responses (excluding responses to the new element of multi-level academic leadership)

Factor drawn from the literature	Whether an individual ('ind') or institutional ('inst') factor	Summary of BME respondent comments on this factor
Academic language	Ind	Six respondents did not feel prepared for the academic challenges of HE and, of the four who did, two had pursued a course that had prepared them.
Intrinsic /extrinsic motivation	Ind	A single respondent cited parental influence as a factor in their selection of their degree subject with the predominant view being that the student had been responsible for their subject choice.
Attendance	Ind	Seven of the students claimed to attend virtually all lectures, missing only because of illness.
Willingness to ask questions in class	Ind	Generally, the interviewees expressed confidence in their ability to ask questions in class.
Culture	Inst	All but one student described themselves as being "very comfortable" at the university.
Sense of belonging	Inst	All but three had a strong sense of belonging.
Sense of diversity	Inst	Diversity was seen as being celebrated by the majority of respondents, there appeared to be a lesser tendency to consider this on courses with low proportions of BME students.
Unconscious bias	Inst	There was a sense that though staff tried to be fair there might be some unconscious bias for example in the way students with accents were treated.
Fair assessment	Inst	Eight of the ten respondents felt assessment criteria were transparent.
Expectations of own ability	Inst	All but two respondents were confident that lecturers shared their own expectations of their abilities.

(Continued)

TABLE 6.5 (Continued)

Factor drawn from the literature	Whether an individual ('ind') or institutional ('inst') factor	Summary of BME respondent comments on this factor
Representation of BME academics	Inst	The majority of the respondents did not feel that the lack of BME academic staff would affect their attainment.
Inclusive curriculum	Inst	Nine of the respondents were satisfied, with just one calling one for a greater diversity of perspectives.
Approachability of lecturers	Inst	Nine of the respondents described lecturers as 'quite' or 'very' approachable.

Leadership and its impact on academic attainment

It can be seen clearly from the summary of interviews in Table 6.5 that the vast majority of students do not have negative experiencs of any of the thirteen factors identified in the previous literature (four individual and nine institutional factors) as largely responsible for the BME attainment gap.

This leaves open the question as to the part played by multi-level leadership in the BME attainment gap, the focus of the final section of the interviews. Here, BME respondents were asked to comment on (a) the level of academic leadership that could impact student attainment, (b) the kind of leadership behaviours that they regarded as ideal, (c) the importance of communications with multi-level leadership, (d) their ability to name leaders at varying levels of the hierarchy and (e) comparison of contacts across the hierarchy at school and at university. These questions had not been posed previously in studies of the BME attainment gap, and responses are shown below.

(a) Level of academic leadership that could impact BME student attainment

In terms of levels of academic leaders that could influence student attainment, four students cited lecturers and three, tutors. References were also made to module leaders, to a professor and to deans of faculty and Vice-Chancellors. Here are some indicative comments to give you a flavour of students' responses:

> Two design tutors have been particularly influential because they work most closely with us. We have a lot of contact with them so it is not a traditional

relationship. They've been very nurturing and they can be harsh but I see the reasoning behind their advice. They are approachable and do not care about sticking to tight regulations. The tutors that I like are flexible.

Lecturers and personal tutors are kind, listen if you have questions and are full of energy and passion for their field. People think that scientists are boring but they can be ecstatic, happy and smiling about their fields.

(b) The kind of leadership behaviours that they regard as ideal

Respondents were asked for their views concerning the ideal characteristics of lecturers and senior academic leaders and were also asked to compare the incidence of these ideal characteristics at university and at school. In terms of ideal characteristics in lecturers and senior staff, interview respondents emphasised:

- Approachability and friendliness
- Kindness, understanding, not being dismissive
- Visibility.

The frequency with which these responses emerged in respect of multi-level leadership (i.e. leadership across the academic hierarchy) can be found in Table 6.6.

Moreover, the way in which BME students' views of ideal leadership relate to the concept of inclusive leadership are shown in Table 6.7, revealing the extent to which their idealised model of multi-level academic leadership is inclusive in character.

Here are some indicative comments:

Comments on lecturers: "Someone approachable who is available and kind and not dismissive"; "Lecturers should be very encouraging; office hours availability; open to questions; friendly; more senior people should be like this too but I never see them or speak to them"; "Happy, passionate person who likes their subject. Not too formal but knowing what the appropriate boundaries are. Approachable".

Comments on senior academic staff: "Would be good if senior staff were more approachable so that if you're walking in the corridor, they could say 'hello' and ask how the course is going. This would make university life more like a family and would make senior people more aware of what is happening. If they don't do this, then students become numbers. All that senior people see is numbers and statistics but if they have more contact with students, they will get a better picture of why things are as they are."

TABLE 6.6 The incidence of behaviours cited as ideal by BME interview respondents

Ideal leadership behaviour characteristic	Number of times this characteristic is volunteered in respect of academic staff		
	Lecturers	Senior academic Staff	Totals
Approachable, friendly	5	3	8
Communication with students	2	1	3
Open-door policy	1	1	2
Frequent checking of emails	2	1	3
Available to answer questions	2	1	3
Kind, understanding, not dismissive	4	2	6
Visible	–	3	3
Encouraging and positive	2	1	3
Practical life experience	1	1	2
Subject enthusiasm	1	1	2
Interested in the student and able to assess their academic abilities and offer advice	1	1	2
Understanding students	1	1	2

TABLE 6.7 How BME students' concepts of idealised academic leadership behaviours relate to inclusive leadership (numbers in brackets show number of respondents mentioning this factor)

Inclusive leadership attributes	Description	Whether from Transformational (Tf) or Servant Leadership (SL) models	Students' concepts of ideal leadership mapped against inclusive leadership attributes, with the number of times cited by students shown in brackets
Individualised consideration	Showing individual interest and offering one-to-one support for followers	Tf	Approachable, friendly (8)
Idealised influence	Having admirable qualities that followers want to identify with	Tf	
Inspirational motivation	Providing an appealing vision that inspires followers	Tf	Subject enthusiasm (2)
Intellectual stimulation	Encouraging followers to develop their ideas and to be challenged	Tf	Available to answer questions (3) Subject enthusiasm (2)

Inclusive leadership attributes	Description	Whether from Transformational (Tf) or Servant Leadership (SL) models	Students' concepts of ideal leadership mapped against inclusive leadership attributes, with the number of times cited by students shown in brackets
Unqualified acceptance	Being inclusive in considering followers	SL	Open-door policy (2) Not dismissive (6)
Empathy	Putting oneself mentally and emotionally into the follower's place	SL	Understanding (6)
Listening	Actively listening to followers	SL	Interested in the student and offering advice (2)
Persuasion	Being able to influence followers	SL	Visible (3)
Confidence building	Providing followers with opportunities and recognition	SL	Encouraging (3)
Growth	Encouraging followers to reach their full potential	SL	Encouraging and positive (3) Able to assess students' academic abilities (2)
Foresight	Having the ability to anticipate events and where they might lead	SL	Life experience (1)
Conceptualisation	Having a vision about possibilities and articulating that vision to followers	SL	Communication with students (3)
Awareness	Being fully open and aware of environmental cues	SL	Open-door policy (2)
Stewardship	Articulating the belief that the organisation's legacy is to contribute to society	SL	
Healing	Helping followers cope with any burdens	SL	Understanding students (2)

"Would be very nice to know the senior people to begin with so that you can put a name to a face. Then, they should have the same characteristics as the lecturers, and even more so since they set an example to the lecturers. They should make themselves more visible to students – walking around the library for example – but we don't know who they are."

(c) The importance of communications with multi-level leadership

In terms of the importance of communications with multi-level academic leadership, six students thought that frequent communications were important with people at the level of lecturer and module leader and half of the sample thought it important at the level of dean and vice-chancellor (V-C) as well.

Where communications with lecturer and module leaders were concerned, one respondent took the view that communication with course leaders was less important than with lecturers and personal tutors but that it was good to know that you could speak to course leaders. Another student spoke of the importance of contact with the personal tutor and course leaders on the basis that the course that they were following (Foundation in Art and Design) demanded that students made many presentations and critiques of their work and plentiful feedback on these was useful. The respondent pointed out that it is possible to easily spend a day going down 'the wrong track' without guidance and feedback.

In terms of communications with more senior people at the level of dean and V-C, half of the respondents identified the importance of communicating with senior people with arguments focused on the fact that (i) this would provide senior staff with student-relevant information, (ii) it would help the students feel part of more than just a department and would provide a joined-up sense of the university, (iii) senior staff were perceived as being able to offer more help than lecturers and (iv) it would give students a sense that senior staff cared for them.

Some of the comments that were typical of students' responses are shown below:

"I had a problem with the course and we were told to bring problems to lecturers and not to senior people. But senior people could have power to help more than the lecturers."

"Very important to be able to communicate with people right up to V-C because it's important to open up channels of communication otherwise people in leadership have no understanding of the student experience. I think that if senior academic leaders don't understand what affects us, they're not best placed to lead. I've never seen the V-C; I've met the dean once in 18 months: we've had a change of dean and I've never seen the new dean. These sort of things are quite important because they affect how much a student feels that they are cared about."

"My course leader knows who I am and she has 30 students to look after and beyond that I don't know what goes on and it is important to have the opportunity to know what goes on beyond the course leader because otherwise I don't see the point of the university – the course might just as well exist on its own."

"I would like a greater number of senior people to inform us more, for example about plans for the campus and would like an opportunity to be spoken to – it should not just be about logging onto the Intranet to get information on what is going on in the faculty."

(d) Ability to name leaders at varying levels of the hierarchy

Respondents were also asked to indicate their ability to put a name to people at different levels of the organisation, from lecturers, personal tutors, course leaders to dean of faculty and vice-chancellor, the assumption being that knowing the name of a senior person would indicate a degree of familiarity with that person. In fact, whereas all respondents could name their lecturers and personal tutors, just three students could name the dean of faculty and only one could name the vice-chancellor (see Table 6.8).

The students' inability to name senior people suggests minimal or perhaps no communication with these senior staff, even though half of the interviewees considered communication with staff at the level of dean and V-C to be essential.

(e) Comparison of contacts across the hierarchy at school and at university

When invited to compare the frequency of contacts with senior people at university and at school, 75% of respondents spoke of more such contacts occurring at school, with only one respondent referring to more such contacts at university and one describing a similar level of activity at school and at university. Comments that were typical of students' views included the following:

"Staff across the hierarchy at school had more engagement with the students."
"More teachers were like this (i.e. experienced, approachable and interactive)."
"Fewer contacts at school. Teachers tended to be relatively older, very nice but formal and old fashioned."
"About the same. Yes, there was a particular teacher at school who was trying to push me and check up on assignments."
"Had a lot more interaction at school and this interaction across the hierarchy made me feel that someone cared about my performance and my doing well."

TABLE 6.8 The incidence with which BME undergraduate students can name multi-level academic leaders

Position	Number of respondents able to put a name to the person at this level
Lecturer	10
Personal tutor	10
Course leader	8
Dean of faculty	3
Vice-chancellor	1

"My contact with the Head was very good and she knew me on a first name basis."

"More contact at all levels at school. The head teacher was informal and widely available. He was passionate about science and the biology teacher recognised and supported that enthusiasm."

"Two or three teachers particularly helped – more approachable, more understanding, a better, more personal relationship than at university."

Summary of interview findings

Prioritisation of institutional and non-institutional factors

In terms of a comparison of the ratings that students gave to the impact of institutional and non-institutional factors on their academic attainment, these are shown in Table 6.9, with the top-rated four factors shown in bold.

As can be seen from Table 6.9, the factors rated by BME students as most likely to influence their academic attainment are those related to self-motivation, fairness of treatment and assessment and the presence of ideal types of academic leaders

TABLE 6.9 Average of students' ratings regarding the impact of certain factors on their academic attainment (top four scores shown in bold)

Topic	Average BME student rating on the extent (on a scale of 1–10 with 10 being the most significant) to which a factor impacts academic attainment
Culture that can connect with a feeling of belonging	7.4
Feeling included	7.8
Students treated fairly and equally by all academic staff	**9.1**
Fair assessments	**9.3**
Lecturers' expectations in line with those of students	8.2
Representation of BME academics on the faculty	4.6
An inclusive curriculum	5.8
An environment in which students are willing to ask questions	7.5
Approachability of lecturers	8.7
Academic language that can be understood	7.8
Self-motivation	**9.4**
Attendance at lectures	8.5
Behaviour of academic leaders at all levels of the hierarchy	8.0
Ideal academic leadership across the hierarchy	**8.8**

across the hierarchy. The priority given to an ideal form of academic leadership shows the importance placed on this by BME students, something not identified in previous literature on the BME attainment gap.

Comparison of school and university experiences

In the course of the in-depth interviews, BME students were asked to compare their experience of university with that of school on each of the factors discussed. Their responses are summarised in Table 6.10.

Table 6.10 shows that university experiences are regarded as more positive than those at school, with the single exception of those relating to 'contacts across the hierarchy'. In this case, university students experience fewer such contacts at university than at school an experience that cannot simply be a reflection of size since the average secondary school in 2016 had 939 pupils (see www.riseinformation-centre.org.uk/statistics), larger than most university departments.

So, the finding that students had significantly greater contact with senior staff at school than at university is perhaps rather surprising given relative pupil/student numbers. For example, one faculty at the respondent university has eight departments and if student numbers are evenly divided across all departments, this would equate to 500 students per department, a number that is almost half that of the average-sized secondary school. So, if close contacts can be maintained between senior staff and pupils at school then it ought to be possible to do something similar at the level of department or faculty and higher than too if a variety of means of communication are used.

So much for the interviews. It is now time to turn our attention to the survey that measured students' perception of inclusive leadership amongst multi-level

TABLE 6.10 BME students' views on the extent to which their experience on particular factors compare at school and university level

Factor	How particular behaviours at school and university are perceived (numbers indicate the number of interviewees making this point)		
	Same	More at University	More at school
Sense of belonging at university	4	3	4
Social inclusion	1	6	2
Unconscious bias	7	–	2
Clear assessment criteria	3	3	2
Own expectations supported by teaching staff	4	3	3
BME teaching staff	3	2	5
Inclusive curriculum	6	2	1
Good confidence	–	5	3
Approachability of teaching staff	–	6	3
Contacts across the hierarchy	1	1	6

academic staff as well as their perceptions of their own productivity, motivation and well-being.

Survey on academic leadership behaviours

After the interviews revealed the fact that students' ideal leadership was inclusive in character, the wording of the survey used in the industry study (see the previous chapter) was modified to suit an audience of university students. Completed survey responses were then received from 104 students of whom 59 were white and 45 BME (Black = 17, Asian = 21, Mixed = 4, Other = 3). It should be noted that the short period in which the survey was available online during the busy winter holiday period may have limited both the size and demographics of the sample, given that students are often busy with deadlines or committed to extra-university affairs over this period. The length of the survey, running to fifty questions, may also have been a limiting factor (Burchell and Marsh, 1992; Galesic and Bosnjak, 2009) although it is unlikely to have affected the quality of responses (Burchell and Marsh, 1992).

It was not possible unfortunately to calculate the response rate since information was not available concerning the number of students who viewed the opportunity. However, the survey responses evidenced a very high level of internal reliability between each of the statements rated by respondents on a 5-point Likert scale (Cronbach's α = 0.964).

Correlation between academic leadership styles and self-rated student outcomes

A comparison by the psychologist on the project, Dr Ceri Sims, of student ratings of academic leadership behaviours on the one hand and student self-perceptions of their own productivity, motivation and well-being on the other reveals a strong and positive linear association with a Pearson product-moment correlation indicating a significant and high positive correlation between ratings of academic leaders as inclusive and self-ratings of productivity, motivation and mentally wellness ($r(104) = 0.854$, $p < 0.001$).

Dr Sims also found significant positive correlations between perceptions of leaders as inclusive and each of the three self-rating sub-scales (performance − $r = 0.855$, motivation − $r = 0.795$, satisfaction − $r = 0.789$, df = 104, $p < 0.001$). In other words, for this student sample, the perception of leaders as inclusive was strongly related to students' self-perceptions as more academically productive, motivated and with positive mental well-being. In fact, a linear regression analysis demonstrated that the ratings for inclusive leadership behaviours accounted for 73% of the variance in self-rated academic performance, motivation and well-being measures.

Whilst this finding demonstrates a correlational rather than causal relationship, an overlap of the strength of the one demonstrated here indicates that students' experience of inclusive leadership behaviours is a strong indictor and predictor of positive student outcomes. Furthermore, Pearson correlations for inclusive leadership behaviours against outcomes for both BME and white subgroups separately showed high and significant correlations for both ethnic groups (BME = 0.83, white = 0.87). It should be noted that the fact that perceptions of inclusive leadership behaviours failed to differentiate between gender, faculty and year of study in this sample indicates that this co-varying pattern is more than just a phenomenon pertaining to a particular student sector or group and signifies instead a pattern representing a broad spectrum of students.

In addressing the issue of whether student ethnicity influences these ratings, statistical tests of differences between groups were conducted. In fact, there were no significant differences between the BME and white subgroups for ratings of IL (BME = 137.6, white = 138.1). Having said that, Asian participants gave lower average IL ratings of their leaders than did black groups but the significance of this finding varied between tests. In this way, a so-called 'analysis-of-variance' fell short of showing significance (F(2,93)−2.96, p = 0.057) while another test (a so-called 'Tukey multiple comparisons test') revealed this difference to be a statistically significant one (p < .05). This indicates that further examination of responses by BME ethnicity is worthy of further investigation with a larger sample. For self-rated outcomes, there were no significant differences (BME = 40.1, white = 41.1).

What is more, there were no significant differences in rated outcomes for gender, disability, religion, year of study or faculty. Where sexuality is concerned, the numbers were too small to be subjected to statistical analysis.

Ability to name leaders at different levels of hierarchy

Other questions in the survey, deriving from the preceeding interview responses, sought to investigate the extent to which students could put a name to academic staff at different levels of the hierarchy, from lecturer to vice-chancellor. The survey results, illustrated in the first column of Table 6.11 show the percentage of students (out of 104) who are able to put a name to academic leaders occupying different roles of the university. This table also displays the data from the interviews (shown earlier in Table 6.8) in the right column by way of comparison.

TABLE 6.11 The extent to which students are able to put a name to academic leaders at different levels of the hierarchy

Position	Survey: proportion of respondents able to put a name to the person at this level (%)	Interviews: proportion of respondents able to put a name to the person at this level (%)
Lecturer	94.3	10
Personal tutor	83.0	10
Course leader	69.8	8
Dean of faculty	12.3	3
Vice-chancellor	5.7	1

What this reveals is that participants can, for the most part, name academic leaders at more junior levels of the hierarchy but are less able to do so for more senior academics, with just 12.3% and 5.7% of students able to name those at the levels of dean and vice-chancellor respectively. These figures suggest that senior academic leaders are largely invisible to students, thereby mirroring some of the qualitative comments made by the BME students. Regrettably, these findings run counter to the wishes expressed by those respondents for more regular contact with senior academic leaders and while questions may remain as to the form that such contact could take, this is perhaps a topic for future research. In moving forward with this, models could perhaps be tested from industry Best Practice where communications (written, audio or video) between customers and senior as well as frontline staff are often regular and two-way, even in large organisations. As a report by the CEO of IBM stated, "Connectedness is the hallmark of our era" (Rometty, 2012, p. 57).

Leadership levels in the minds of survey respondents

It is perhaps students' limited direct or indirect contact with senior academic leaders that accounts for their perceptions of leadership behaviours as linked largely to lower level leaders. Thus, when asked which members of staff they had in mind when completing the questionnaire on inclusive leadership, 90% referred to lecturers, 70% to module leaders and 67% to personal tutors. Only a small proportion of ratings related to those at dean or vice-chancellor levels (8.5% and 5.7% respectively) and this could well highlight the tendency for students' interactions to be limited largely to the lower-level academic leaders with whom they are in regular contact for their teaching and learning.

Such a conclusion, like that relating to the small proportion of students able to name the dean and V-C, would highlight the absence of multi-level inclusive leadership, something that would prevent the establishment of an inclusive culture since, as we have seen, this to be modelled from the top of an organisation (Schein, 2010; Moss *et al*, 2016).

Discussion

This is a single-institution study exploring whether academic leadership behaviours could be a factor in the BME attainment gap. The in-depth interview results show that BME students prioritise inclusive leadership as one of four sets of factors influencing academic attainment, while the survey reveal a correlation (0.85) between the perception of academic leaders as inclusive and student self-perceptions as academically productive and motivated, with a high level of well-being. This correlation mirrors closely that obtained in the industry-based survey reported in Chapter 5 when a similar survey instrument and responses from 966 employees produced a correlation of 0.87. (Moss, 2016; Moss *et al*, 2016).

In terms of comparisons between school and university experiences, the interview responses from BME students showed that contacts with senior staff occurred more frequently in secondary schools than at university, suggesting that leadership in secondary schools may be more inclusive than at university. This is a potentially important finding given that the BME attainment gap is absent at the level of school GCSEs. Moreover, although both BME and white student survey responses revealed a strong correlation between the perception of academic leaders as inclusive and self-perceptions as academically productive and motivated with high levels of well-being, the presence of IL in multi-level leadership may be more highly prioritised by BME than white students, given:

(i) the emphasis in the previous literature on BME concerns to achieve a sense of belonging and connection with the culture of the university (Gonzalez, 2003; Leathwood and O'Connell, 2003; Davies and Garret, 2012; Harper, 2013; Meeuwisse *et al*, 2014; Mountford-Zimdars *et al*, 2015) and

(ii) the very high priority that BME interview respondents give to self-motivation as a factor in their academic attainment, with this factor emerging as the most highly ranked of the factors rated in the interviews. Since the presence of inclusive leadership (IL) was highly correlated with motivation in the student survey results, the presence of multi-level IL would have an impact on student motivation and through that, their attainment.

Further research would be needed on a larger sample to test the relative importance of belonging and motivation to academic achievement for BME and white students.

Conclusions

It appears that multi-level inclusive leadership may have an important role to play in enhancing BME as well as white student academic achievement. This finding complements an earlier call for new approaches to leadership in HE in order to ensure a sustainable and successful future for HEIs. For example, one researcher (Tysome, 2014) proposed a 'light-touch' approach to leadership using good communication, persuasive argument and effective interpersonal skills. Other researchers, meanwhile, have proposed a "consultative and collaborative bottom-up approach" in preference to "an authoritative, top-down approach" (Peters and Ryan, 2014, p. 41) with others proposing a "distributed, plural, or collective and relational leadership" (Dopson *et al*, 2016, p. 56). Regrettably, the only study of leadership styles conducted across one or more HEIs in the UK in the last fifteen years depicted a sector distinguished by autocratic leadership (Davies, 2002), a finding very different to that proposed by these commentators. What is more, the small study reported here appears to mirror this finding through a finding of an absence of IL.

Next steps? Inclusive leadership of students should be central to leadership and management development programmes for all levels of academic staff in HE as well selection criteria for all roles, particularly middle and senior academic managers. Boards of Governors and vice-chancellors who are taking the attainment gap seriously need to set high expectations of themselves and their senior teams in terms of IL just as sector bodies delivering their Public Sector Equality Duty under the Equality Act, 2010, through regulatory frameworks, Access Agreement guidance and monitoring and impact exchange mechanisms.

It is for discussion moreover as to where the push to instigate these changes is likely to originate from, since there is little evidence of cross-sector initiatives to make leadership in HEIs more inclusive, both in a generic sense and a diversity-specific sense.

References and further reading

Barton, A. C. and Tan, E. (2009). Funds of knowledge and discourses and hybrid space. *Journal of Research in Science Teaching*, 46 (1), 50–73.

Bennett, N., Wise, C., Woods, P. and Harvey, J. A. (2003). *Distributed leadership: A review of literature*. National College for School Leadership, http://oro.open.ac.uk/8534/1/bennett-distributed-leadership-full.pdf

Bennis, W. (2002). Becoming a tomorrow leader. In Spears, L. C. and Lawrence, M. (eds.), *Focus on leadership: Servant leadership for the twenty first century*, pp. 101–110. New York, NY: John Wiley & Sons.

Bolden, R., Gosling, J., Maturano, A. and Dennison, P. (2003). *A review of leadership theory and competency frameworks*. University of Exeter: Centre for Leadership Studies, working paper.

Bolden, R., Jones, S., Davis, H. and Gentle, P. (2015). *Developing and sustaining shared leadership in higher education: Stimulus paper*. London: Leadership.

Bolden, R., Petrov, G. and Gosling, J. (2008). *Developing collective leadership in higher education: Final report*. London: Leadership Foundation for Higher Education.

Bolden, R., Petrov, G. and Gosling, J. (2009). Distributed leadership in higher education: Rhetoric and reality. *Educational Management, Administration and Leadership*, 37 (2), 257–277.

Braun, V. and Clarke, V. (2006). Using thematic analysis in psychology. *Qualitative Research in Psychology*, 3 (2), 77–101.

Bristol Students Union. (2016). *The BME attainment gap report*, www.bristol.ac.uk/media-library/sites/sraa/bme-attainment-gap-report.pdf, accessed on 1 August 2018.

Broecke, S. and Nicholls, T. (2007). *Ethnicity and degree attainment*. DfES Research Report No RW92. London: DIUS.

Burchell, B. and Marsh, C. (1992). The effect of questionnaire length on survey response. *Quality and Quantity*, 26 (3), 233–244, doi:10.1007/BF00172427, https://link.springer.com/article/10.1007/BF00172427, accessed on 6 November 2017.

Canwell, A., Dongrie, V., Neveras, N. and Stockton, H. (2014). *Leaders at all levels: Close the gap between hype and readiness*. Deloitte University Press, 7 March, https://dupress.deloitte.com/dup-us-en/focus/human-capital-trends/2014/hc-trends-2014-leaders-at-all-levels.html, accessed on 20 November 2017.

Cockley, K. O. (2003). What do we know about the academic motivation of African American college students? Challenging the 'anti-intellectual myth. *Harvard Educational Review*, 73, 524–558.

Cotton, D., George, R. and Joyner, M. (2010). *The gender and ethnicity attainment gap project: Executive summary.* www1.plymouth.ac.uk/research/pedrio/Documents/PedRIO%20 Paper%202.pdf, accessed on 21 April 2015.

Cotton, D., George, R. and Joyner, M. (PedRIO with Plymouth University) (2013). *The gender and ethnicity attainment gap research project* [online], www1.plymouth.ac.uk/research/pedrio/ Documents/PedRIO%20Paper%202.pdf, accessed on 5 November 2014.

Cousin, D. and Cuerton, G. (2012). *Disparities in student attainment* [online], Higher Education Academy, www.heacademy.ac.uk/system/files/hub/download/worlverhampton_2010_ disa_final_report_copy_1.pdf, accessed on 28 December 2017.

Cowden, S. and Singh, G. (2012). Multiculturalism, 'race', 'post-race': Implications for peda- gogy. In *Workshop proceedings: Debating multiculturalism 2.* London: The Dialogue Society, www.dialoguesociety.org/publications/debating-multiculturalism-2.pdf, accessed on 27 September 2012.

Crimp, M. and Wright, L. (1995). *The market research process.* London: Prentice Hall.

Davies, C. and Garrett, M. (2012). The BME student experience at a small northern univer- sity: An examination of the experiences of minority ethnic students undertaking under- graduate study within a small northern university. *Compass: The Journal of Learning and Teaching at the University of Greenwich,* 5, 57–66.

Davies, J. K. (2002). *Managing the effect in higher education: Valuing staff to enhance performance,* Higher Education Staff Development Agency (HESDA), briefing paper, January.

DfE (2015) GCSE and equivalent attainment by pupil characteristics: 2015 [Online], Department for Education. Available at https://www.gov.uk/government/ statistics/gcse- and-equivalent-attainment-by-pupilcharacteristics- 2014 (accessed 4 December 2017).

Dhanda, M. (2009). *Understanding disparities in student attainment: What do black and minority eth- nic students say?* www2.wlv.ac.uk/equalopps/mdreport.pdf, accessed on 18 February 2015.

Dopson, S., Ferlie, E., McGivern, G., Fischer, M., Ledger, J., Behrens, S. and Wilson, S. (2016). The impact of leadership development in higher education: A review of the literature and evidence. *Leadership Foundation for Higher Education,* April.

Equality Challenge Unit. (2017). *Equality in higher education: Students statistical report 2017* [online]. Equality Challenge Unit, www.ecu.ac.uk/publications/equality-in-higher-edu cation-statistical-report-2017, accessed on 10 April 2017.

Forde, C., Mcmahon, M. and Dickson, B. (2011). Leadership development in Scotland: After Donaldson. *Sottish Educational Review,* 43 (2), 55–69.

Galesic, M. and Bosnjak, M. (2009). Effects of questionnaire length on participation and indicators of response quality in a web survey. *Public Opinion Quarterly,* 73 (2), 349–360, doi:10.1093/poq/nfp031.

Glaser, B. G. and Strauss, A. L. (1999). *Discovery of grounded theory: Strategies for qualitative research.* New Brunswick and London: Aldine Transaction.

Gonzalez, K. P. (2003). Campus culture and the experiences of Chicano students in a predomi- nantly white university. *Urban Education,* 37 (2), 193–218, doi:10.1177/0042085902372003

Guetterman, T. (2015). Descriptions of sampling practices within five approaches to qualitative research in education and the health sciences. *Forum: Qualitative Social Research,* 16 (2), May.

Gummesson, E. (1991). *Qualitative methods in management research.* Revised edition. London: Sage.

Harper, S. R. (2013). Am I my brother's teacher? Black undergraduates, racial socialization, and peer pedagogies in predominantly white post-secondary contexts. *Review of Research in Education,* 37, 183–211.

HEFCE. (2013). *Higher education and beyond: Outcomes from full-time first degree study.* Issues paper 2013/15. Bristol: HEFCE, www.hefce.ac.uk/media/hefce/content/pubs/2013/201315/

Higher%20education%20and%20beyond%20Outcomes%20from%20full-time%20 first%20degree%20study.pdf

HEFCE. (2015). *Differences in degree outcomes: The effect of subject and student characteristics*. Issues paper 2015/21. Bristol: HEFCE.

Hyde, K. F. (2000). Recognising deductive process in qualitative research. *Qualitative Market Research: An International Journal*, 3, pp. 82–89, doi:10.1108/13522750010322089

Jabbar, A. and Mirza, M. (2017). Managing diversity: Academic's perspective on culture and teaching. *Race Ethnicity and Education*, doi 10.1080/13613324.2017.1395325

Kellerman, B. (2012). *The end of leadership*. New York, NY: Harper Collins.

Kellerman, B. (2015). *Hard times: Leadership in America*. Stanford, CA: Stanford Business books.

Leathwood, C. and O'Connell, P. (2003). It's a struggle: The construction of the 'new student' in higher education. *Journal of Education Policy*, 18 (6), 597–615, doi:10.1080/02680930 32000145863.

Levačić, R., Steele, F., Malmberg, L. and Smees, R. (2003). The relationship between school climate & head teacher leadership, and pupil attainment: Evidence from a sample of English secondary schools, paper presented at *British Educational Research Association Annual Conference*, Heriot-Watt University, Edinburgh, 11–13 September.

Lincoln, Y. and Guba, E. (1986). *Naturalistic inquiry*. Beverly Hills, CA: Sage.

Mazzucchelli, T. and Purcell, E. (2015). Psychological and environmental correlates of well-being among undergraduate university students. *Psychology of Wellbeing*, 5 (6), 1–18, doi 10.1186/s13612-015-0033-z

Meeuwisse, M., Born, M. and Severiens, S. (2014). The family-study interface and academic outcomes: Differences and similarities between ethnic minority and ethnic majority students. *Cultural Diversity and Ethnic Minority Psychology*, 20 (3), 401–412.

Milkman, K. L., Akinola, M. and Chugh, D. (2014). What happens before? A field experiment exploring how pay and representation differentially shape bias on the pathway into organizations. *Social Science Research Network*, 100 (6), 1678–1712.

Moss, G. (2016). Inclusive leadership: Boosts engagement, productivity and organisational diversity. *Equal Opportunity Review*, 268, June, 5–8.

Moss, G., Sims, C., Dodds, I. and David, A. (2016). *Inclusive leadership . . . driving performance through diversity*. London: Employers Network on Equality and Inclusion.

Mountford-Zimdars, A., Sabri, D., Moore, J., Sanders, J., Jones, S. and Higham, L. (2015). *Causes of differences in student outcomes*, HEFCE, www.hefce.ac.uk/media/HEFCE,2014/ Content/Pubs/Independentresearch/2015/Causes,of,differences,in,student,outcomes/ HEFCE2015_diffout.pdf

Nulty, D. (2008). The adequacy of response rates to online and paper surveys: What can be done? *Assessment and Evaluation in High Education*, 33 (3), 301–314, https://www.uaf.edu/ files/uafgov/fsadmin-nulty5-19-10.pdf

NUS. (2011). *Race for equality: A report on the experiences of Black students in further and higher education*. London: National Union of Students, www.nus.org.uk/PageFiles/12350/ NUS_Race_for_Equality_web.pdf

Oshagbemi, T. and Gill, R. (2004). Differences in leadership styles and behaviour across hierarchical levels in UK organisations. *Leadership & Organization Development Journal*, 25 (1), 93–106, doi.org/10.1108/01437730410512796

Patton, L., McEwen, M., Rendón, L. and Howard-Hamilton, M. (2007). *Critical race perspectives on theory in student affairs*, http://works.bepress.com/cgi/viewcontent.cgi?article=10 03&context=loripattondavis

Peters, K. and Ryan, M. (2014). *Higher Education Leadership and Management Survey (HELMS), Leading Higher Education*, Leadership Foundation for Higher Education.

Podsakoff, P. and Organ, D. (1986). Self-reports in organizational research: Problems & prospects. *Journal of Management*, 12, 531–544, doi:10.1177/014920638601200408

Rathi, A. and Ware, G. (2014). *Race and academia: Diversity among UK university students and leaders*, https://theconversation.com/race-and-academia-diversity-among-uk-university-students-and-leaders- 24988, accessed on 1 August 2019.

Richardson, J. (2008). The attainment of ethnic minority students in UK higher education. *Studies in Higher Education*, 33 (1), 33–48.

Rometty, G. *Leading through connections*, IBM, www-935.ibm.com/services/multimedia/anz_ceo_study_2012.pdf

Schein, E. (2010). *Organisational culture and leadership*. 5th edition. San Francisco, CA: John Wiley & Sons.

Sims, C., Moss, G., Dodds, I. and David, A. (2016). Can inclusive leadership bring benefits to organisations? Presentation at *8th European Conference on Positive Psychology*, Angers, France.

Smith, D. and Fletcher, J. (2001). *Inside information: Making sense of marketing data*. Chichester: John Wiley & Sons, http://socioline.ru/files/5/283/D._Smith_Inside_Information.pdf, accessed on 1 August 2018.

Snieder, R. and Larner, K. (2009). *The art of being a scientist: A guide for graduate students and their mentors*. Cambridge: University Press.

Stevenson, J. (2012). *Black and minority ethnic student retention and degree attainment: Interviews with staff and students. HEA Black and Minority Ethnic (BME) students learning and teaching summit: Accompanying documents*, www.heacademy.ac.uk/events/detail/2012/academy-events/bme_student_summit_april, accessed on 22 June 2012.

Stevenson, J. and Whelan, P. (2013). *Synthesis of US literature relating to the retention, progression, completion and attainment of black and minority ethnic (BME) students in HE*. New York, NY: Higher Education Academy.

Stuart, M., Lido, C. and Morgan, J. (2009a). *The impact of social identity and cultural capital on different ethnic student groups at university: Full research report ESRC end of award report* [online]. RES-000–022–2485. Swindon: Economic and Social Research Council, https://s3-eu-west-1.amazonaws.com/esrc-files/outputs/V98stuXupEOgSRdhDkrT7A/Vnz4RGjHzU6M16YK99hoDQ.pdf, accessed on 4 December 2017.

Stuart, M., Lido, C., Morgan, J. and May, S. (2009b). *Student diversity, extra curricular activities and perceptions of graduate outcomes* [online], Project report for the Higher Education Academy, http://gala.gre.ac.uk/3232/1/HEA_project_report_2007_8.pdf, accessed on 4 December 2017.

Tate, S-A. and Bagguly, P. (2017). Building the anti-racists university: Next steps. *Race, Ethnicity and Education*, 20 (3), 289–299, doi:10.1080/13613324.2016.1260227

Tatlow, P. (2015). *Participation of BME students in Higher Education*, in Aiming Higher, Runnymede Trust, www.runnymedetrust.org/uploads/Aiming%20Higher.pdf, accessed on 17 November 2017.

Tysome, T. (2014). *Leading academic talent to a successful future: Interviews with leaders, managers and academics, Leadership Foundation for Higher Education*, file:///C:/Users/gmoss01/Downloads/tysome_-_academic_talent.pdf, accessed on 16 June 2015.

7

ACADEMIC LEADERSHIP STYLE AND ITS ASSOCIATIONS WITH STUDENT ATTAINMENT, MOTIVATION AND WELL-BEING IN NORWAY AND THE UK

Introduction: a comparison of Higher Education in Norway and the UK

In the last chapter, we looked at the impact of academic leadership style on university students' outcomes in a UK university. In this chapter, the research team consisting of Gloria Moss, Dr Ceri Sims and Benja Stig Fagerland turn the spotlight on Norway, a country with similar and also dissimilar experiences of higher education (HE). What the two countries have in common is a similar proportion of graduates in the population – Norway at 34% and the UK at 32% (2007, www.statista.com/statistics/232951/university-degree-attainment-by-country/) but what divides them is the political will to fund the HE sector, with study in Norway for the most part free to students and study in the UK running to £9,250 per annum for undergraduate study.

For in fact, education in Norway is generously endowed. Overall, expenditure there per student from primary to tertiary level is the third highest across the OECD countries, after Switzerland and the United States with spending per student exceeding the OECD average for primary through tertiary education (OECD, 2014). In terms of lifelong learning, moreover, this is also very well developed in Norway in comparison to other OECD countries, with the level of participation in formal and non-formal education among 25–64 year olds amongst the highest across OECD countries, at 64%. Generally, most of those engaged in lifelong learning are employed, and this is the case in Norway with 70% of the employed population engaged in formal and/or non-formal education (*ibid*). In 2017 in the UK, by contrast, part-time university students were down 44% and mature students down 29% compared to 2008–2009 (Stanton, 2017).

How do student outcomes compare in the two countries? A comparison in 2016 of student satisfaction amongst international students in twenty-one European countries put Norway in top position with an average score of 9.25, and the UK ranked fifth in the same exercise with an average score of 9.05 (Study Portals, 2016). So the scores of the two countries were not dissimilar – the lowest score came from France with 8.19 – with similar levels of satisfaction in both. It should be pointed out, however, that although Norwegian universities emerge with a clean bill of health from the Study Portals exercise, research by the Norwegian Research Institute, the NIFU, found satisfaction amongst social science and education masters students to have the lowest levels of satisfaction. Moreover, satisfaction figures amongst students of technical subjects and natural sciences in Norway showed a drop in satisfaction figures of ten percentage points (NIFU, 2018).

Academic leadership and student outcomes

As we have seen, leadership is credited with having a major role in setting a vision that supports an organisation's goals and creating a motivating environment to facilitate achievement of those goals. How might student outcomes in the UK and Norway be associated with academic leadership in HE? Before looking in detail at this question, we will consider the changing context to academic leadership today and then views on the nature of academic leadership and how this may be associated with employee and student outcomes.

Context to higher education

HE is thought to be facing new pressures in OECD countries, with Vincent-Lancrin (2004) speaking of increasing demands on higher education institutions (HEIs) to generate income, a factor that will, in his view, produce greater autonomy in a market with a broader range of educational providers but also greater scrutiny from a range of stakeholders. He also refers to changing student demographics with a decline in the traditional student cohort of young learners and an increase in lifelong, part-time, international and older 'leisure' learners. Alongside this, he refers to increasingly liberalised conditions for the trade of higher educational services across national borders together with advances in technological developments. Another more recent commentator has described pressures from quality assurance, performance management and continuous improvement (Moore, 2008).

Academic leadership in HE

What sort of leadership currently exists in higher education and what form should it take in order to deal with competitive pressures and developments now and in the future? It may come as a surprise, given the importance both of leadership and of HE, to learn as we did in Chapter 6 that there have been few studies of the leadership style in higher education institutions. One commentator (Bryman, 2007) attributed the general lack of research on leadership in HE to the rather self contained nature of the literature on HE leadership and the relatively little cross-referencing in this literature to wider leadership theory and research.

The consequence of this neglect is that there are just two pieces of research describing the nature of leadership styles in HEIs. The first, from 1992, described the styles of university presidents in the US, finding that, most of the time, these leaders were transactional rather than transformational in their leadership style (Birnbaum, 1992). Ten years later, research in the UK (Davies, 2002) described the prevailing style in HE, based on a study of fifteen higher education institutions as one featuring an emphasis on management by exception, a feature, as we have seen, of 'transactional' leadership. The researcher noted an absence of inspirational motivation and individual consideration, elements that are part of the contrasting 'transformational' style as we know.

So, the two studies of academic leadership found it to be transactional in character. Is this the style of choice? We can answer this question with reference to information on (i) employee preferences, (ii) Best Practice and finally (iii) research on the association between academic leadership style and student outputs. In considering this last point, it is important to be aware of the fact that leadership is considered to be a multi-level activity both in education and industry-related studies (Forde et al, 2011; Canwell et al, 2014, respectively) with the consistency (Oshagbemi and Gill, 2004) and 'connectedness' (Forde et al, 2011, p. 57) of leadership across a given hierarchy creating the defining culture of organisations (Schein, 2010; Moss et al, 2016). For this reason, any study of leadership needs to consider the behaviours of leaders at all levels of the organisation.

It is important also to be aware of the view that HEIs should be measured against categories of leader behaviour that are specific to HE (Bryman, 2007), an opinion based on the notion that the field of HE research is an 'atheoretical' community of practice (Tight, 2004). However, to follow this line of thinking is to ring-fence the sector, distancing it from the rich literature on leadership without any obvious justification, not least because subsequent studies have satisfactorily discussed HEI practices in the light of well-accepted concepts of leadership (Webb, 2009; Alonderiene and Majaiskaute, 2016; Moss et al, summarised in LFHE *Insight Report*, 2018).

Is inclusive leadership, then, the style of choice for multi-level academic leadership in HE? One study (Peters and Ryan, 2014) identified a preference on the part of academics for an inclusive style of leadership with *agentic* and *communal* attributes such as 'warmth and morality' (*ibid*, p. 41). Moreover, the deep ambivalence expressed by many academics towards leadership and management in their organisations (Raelin, 1995, p. 17) may reflect an antipathy to the 'management of autonomy' that HE leadership engages in (Bryman, 2007).

In terms of Best Practice academic leadership, two studies in the UK (Bryman, 2007; Tysome, 2014) called for new approaches to HE leadership to ensure a sustainable and successful future for institutions. In the first case, Bryman suggested that academic leadership should reflect a number of capabilities:

- creating strategic vision
- communicating the vision
- creating a positive organisational climate

- being considerate and treating staff fairly and with integrity
- involving academic staff in key decisions
- being persuasive
- preserving personal and professional autonomy
- providing feedback on performance

Then, Tysome (2014) suggested that academic leaders employ a 'light-touch' approach using good communication, persuasive argument and interpersonal skills to achieve clearly articulated outcomes. In fact, there seems similarities between the models proposed by Bryman and Tysome and similarities too between their models and that of inclusive leadership. So, in a sector which appears to have transactional leadership as the norm, these commentators seem to be recommending an inclusive form of leadership constituted of elements from transformational and servant leadership.

Does existing research on the associations between HE leadership style and outputs justify a recommendation to use an inclusive rather than transactional style of leadership in HE? There is one view arguing against this and three studies supporting this view: of these, one follows an employee perspective and two a student perspective, employees and students being the two main stakeholders in HE (Siddique *et al*, 2011). How valid are these two contrasting views?

The view that argues against deviations from traditional, transactional leadership supports maintenance of the *status quo* culture in the belief that were transformation to be so deep as to disrupt cultural patterns, a great deal of damage could be inflicted on faculty support within HEIs (Birnbaum, 1992). It is not obvious, however, that with the systemic changes predicted in the HE sector (Vincent-Lancrin, 2004; Moore, 2008), a style can be maintained based on preserving existing cultural patterns rather than on producing effective change and adaptation.

Then, in terms of employees, one recent study in Lithuania (Alonderiene and Majaiskaute, 2016) found that a servant leader style was more likely to enhance employee (academic) satisfaction than a transactional style.

In terms of impact on students, and contextualising the HE studies, most studies on school leadership and pupil attainment estimate a direct impact of leadership behaviours on student attainment (Levačić *et al*, 2003), with a study in schools showing that pupils' assessment of 'headteacher leadership' and the adults' rating of 'warm teacher–pupil relationships' had positive and significant effects in six out of the seven attainment measures. Where the specific instance of HE is concerned, two pieces of research are relevant. The first, conducted in North America in 2011, studied the behaviours of college and university presidents within the 105 HEIs that fall within the Council for Christian Colleges and Universities (CCCU) and found that the transformational model accounted for 75% of the variance in employee job satisfaction (Webb). Then, as the reader who has read the last chapter will know, the study that the first author of this chapter led for the Leadership Foundation for Higher Education in the UK (Moss *et al*, 2018, see https://tinyurl.com/y836mly6) found a strong association between students' perceptions of academic leadership as inclusive and enhanced self-perceptions of their own performance, motivation and mental well-being.

So, educational research, including HE-based research, appears to support inclusive leadership (IL) based not only on positive associations between this and employee satisfaction and performance but also on positive associations between IL and student satisfaction, the single variable measured in a US study (Webb, 2009), and between IL and performance, motivation and satisfaction, the three elements measured in a UK study (see Moss *et al*, 2018). Importantly, boosts to satisfaction can be assumed to co-exist with boosts to effectiveness, according to the substantial literature linking the two (Jones *et al*, 2008; Zhang and Zheng, 2009).

Nevertheless, the literature on academic leadership styles and their effects on employees and students is patchy, so this chapter reports on a small-scale study in Norway that extends our understanding of the impacts of academic leadership on student outcomes while allowing a comparison to be made with the similar study in the UK (see Chapter 6).

Methodology

The survey used in the study reported on in the previous chapter was used with only minor modifications in this second study in Norway. It was administered in English since the level of English in Norway is extremely high, with the country, in 2016, having the fourth highest non-native grasp of English in the world as measured by the English Proficiency Index (EPI) from global language training company Education First (EF) (Cremer, 2016).

The survey, created by the first two authors, like that used in industry and described in chapter 5, is in two parts with the thirty-eight questions in the first part inviting comments on the academic style of leadership in their university (seeking to establish whether students perceived this as inclusive or not) and the second part posing questions as to students' perceptions of their personal performance (Factor 1), motivation (Factor 2) and well-being (Factor 3). The purpose of the survey was to measure the extent to which there was an association between the two parts of the survey, something that had been found to be present both in the study of employees in industry (see chapter 5) and in the study of university student responses in the UK.

Ethics approval for using the survey with students in the Norwegian university was obtained by the Norwegian co-author of this study. Once obtained, the survey was sent to a cohort of 750 students who had taken further education at a School of Business in a large, newer university. A high proportion of the students were studying part-time alongside a working career – a sign of the growing trend to lifelong learning (Vincent-Lancrin, 2004) found in Norway (OECD, 2014) – with the average age of respondents therefore higher than in a typical undergraduate cohort. The survey was available online for nine days before a decision was made to take it down in order to complete the data analysis in time for publication.

Results

Responses

Completed responses were received from seventy-seven students, seventy-one of whom were Norwegian, four Danish and two Swedish. The vast majority of the participants were white ($n = 74$), with two Chinese participants and one Asian participant. Of the seventy-seven participants, sixty were female and seventeen male and, of the sixty-three participants who gave their age, the range was 31 to 58 years with a mean age of 45.68. It should be noted that the short period in which the survey was available online (Quinn, 2002 quoted in Nolty, 2008), together with the length of the survey, extending to fifty questions (Burchell and Marsh, 1992; Galesic and Bosnjak, 2009), may have limited the size of the sample, though not the quality of responses (Burchell and Marsh, 1992). These two points applied equally to the survey posted a year or so earlier in the UK.

In terms of response rate, it was not possible to calculate a response rate since information was not available on the number of students who viewed the survey opportunity. However, as in the case of the UK survey, responses evidenced a very high level of internal reliability as shown by consistency in responses to survey items rated by respondents on a 5-point Likert scale, indicating that the items within each scale were closely related (see Table 7.1 for these statistical figures).

Correlation between academic leadership styles and self-rated student outcomes

A comparison of student ratings of academic leadership behaviours on the one hand and student self-perceptions of their own performance, motivation and mental well-being on the other reveals a strong and positive linear association ($r(75) = 0.83$, $p < 0.001$) between these two variables. The analytical tool was a Pearson product-moment correlation, and significant high positive correlations were also found between IL and each of the three self-rating sub-scales (performance $-r = 0.73$, motivation $-r = 0.70$, satisfaction $-r = 0.81$, df $= 75$, p < 0.001). These results show that the ratings for inclusive leadership behaviours accounted for 73% of the variance in self-rated academic performance, motivation and mental well-being measures.

TABLE 7.1 Degrees of internal reliability in the UK and Norwegian data

	Cronbach's alphas for Part 1 of the survey	*Cronbach's alphas for Part 2 of the survey*
UK survey data	0.97	0.96
Norwegian survey data	0.89	0.92

Where the effect of gender is concerned, mean ratings of academic leadership styles were similar for both gender groups (female = 140.45, male = 137.77), with an independent groups t-test showing no significant effect of gender either on ratings of academic leadership styles (t(75) = 0.46, p = 0.65, ns, equal variances assumed) or on self-ratings (t(75) = −0.76, p = 0.45 equal variances assumed). In terms of the effect of age, likewise, there was no significant Pearson correlation between age and either ratings of academic leadership style (r(61) = 0.03, p = .80, ns) or self-rated outcomes (r(61) = 0.05, p = 072, ns).

In other words, for this student sample, the perception of leaders as inclusive in their behaviours was strongly related to their own perceptions of themselves as more academically productive, motivated and satisfied as a student. Whilst this finding demonstrates a correlational rather than causal relationship, an overlap of the strength of the two variables demonstrates that students' experience of inclusive leadership behaviours is a strong indicator and predictor of positive student outcomes. It should also be noted that the fact that perceptions of inclusive leadership behaviours and self-perceptions of outcomes fail to differentiate between gender and age in this sample, indicates that this co-varying pattern is more than just a phenomenon pertaining to a particular student sector or group, signifying instead a pattern representing a broad spectrum of students.

Clustering of concepts

Do the inclusive leadership scale items involve one or more factors? In order to answer this question, a principal component analysis (factor analysis) of the thirty-eight item IL questionnaire indicated a good degree of unidimensionality, with one component accounting for 47.39% of the variance in the data with any further factors identified accounting for less than 6% of the variance in the data. This shows the extent to which the fifteen factors underlying the definition of IL used in this survey were clustered together.

Educational background of the students

As mentioned, the age range of the respondents who volunteered information on age range was 31 to 58 years with a mean age of 45.68. Half of the cohort had already completed a first degree and 20% had a master's degree, and these facts, together with the mature age range of the students, presents an example of lifelong learning in these Norwegian students.

Comparison of Norwegian and UK results

The strength of the correlations between perceptions of leadership style and self-perceptions of outputs (performance, motivation and mental well-being) reach the same high level of statistical significance in the Norwegian study presented here as in the UK study presented in Chapter 6, with the two sets of results shown side by side in Table 7.2 below.

In terms of demographic responses, it should be noted that where gender is concerned, both the enei research (Chapter 5) on IL and employee outputs (performance, motivation and satisfaction) and the UK university research on IL and student outputs (Chapter 6), showed no significant differences in response by gender. For the curious reader, Table 7.3 shows the Norwegian and UK results by gender set alongside each other.

Clustering of concepts

The close clustering of IL concepts manifest in students' responses in Norway, with one component accounting for 47.39% of the variance in the data, mirrors the finding in the UK university study where a single factor accounted for 39.37% of the variance. These findings, corroborated by both the Norwegian and the British HE survey as well as by the industry study (see chapter 5, p.110).

TABLE 7.2 Correlations between perception of academic leadership as inclusive and output measures in a Norwegian and British university

	Objects of the measures of correlation	
Country in which the survey was administered with respondent (R) numbers	*Leadership style and outputs overall*	*Leadership style and individual outputs* *Performance Motivation Satisfaction*
Norway R = 77	r(75) = 0.83, p < 0.001	r = 0.73 r = 0.70 r = 0.83 Overall significance: df = 75, p < 0.001
UK R = 106	r(104) = 0.85, p < 0.001	r = 0.86 r = 0.80 r = 0.80 Overall significance: df = 104, p < 0.001

TABLE 7.3 Correlations between perception of academic leadership as inclusive and output measures in a Norwegian and British university

Country in which the survey was administered	*Mean ratings of academic leadership style by gender* *Male*	*Female*
Norway R = 77	137.77	140.45
UK R = 106	140.91	137.22

Combining the Norwegian and UK samples

If we combine the Norwegian and UK samples (Norway $n = 77$; UK $n = 106$ – total $= 183$) and perform a Pearson correlation between IL rating of academic leaders and student self-ratings, a very high and significant positive correlation of 0.82 ($df = 181$, $p<0.001$) between these elements is found. In fact, Figure 7.1 shows the scatterplot for the association between these two measures for the combined Norwegian and UK samples while Figure 7.2 shows a preliminary model of the impact

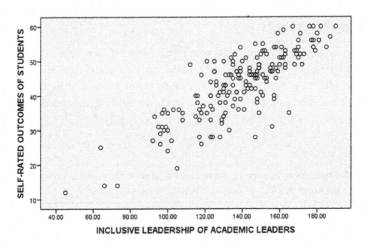

FIGURE 7.1   Scatterplot showing the linear relationship between ratings of inclusive leadership of academic leaders and student self-ratings of the outcomes of performance, motivation and satisfaction in a Norwegian and British university ($n = 183$)

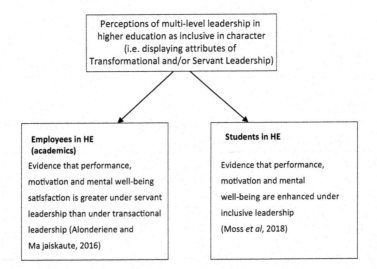

FIGURE 7.2   Preliminary model showing the impact of multi-level inclusive academic leadership on employees and students

of Transformational and/or Servant leadership on employees as well as students in Higher Education:

Discussion and conclusions

The results of the survey among a group of mature, Norwegian students pursuing studies at a large, newer Norwegian university provide information for the first time on the association between multi-level inclusive leadership and students' self-perceptions of their outcomes in Norway. The results show a strong association between perceiving academic leaders as inclusive and students experiencing enhanced self-perceptions of their performance, motivation and mental well-being, with gender and age not affecting these findings. The results also show unidimensionality of leadership components with a strong tendency for them to cluster together.

Importantly, these findings mirror those obtained with a sample of younger university students in the UK, with a combined sample showing highly significant associations between students' perceptions of leadership as inclusive and student self-perceptions as highly productive and motivated and with good mental well-being. These findings in fact mirror those obtained with a similar version of the survey in industry, producing evidence of a strong association (of 0.87, $p < 0.001$) between employees' perceptions of leaders as inclusive and employess self-ratings as more productive and motivated with good mental well-being (Moss *et al*, 2016; Moss, 2016; Sims *et al*, 2016).

It remains to be seen, through future research, whether the industry-based findings concerning the positive impact of inclusive leadership on *employee* performance, motivation and mental well-being would be matched in HEIs. To date, as we have seen, there has been research in Lithuania showing the positive impact of servant leadership on academic satisfaction (Alonderiene and Majaiskaute, 2016) but as yet there has been no research on the extent to which the broader concept of inclusive leadership has a positive impact on the performance, motivation and mental well-being of employees in HEIs.

Conclusions

The correlations between Norway- and UK-based studies in higher education suggest that multi-level academic leadership behaviours are a significant and overlooked factor in student performance, motivation and mental well-being. As a result, future research could usefully focus on the reactions of students across a range of universities, ages, geographies, subjects and levels of study in order to gauge the extent to which results may be influenced by age, geography, and level and subject of study. Future research could also usefully examine the extent to which the enhancements to students' performance, motivation and mental well-being associated with the perceived presence of inclusivity in academic leadership may be mirrored by that of academic and administrative employees in HE, a topic on which to date there has been no research.

In terms of HR and leadership policies in Norwegian and UK HEIs, it may make sense for these to reflect the important associations reported here between inclusivity in academic leadership and enhancements to student performance, motivation and mental well-being.

References

Alonderiene, R. and Majaiskaute, M. (2016). Leadership style and job satisfaction in higher education institutions. *International Journal of Educational Management*, 30 (1), 140–164.

Birnbaum, R. (1992). *How academic leadership works: Understanding success and failure in the college presidency*. San Francisco, CA: Jossey-Bass.

Bryman, A. (2007). *Effective leadership in higher education*, Leadership Foundation for Higher Education, Research Report, June, https://hr.ku.dk/strategi_og_projekter/effectiveleadershipinhighereducation.pdf

Burchell, B. and Marsh, C. (1992). The effect of questionnaire length on survey response. *Quality and Quantity*, 26 (3), 233–244, doi:10.1007/BF00172427, https://link.springer.com/article/10.1007/BF00172427, accessed on 6 November 2017.

Canwell, A., Dongrie, V., Neveras, N. and Stockton, H. (2014). *Leaders at all levels: Close the gap between hype and readiness*. Deloitte University Press, 7 March, https://dupress.deloitte.com/dup-us-en/focus/human-capital-trends/2014/hc-trends-2014-leaders-at-all-levels.html, accessed on 20 November 2017.

Cremer, J. (2016). *Norway moves up English-speaking ranks*, 15 November, www.thelocal.no/20161115/norway-moves-up-english-speaking-ranks, accessed on 1 August 2018.

Davies, J. K. (2002). *Managing the effect in higher education: Valuing staff to enhance performance*, Higher Education Staff Development Agency (HESDA), briefing paper, January.

Department for Education (DfE), Statistics: GCSEs (Key stage 4), https://www.gov.uk/government/collections/statistics-gcses-key-stage-4, accessed on 17 January 2019.

Forde, C., Mcmahon, M. and Dickson, B. (2011). Leadership development in Scotland: After Donaldson. *Sottish Educational Review*, 43 (2), 55–69.

Galesic, M. and Bosnjak, M. (2009). Effects of questionnaire length on participation and indicators of response quality in a web survey. *Public Opinion Quarterly*, 73 (2), 349–360, doi:10.109

Jones, M., Jones, R., Latreille, P. and Sloane, P. (2008). *Training, job satisfaction and workplace performance in Britain: Evidence from WERS 2004*, http://ftp.iza.org/dp3677.pdf, accessed on 1 August 2018.

Levačić, R., Steele, F., Malmberg, L. and Smees, R. (2003). The relationship between school climate & head teacher leadership, and pupil attainment: Evidence from a sample of English secondary schools, paper presented at *British Educational Research Association Annual Conference*, Heriot-Watt University, Edinburgh, 11–13 September.

Moore, T. (2008). Three jeers for managerial jargon. *The Australian Higher Education Review*, 30 April, 30.

Moss, G. (2016). Inclusive leadership: Boosts engagement, performance and organisational diversity. *Equal Opportunity Review*, 268, June, 5–8.

Moss, G., Sims, C., Dodds, I. and David, A. (2016). *Inclusive leadership . . . driving performance through diversity*. London: Employers Network on Equality and Inclusion.

Moss, G., Sims, C., Tatam, J. and McDuff, N. (2018). The impact of academic leadership behaviours on BME student attainment, *Insight Report,* Leadership Foundation for Higher Education, https://tinyurl.com/y836mly6, accessed on 1 July 2018.

NIFU. (2018). www.forskerforum.no/undersokelse-disse-studentene-er-minst-fornoyde/, accessed on 1 August 2018.

OECD. (2014). *Education at a glance*, www.oecd.org/education/Norway-EAG2014-Country-Note.pdf, accessed on 1 August 2018.

Oshagbemi, T. and Gill, R. (2004). Differences in leadership styles and behaviour across hierarchical levels in UK organisations. *Leadership & Organization Development Journal*, 25 (1), 93–106, doi:10.1108/01437730410512796

Peters, K. and Ryan, M. (2014). *Higher Education Leadership and Management Survey (HELMs)*, *Leading Higher Education*, Leadership Foundation for Higher Education.

Raelin, J.A. (1995). How to manage your local professor. *Academy of Management, Proceedings*, (1), 207–211.

Schein, E. (2010). *Organisational culture and leadership*. 5th edition. San Francisco, CA: John Wiley & Sons.

Siddique, A., Aslam, H., Khan, M. and Fatima, U. (2011). Impact of academic leadership on faculty's motivation, and organizational effectiveness in higher education system. *International Journal of Business and Social Science*, 2 (8), 184–191, www.ijbssnet.com/journals/Vol._2_No._8%3B_May_2011/23.pdf, accessed on 1 August 2018.

Sims, C., Moss, G., Dodds, I. and David, A. (2016). Can inclusive leadership bring benefits to organisations? Presentation at *8th European Conference on Positive Psychology*, Angers, France.

Stanton, K. (2017). *Lifelong learning is back in focus: How do we rise to the challenge*, Universities UK, www.universitiesuk.ac.uk/blog/Pages/Lifelong-learning-is-back-in-focus-how-do-we-rise-to-the-challenge.aspx, accessed on 1 August 2018.

Study Portals. (2016). September, www.studyportals.com/press-releases/norway-climbs-to-the-top-of-international-student-satisfaction/, accessed on 1 August 2018.

Tight, M. (2004). Research into higher education: An a-theoretical community of practice? *Higher Education Research and Development*, 23 (4), 395–411.

Tysome, T. (2014). Leading academic talent to a successful future: Interviews with leaders, managers and academics. *Leadership Foundation for Higher Education*, file:///C:/Users/gmoss01/Downloads/tysome_-_academic_talent.pdf, accessed on 16 June 2015.

Vincent-Lancrin, S. (2004). Building futures scenarios for universities and higher education: An international approach. *Policy Futures in Education*, 2 (2), 245–263.

Webb, K. S. (2009). Creating satisfied employees in Christian higher education: Research on leadership competencies. *Christian Higher Education*, 8 (1), 18–31, www.tandfonline.com/doi/full/10.1080/15363750802171073

Zhang, J. and Zheng, W. (2009). How does satisfaction translate into performance? An examination of commitment and cultural values. *Human Resource Development Quarterly*, 20 (3), 331–351.

8

INCLUSIVE LEADERSHIP IN ROYAL MAIL SALES

1. Overview of the organisation and its markets

Background: Royal Mail

The Royal Mail Group delivers more letters and parcels, to more addresses in the UK, than do all of its competitors. Under the Postal Services Act 2011 Ofcom became the regulator for postal services in the UK, designating it the UK's sole universal service provider with a 'one-price-goes-anywhere' service on a range of letters and parcels to around 30 million addresses, six days a week. The then Royal Mail was privatised in 2013 on the advice of reviews by Richard Hooper, who determined that with a fall in the number of letters sent via Royal Mail, a consequence of the rise of email and the internet, private capital should be introduced to Royal Mail.

In fact, change had been underway in Royal Mail since 2007 when the regulator afforded the organisation greater commercial freedom. Internal restructuring took place under the then chairman of Royal Mail Alan Leighton, who spoke of the need to remove the 'treacle', the middle managers, who were perceived as slowing down the organisation. Alongside this, the then (and current) Group sales director, Graham Davis, took steps to create an inclusive sales organisation that brought the customer into the heart of the operation. At that point, there were just 2,000–3,000 managed business customers (compared to the 18,000–19,000 in 2018), and an initiative was taken to move from serving customers to helping customers thrive, bringing their voice into Royal Mail.

Alan Leighton's leadership gave way to that of Adam Crozier, former CEO of the Football Association, and following his departure Donald Brydon took on the role until Moya Greene, former CEO of Canada Post, was appointed. She continued the process of creating a responsive and more efficient organisation until 2018.

Royal Mail turnover

Royal Mail turnover in 2018 was £10.2bn, 75% (£7.6bn) of which was through UK activity. Royal Mail Sales operates through UK Parcels, International and Letters. The non-UK activity is generated through Royal Mail's pan-European parcels business, General Logistics Systems, which operates one of the largest, ground-based deferred parcel delivery networks in Europe with operations in forty-one European countries. Royal Mail also operates in seven states in the US.

Changing markets

While letters continue to hold an important place in Royal Mail's product offering, accounting for around 45% of the Group's revenue and almost 60% of its UK revenue, e-substitution continues to drive a decline in UK-addressed letter volumes. Meanwhile, in the domain of parcels, e-retail continues to fuel overall growth in parcel volumes, with some of this being cross-border trade. Overall, the organisation continues to face significant competition both from companies with established delivery capabilities and from new entrants.

People

Royal Mail employs about 159,000 people across the Group, the vast majority of whom are on permanent contracts; with just 300 people employed in Sales. Its people strategy supports the business through a number of policies:

- Celebrating diversity and creating an inclusive environment
- Creating a customer-focused culture
- Maintaining a stable industrial relations climate
- Using technology and data to enhance decision-making
- Investing in people and providing opportunities for all

Customers

Royal Mail Group has a wide range of customers for its letters, parcels and data services. Customers include consumers; small and medium-sized enterprises (SMEs); some of the UK's largest businesses and retailers; and other postal operators who use its downstream network (this is where a postal operator other than Royal Mail collects mail from the customer, sorts it and then transports it to Royal Mail for delivery). Then a separate operation, General Logistic Systems (GLS), provides a range of business-to-business (B2B) and business-to-consumer (B2C) services across continental Europe.

In terms of customer satisfaction, an IPSOS MORI survey (2016) found 78% of customers to be favourable to the Group and 88% satisfied. Royal Mail also ranks as the most trusted and preferred delivery company in Business CSI's Brand

Tracker 2016–2017 surveys, a result attributable perhaps to Royal Mail's following of a stringent set of regulatory standards for parcels and letters delivery, with other providers offering limited or no regulatory consumer protection.

Shareholders

Following the Group's flotation on the London Stock Exchange in 2013, institutional investors were based in the UK and also overseas. In terms of employees, a record 12% of the company has been awarded to eligible colleagues on a *gratis* basis.

Royal Mail Group's transformation

As part of Royal Mail's universal service mission, it offers a delivery to every household and business in the UK, Monday to Saturday, and the business as a whole benefits when it delivers parcels alongside letters as part of its core network. Of course, if it is to retain its preferred provider status, it needs to stay ahead of the competition in both letters and parcels, and initiatives to help achieve this include an enhanced range of pick-up and drop-off points; better systems integration with retailers; and extending acceptance times at Mail and Regional Distribution Centres.

The Group is also seeking to enhance its overall e-commerce capability and this involves changing the way it uses technology and data, and changing its internal and external processes. In doing this, an overall aim is to digitise as many processes as possible, helping its customers with every step from purchase, to delivery, to returns. It also plans to operationalise its vision of being recognised as the best delivery company in the UK and Europe while delivering sustainable shareholder value and continuing to honour its universal service commitment.

Strategic priorities

The competitive environment faving Royal Mail has resulted in fresh initiatives in the areas of parcels, letters as well as in new areas of activity.

Where these three areas are concerned, the objective has been:

1 *Parcels*: to maximise ease of use by consumers, SMEs and marketplace sellers through investments in tracking and automation in order to improve delivery management and improved labelling
2 *Letters*: to seek new efficiencies in order to enhance returns
3 *New Areas*: to increase its digital capability in e-commerce and to expand GLS into new markets as part of the Group's focused geographic expansion.

In order to facilitate these strategic priorities, the Group has placed a focus on cost control, the use of technology to obtain greater efficiencies and the motivation of its workforce. It is the drive for greater motivation that has fuelled a move to a more inclusive approach in Royal Mail Sales, an initiative that is described in the next section.

2. The sales challenge

As described earlier, Royal Mail moved from a monopoly position in the public sector to a company operating in a deregulated environment, and this change demanded that the Sales organisation move from an exclusive focus on serving customers to one focused on the three aims of selling, defending existing customer revenues and growing new business. This change of focus was achieved through four major initiatives, which are described below.

Vision

The first step of the change process involved establishing a new vision together with new values for Royal Mail Sales. This was important because many staff had worked in the organisation for many years, and establishing a vision was vital to setting out the new landscape and objectives. In order to create the vision, sales teams were asked to envisage the future demands of customers, stakeholders and colleagues. Critical to this was the development and introduction of three new Royal Mail core values around which the organisation would coalesce:

- Be Positive
- Be Brilliant
- Be Part of it

This process led to a new vision of Sales, which put customers at the very centre. This required focus and change in four key areas, namely customer segmentation, sales structure, sales competencies and mind-sets. Details of the priorities in each of these four areas follows.

Customer segmentation

Royal Mail needed to create a future-focused segmentation of its customer based on the opportunities and threats present in the market. Once the customer base was segmented, it was necessary to consider *how* each of these segments should be served.

Sales structure

The Sales organisation and the teams within it needed to be able to support the new Sales vision, so it was important to understand the kind of sales teams and sales specialists needed. In 2018, Royal Mail Sales had over 300 full-time sales people to support its UK operations with, in addition, the use of agency sales resources in the UK, EMEA and US markets.

Sales competencies

It was important to draw up a people plan detailing the knowledge, skills and behaviours needed in any future sales organisation, an initiative that led to the creation of new professional salesforce competencies. An external organisation assessed Royal Mail sales staff against these competencies, and this initiative led 20% of staff to offer voluntary resignations with a further 20% of staff leaving because they were not judged as having met the required level of the new competencies. Many of the 60% of people who remained at Royal Mail suffered survivor syndrome (many of their friends and work colleagues having left), and the effect was to produce a demotivated and emotionally fragile sales workforce.

Changing mindsets

Before and following privatisation, it was important to create a winning mindset, a 'can do' attitude and a sense that anything was possible whether at home or at work. So, Royal Mail Sales initiated a new training programme – which ran for a period of two years and some remarkable changes took place. For example, one female employee who had never flown before set herself the target not only of flying but flying on the wings of a biplane! Another woman said that she would set up a charity to help young people in Gambia gain an education, and her success at doing this in the following years led to her being recognised with an MBE.

How could the training have such a dramatic effect? It was designed to create a sense in staff that anything was possible and, in the words of Group Sales Director Graham Davis, people became 'go-getters' and 'can do' people and ultimately 'became extremely loyal in the process'.

3. Sales leadership and coaching

Creation of the Sales Leadership Programme

In the view of the Group sales director of Royal Mail, professional sales leadership and the ability to coach direct reports are major drivers of performance with command and control leadership no longer having a place. As he says,

> Under a hard command and control leadership style, we don't help people; we just give them a rollicking if they don't achieve. So, we decided that the world is evolving and that people won't tolerate hard command and control by managers any more. What is more, the hard command and control climate encourages people to leave their brains at home so our Sales leaders need to coach people to be the best they can be.

Interestingly, a study of the sales leadership community using activity vector analysis (AVA) reached similar conclusions. AVA was used in order to help determine the attributes of the ideal leader, and a mapping exercise showed that a variety of traits could be demonstrated by the successful leader so long as they were embedded in an inclusive leadership style. This finding led Royal Mail Sales to introduce performance coaching and inclusive leadership training in 2015, the objectives of which were to:

1   professionalise sales leadership, encouraging leaders to respect their profession and, through demonstrable actions with their teams and colleagues, inspire, motivate and lead others to deliver results
2   provide sales leaders with the ability to coach their direct reports using a style of coaching that is results orientated and consistent with the standards expected at Royal Mail Sales
3   build the confidence and skills of sales leaders to deliver inspirational communications and effective messages with a view to engaging different audiences.

The sales leadership training that followed the AVA exercise emphasised the importance of a number of behaviours, with the following five prioritised for leaders:

i   demonstrating non-biased behaviour in order to ensure equal opportunities and the free expression of opinion
ii   giving more attention to team members than to themselves
iii   viewing tasks as developmental opportunities for team members
iv   adapting to the people in the team and ensuring that all members of the team have an equal amount of time in which to express their views in meetings
v   giving people the confidence to 'be themselves' at work.

Moreover, other interventions to support/enable an inclusive approach in the sales organisation were included, in particular:

i   Executive management development through Oxford Said Business School for senior sales leaders
ii   Unconscious bias training for all members of the sales organisation, including sales leaders
iii   Diversity training within Royal Mail alongside the formation of a Sales Diversity Group

At the end of the leadership training, leaders were invited to write about their leadership journey and the learning involved, and this was subsequently reinforced through the quarterly sessions of the Sales Leadership forum.

In terms of coaching skills, all sales leaders in Royal Mail followed a regular programme of training to become a qualified coach, and each sales leader then coached

Individual team members for up to 7.5 hours per week, a volume of coaching that meant that sales leaders were spending half of every month in coaching activities. This volume of coaching vastly exceeded the typical benchmark in the sales sector of four hours per month and was justified, according to the Group sales director, by the fact that "The coaching environment and culture makes people want to come and work for you".

Moreover, in an environment aspiring to inclusive leadership, it is important for managers and leaders to "walk the talk" and to be seen to be doing this. In this way, Sales Director Graham Davis made the decision not to have an office but instead work around the country – being visible, engaging with the teams and removing the physical barrier of the office door. Inclusive leadership starts at the top, and being visible, engaging and building trust and rapport with the teams are just some of the ways of successfully embedding inclusive leadership.

4. Summary of the timeline of sales leadership and engagement activities

Preparing for Privatisation 2012/13

As part of the preparation for the privatisation of the Sales organisation and the development of an inclusive culture, Royal Mail took a number of steps that included:

- Development of an in-house 'Sales Academy' to provide all sales people with a consistent platform of skills and techniques, built on external benchmarking and Best Practice
- In parallel, introduction of a Sales Coaching Programme to help sales managers develop their teams and maximise their potential
- Production of a sales competency development builder for sales people and sales managers to assess their capability gaps and development needs
- Introduction of a quarterly Inclusive Sales Leadership Forum to foster a sales leadership network, build a culture and community, develop leadership capability and share and inform strategy and planning
- Introduction of an ongoing programme of road shows to engage (*include*) sales people, share plans and invite their feedback about what it could do better.

Royal Mail post privatisation – 2014–17

In terms of initiatives taken to encourage an inclusive culture in Sales following privatisation, these included:

- 'Winning Minds' training across Sales embedding a step-change mind-set of high achievement using expertise and techniques used by leading sports/sales organisations
- Introduction of an ILM (Institute of Leadership & Management) recognised Sales Leadership programme with external accreditation of the training

- First of yearly Sales Leaders Coaching frontline external benchmark survey and Sales Leaders Functional Diagnostic Surveys (CEB Gartner)

- Becoming a founding member of the Association of Professional Sales (APS) and playing a key role in seeking chartered status for sales professionals.

Today – 2018/19
- Introduction of degree-level B2B Sales Apprentices programme through a partnership with Middlesex University and the Consalia Partnership. This degree is the first of its kind and recognised as a benchmark for industry sales organisations
- Recognition by the APS (Association of Professional Sales) through an 'Investor in Sales' Training Award
- APS "Professional Registration" exam and award to over 200 Sales individuals.

5. Definitive outcomes

The initiatives taken to develop an inclusive culture at Royal Mail Sales involved major change, and one of the ways of measuring the impact of this change was through the performance of Royal Mail Sales on a number of indices. Over the period 2017–2018, these showed some extremely positive figures:

- Sales Employee Engagement Index score of 78% vs 59% Ipsos UK Large Organisation benchmark and best in class across Royal Mail Group
- Sales Culture Index score of 68% and in upper quartile across Royal Mail Group
- Sales Customer Index score of 91%.

Moreover, the extent to which managers and those without leadership responsibilities perceived Royal Mail Sales to be inclusive can be gauged from the *verbatim* qualitative comments obtained from conversations that took place between Royal Mail Sales personnel (both managers and non-managers) and the author. The substance of these conversations are shown below in full.

Qualitative evidence of impact

As mentioned, conversations took place with staff within Royal Mail Sales, with the focus being their experience of working for Royal Mail Sales and the extent to which they believed inclusive leadership was practised. The comments of individuals are quoted *verbatim* and merged in order to create seamless text. It will be apparent, reading this, that both non-managers and managers have a clear understanding of inclusive leadership and perceive it to be widely practised in Royal Mail Sales.

The richness and fullness of people's responses was one reason for this and another was the opportunity that this offered you, the reader, to hear directly form respondents since this is not only more inclusive of your views but also allows you to be involved in interpreting the evidence. You can then consider, when you arrive at the discussion and conclusding section after these verbatim comments whether you agree with the conclusions presented there

A. *Comments from staff without management responsibility*

What follows are the responses of those without management responsibilities:

1 In your opinion, what leadership behaviours and skills are needed to get the most out of a diverse talent pool?

It is important to know what drives individuals on a team so that they can give of their best. In fact, the coaching approach that managers adopt here at Royal Mail takes account of the needs of individuals, allowing people to be viewed in the round, with management varying their approach in the light of this.

2 To what extent do you see inclusive leadership behaviours and skills exercised and practised in Royal Mail Sales?

We're starting to see these behaviours increasingly demonstrated. We conduct Belbin's team roles in order to understand how to get the best out of individuals and we are always being challenged to develop the skills and talents that we have. With the inclusive leadership that we have now in Royal Mail Sales, we have seen people speak up who might not have done so before when the leadership was less inclusive, and the consequence is that their views are now being taken into account and they can be considered for promotion.

Our sales manager was promoted from within team and we trust his opinion since he guides us, leaves us to get on with what we need to do and does not micromanage us. We still have to be sure that we get to the end result but he trusts us, giving us a lot of room in which to be creative. Because of the sales manager's leadership style, there is a strong team spirit here.

3 Inclusive leadership (IL) and gender/nationality

Don't know whether there are differences by gender or ethnicity.

4 Benefits of inclusive sales leadership

Inclusive leadership allows people to strive and be creative in their own way. Moreover, if people come up with ideas, making people aware that their ideas are used makes people feel significant.

5 To what extent do you think that Royal Mail Sales places emphasis on delegating power?

There are a lot of platforms where our feedback is requested, for example, there are sessions with sales directors at which people can put forward ideas. There are champions from the team who can get involved and ideas progressed so there are definitely mechanisms for getting involved and offering feedback.

6 To what extent do you feel that a diversity of people are valued and respected in this organisation?

People are hugely valued and so too is the achievement of a diverse workforce. We're doing more and more to make this apparent with the establishment of a Sales Diversity Group. This consists of volunteers from different ethnic, gender and religious backgrounds and the Group is constantly look at ways of engaging the wider sales team with diversity issues.

7 In what ways might the current styles of leadership in Royal Mail Sales need to change in the future and why?

The sales leadership I've experienced has been positive since it does not work in too structured a way. Many years ago, it was different since it was very structured and people were largely managed on KPIs, for example the number of calls made. Now, we have PDRs and it's more about the person and what they have been doing, with the focus of the review being People, Performance and Process. The sales targets are still there and they are important but they are not the main driver. Now, the emphasis is on quality rather than quantity, so a long conversation with a single client may be encouraged where, in the past, you may have been asked to speak to ten customers in the time that you now spend with one. Yes, we've still got targets but they are presented to us in a different way from the past.

8 What proportion of roles are filled from within the organisation as a consequence of developing existing personnel?

A large proportion of roles are filled from within and people then move around in different sales roles. Given the strong emphasis on recruitment from existing staff and the low attrition rate, Royal Mail Sales has a mature salesforce so the introduction of the Sales Apprentice programme that has brought new people into the business is most welcome. In fact, the aim is to have 10% of sales workforce undertaking a Sales Apprenticeship, something that will future-proof the ageing sales teams.

9 Do employees tend to trust the leaders?

I would say so – a lot of employees respect their sales managers.

10 Your organisation – strategy: more adventurous or more careful?

The last one or two years have been a lot more adventurous. Moving to Sales, I've put forward ideas that have been taken up whereas, in the past, there was more red tape and it was slower to progress things. Now, we're putting forward ideas and they're being implemented more quickly. We've become more adventurous and we can now challenge how things are done, with management willing to change.

11 Are most of the tasks you are involved in highly structured and tightly defined? Or does most of the work involve tasks that cannot be easily structured?

A mixture of the two.

12 Influence of the top person

The Group sales director and his leadership team are highly respected both within Royal Mail and across the sales industry. Recent developments in getting the apprenticeship programme in place, the first of its kind in sales in the country, does makes us feel proud. What is more, the sales leadership team wants us all to succeed and supports us all and this inspires us to do well.

13 What does it feel like to work at Royal Mail Sales?

I am quite proud to work in a company that is so diverse and one that has given me so many opportunities. What is more, knowing that I can put forward ideas that will be progressed makes me aware that I am valued as an employee. An example is when I suggested putting a tape measure on a lanyard and the idea was taken up across the whole of the Royal Mail Group.

The inclusive style of leadership works well since we are all aware that we need to keep up with a customer base that is increasingly knowledgeable and so need to adapt and speak to customers in a different way. In order for employees to do this, companies need to treat their employees in a way that will allow them and their teams to adapt. If everything was tightly structured, you couldn't be so adaptable with customers – for example, you might focus on making several phone calls rather than on being flexible with a single customer.

B. Comments from staff with management responsibility

What follows are the responses of those with management responsibilities:

1 What does inclusive leadership mean to you?

It means non-biased behaviour so that you can be sure that everyone is given an equal opportunity and those members of the team can express their ideas and thoughts. This means giving every person an equal amount of time in meetings and also giving equal consideration not just to the top performers but to those who have not advanced as far in the development cycle. It would be very easy for the top performers to be vociferous in meetings so it is important that others feel that they are able to offer and bring in their own thoughts/ideas as well.

The inclusive leader does not push themselves forward but rather gives greater consideration to the team than to themselves. For example, you might give a task to someone who may not be the obvious person (namely someone more competent who delivers every time) since giving it to that person will help him or her grow.

A lot depends on being adaptable as a leader, both to scenarios and to individuals and giving people a sense of empowerment. Being adaptable is key to allowing everyone the chance to feel that they're part of a team and can be themselves regardless of their background. This last point is very important since allowing people to 'be themselves' at work allows organisations up and down the country, regardless of size, to flourish. A lot of our business is about developing relationships with customers and so empowering staff and allowing people to be themselves is an important part of developing positive relationships with customers.

2 In terms of the definition of inclusive leadership offered, to what extent do you see these leadership behaviours encouraged and practised in Royal Mail Sales?

The Group director of sales has encouraged inclusive leadership throughout the Sales organisation and this would not have occurred in the Operations part of the company which, in fact, offers more of a manufacturing environment and a hard command and control style.

I feel that I live and breathe inclusive leadership both in the way that I am treated and the way that I treat my staff. A lot of what we do is through people, through relationships and dialogue – we're not in a factory situation – and the trust and empowerment that is part of inclusive leadership helps us achieve results through people. Honesty is high up there as well. As sales leaders, we sometimes have to deliver messages that we may not like but we need to present a rationale that is both honest and gets the team on board. Everyone in sales is encouraged to put forward new ideas however short a time they have worked in sales.

3 Do you think that men and women are equally likely to lead in an inclusive way?

Yes.

4 Are people from different national and ethnic backgrounds equally likely to lead in an inclusive way?

One manager had no personal experience with which to answer this. On the other hand, another manager with a minority ethnic background suggested that an ethnic minority background may actually produce stronger incentives for being inclusive than for people from a mainstream background since those from a minority background may have had the experience of feeling excluded. A third manager considered that there were no differences.

5 What, if any, are the benefits of inclusive leadership?

Under inclusive leadership, people contribute more than they would in a hard command and control culture, whether it is ideas, creative approaches, solutions or buy-in. People tend to want to work harder in a climate of inclusive leadership and this can create more healthy competition between people since people want to be seen to do things differently. So, if employees are more positive, they'll do more, they will be more creative and the customer will see that things are progressing more quickly, more creatively. Moreover, other parts of the organisation will notice and we may be able to influence them as well.

Inclusive leadership, of the type that we have here in Royal Mail Sales, creates a culture of positivity, of empowerment. It creates an entrepreneurial culture within Sales in which people feel valued and in which they sense that what they do is valued. People will do the best that they can for their organisation so there are huge positives. It also ensures that you have a broader range of ideas than you would have under a command and control system in which people are much less likely to share their ideas. Under a system of command and control leadership, organisations will be missing out on something vital and this will stunt their ability to grow and progress.

6   What, if any, are the negative outcomes of inclusive leadership?

There are situations where you need 'softer' command and control approach and so you need to take this into account. What is more, where the specific case of diversity is concerned – just one element in inclusive leadership – it would be unfair and divisive to promote certain people on the basis of protected characteristics in order to get the numbers right.

If inclusive leadership is conducted in an artificial way then it becomes disingenuous. For example, if a leader is trying to be inclusive but their behaviour and results go against this, it will have a negative impact and may actually encourage resistance by followers through mistrust of their leader.

7   What, if any, are the outcomes for diversity?

There will be people in the team, often those who are more extrovert, who will come up with ideas straight away while others may operate in a different way, producing ideas at a later stage for example. Being inclusive means being aware of these tendencies and making allowances. All the while, you should always allow people to be themselves in a work environment since this can only have a positive impact.

One of the things I do encourage the team to realise is that everyone is different and that people work and socialise in different ways.

8   Is power delegated?

Yes, to a fair degree, power is delegated. In some cases, it depends. When it comes to the way that our team manage their customers, there's a lot of delegation there but also a lot of rules and regulations on account of the highly regulated nature of the business. For example, decisions relating to pricing all need to go through a process. Having said that, more and more delegated authority is being transferred across Sales and people are increasingly empowered to make decisions that affect them, avoiding layers of approval. The trend is increasingly in this direction rather than in restricting empowerment.

9 In what ways might the current style of leadership in your organisation need to change in the future and why?

If you look at the demographics of Sales the average age is 50 including both leaders and non-managers, with 1%–2% of the workforce being ethnic minorities. Considering selling today, and the importance of digital and social media, it is possible that Royal Mail Sales would benefit by employing younger leaders since they may know more about using social media (not to mention living and breathing customer apps!) than older people.

In fact, our model of leadership is changing. Up until 2015, the senior team had fixed ideas of what a leader should look like – outgoing and extrovert for example – but we are now starting to see, from the Sales Leadership Forum for example, that it is acceptable to behave in different ways, particularly where people have proven that they have got results. In fact, it has been realised that having these differences can give you more.

10 Is inclusive leadership rewarded?

Extroverted people tend to get promoted quickly while those who are more introverted may be less likely to. I was promoted recently and some of the reasons offered were related to the characteristics that I had displayed, for example how I interacted with the team, was a member of the Diversity and Inclusion group and other aspects. Overall, I have noticed that those people given bigger roles tend to be inclusive in their leadership styles.

11 What is the influence of the person at the top?

The person at the top has huge influence and this comes out loud and clear in communications, in meetings and in conference calls. The Group Sales director and the sales leadership team is challenging us (the sales leaders) and the business to do more for our customers and this is filtering across Sales, encouraging us to resolve internal obstacles.

People can influence others through their interactions. For example, my line manager comes to my team meetings and the way that he interacts with the team (he is very inclusive) influences the team's behaviour. For example, the team will know, from his behaviour, that it is completely fine to ask lots of questions and to challenge. It is also interesting to see that the top people become role models and those who have won Sales Leader awards often find people coming to them for advice.

12 Tasks – Are a high proportion of tasks tightly defined or not?

It is a mixture since there are some regulated products with strict criteria and some less regulated products where you can be more creative. For example, there are cases where you can structure a commercial agreement or suggest that the parcel is presented in a different way. So, although we need quite robust processes, there can be variations in how team members manage their customers. Some will spend relatively little time contacting all their customers while some will not want to progress beyond the first customer until all the issues associated with that customer have been resolved.

13 Describe your organisation's strategy and whether it prioritises the development of new services as against existing ones

We're getting better at developing new services since competition in the last four to five years has forced progress and we are listening to customers and looking at the marketplace. I'd say that we've changed from sticking to what we know and do best to being flexible in the marketplace, something that we've had to do. So, we do now prioritise the development of the new.

14 To what extent does it prioritise cost control as against developing new products?

In terms of front-line sales, there's an attitude of let's find a way of getting the deal done so we have a balanced approach. We sanctioned investment for an eye-watering amount in IT but on the whole, we have to control costs since we are not the cheapest, so there is a phenomenal emphasis on costs otherwise we would be uncompetitive.

15 Would you describe the organisation as adventurous when making decisions about new developments or careful and reluctant to take risks?

A mixture of the two, though we are closer to being adventurous than reluctant in decision-making.

16 How are people rewarded?

Some teams are not measured on results but on behaviour while in sales teams there are rigid criteria.

17 What does it feel like to work at Royal Mail Sales?

It is hugely empowering when you look at what we're in control of. For example, I'm responsible for bringing in more than £100m in revenue and I am the voice of the customer within Royal Mail. It feels as if you are part of a team that wants to do the best it can for the organisations, customers and shareholders, one that works well to deliver. What is more, there's a good atmosphere here with no nastiness and back-stabbing. Indeed, the fact that there are people who have worked here in Sales for many years and want to continue to do so is very positive. Each day raises new problems and people are passionate about the Royal Mail and about their customers, and that is an important mix to have. On the whole, people will go home feeling proud to work for Royal Mail Sales.

6. Discussion and conclusions

Discussion

As described earlier, Royal Mail was granted commercial freedoms in 2007 and in 2013 was privatised. With these changes, the Group moved from a monopoly position in the public sector to a company operating in a deregulated environment, and this change demanded that the Sales organisation move from an exclusive focus on serving customers to one focused on the three aims of selling, defending existing customer revenues and growing new business.

Activity vector analysis showed that inclusive leadership would be the style of choice for Royal Mail Sales, and relevant training started to be offered in 2015. By 2018, the time at which the conversations recorded here took place, inclusive leadership was well enough embedded for a manager to speak of the situation at the Royal Mail in which it flourished with remarkable results:

> Inclusive leadership, of the type that we have here in Royal Mail Sales, creates a culture of positivity, of empowerment. It creates an entrepreneurial culture within Sales in which people feel valued and in which they sense that what they do is valued. People will do the best that they can for their organisation so there are huge positives. It also ensures that you have a broader range of ideas than you would have under a command and control system in which people are much less likely to share their ideas. Under a system of command and control leadership, organisations will be missing out on something vital and this will stunt their ability to grow and progress.

As we saw, the form of IL in Royal Mail Sales is rooted in a coaching approach to staff with an emphasis on the growth of the whole person and the fostering of a team culture in which everyone has a voice. If in fact we map the behaviours mentioned in the conversations with sales staff against the defining attributes of IL that we have used in this book, then we find nine skills emphasised from across transformational (Tf) and servant leadership (SL). Table 8.1 presents these alongside their definitions plus the words of staff that exemplify the attributes. We also include behaviours that were referenced by Royal Mail Sales personnel in the course of preparing this case study.

We saw earlier in Chapters 5, 6 and 7 when reporting on the study of IL in eleven organisations and in two universities that the fifteen attributes used to define inclusive leadership evidenced a high level of unidimensionality and coalesced into a single construct, so the fact that the emphasis in Royal Mail is on nine rather than

TABLE 8.1 The main attributes of IL referred to by Royal Mail respondents

IL attribute and whether Tf or SL	Definition of attribute	Words of respondents /facts
Idealised influence (Tf)	Having admirable qualities that followers want to identify with	"The top people become role models and those who have won Sales Leader awards often find people coming to them for advice"
Individualised consideration (Tf)	Showing individual interest and offering one-to-one support for followers	"The coaching approach takes account of the needs of individuals, allowing people to be viewed in the round"
Inspirational motivation (Tf)	Providing an appealing vision that inspires followers	"The sales leadership team wants us all to succeed and supports us all and this inspires us to do well"
Unqualified acceptance (SL)	Being inclusive in considering followers; being non-judgemental and accepting each follower as a unique individual	"We can now challenge how things are done, with management willing to change" "It means non-biased behaviour so that you can be sure that everyone is given an equal opportunity and those members of the team can express their ideas and thoughts. This means giving every person an equal amount of time in meetings and also giving equal consideration not just to the top performers but to those who have not advanced as far in the development cycle".
Growth (SL)	Encouraging followers to reach their full potential by providing opportunities for them to make autonomous and unique contributions	"With the IL we have now, we have seen people speak up who might not have done so before and their views are now taken into account and they can be in the frame for promotion" "IL allows people to be creative in their own way" "You give a task to someone who is not the obvious person to help him or her grow"
Listening (SL)	Actively listening to followers that involves not only listening to the content but also the underlying meaning and emotional significance	"we are listening to customers and looking at the marketplace"

IL attribute and whether Tf or SL	Definition of attribute	Words of respondents/facts
Conceptualisation (SL)	Having a vision about possibilities and articulating that vision to followers	One of the first steps in changing the Sales culture at Royal Mail was setting a vision.
Confidence building (SL)	Providing followers with opportunities and recognition so that they see themselves as valuable contributors to the team and organisation	One person was asked to speak at the Group's internal 'Sales Leadership Forum' and she developed great confidence as a result.
Healing (SL)	Helping followers cope with any burdens or personal troubles in their lives	Sales leaders and teams are encouraged to engage beyond their own work environment championing work, Best Practice or other areas such as Sales Diversity and Inclusion. One employee with terminal cancer was kept on a full-time contract while gradually reducing the actual time that he spent at work. Many of his colleagues volunteered to pick up his work with no additional reward.

fifteen attributes is a good example of the way that a selection of attributes – in this case a large one – may be the focus of IL in any one organisation.

Where strategy is concerned, this organisation appears to have elements of an 'analyser' and also a 'prospector' strategy, with an emphasis on following procedures but also being adventurous.

Conclusions

The privatisation of Royal Mail and plans leading up to that favoured the introduction of inclusive leadership into the Sales area of Royal Mail. Interviews with staff, both those with and without management responsibilities, reveal the extent to which this style has been embedded in the Sales arena with people a encouraged to challenge, put forward new ideas and be themselves at work. For all of this, the impetus has come very much from the top.

From a strategy perspective, Royal Mail Sales appears to have elements of an 'analyser' as well as a 'prospector' strategy, with an emphasis on following procedures but also being adventurous. According to the literature on organisational strategy, the most appropriate leadership style in this situation would be a management style that is high on delegation as well as exploration, and this is exactly what appears to be present in Royal Mail Sales. To this extent, the inclusive leadership present in Sales seems to be a best fit solution to the competitive environment in which Royal Mail finds itself.

References

Business CSI's Brand Tracker survey (2016–2017).
Ipsos MORI Corporate Image Survey (2016–2017).
Ofcom, Consultation on Review of the Regulation of Royal Mail, 25 May 2016, Para 4.12.
Ofcom, Review of the Regulation of Royal Mail, 1 March 2017, Paragraph 3.17.
Royal Mail Group – Sales leadership 2018.

9

INCLUSIVE LEADERSHIP IN PAGEGROUP

1. Overview of the organisation

Background: PageGroup

PageGroup is a leading global recruitment business, which for over forty years has been built on strong organic growth. Established in the UK in 1976, it now spans 140 offices in thirty-six countries providing permanent, contract and temporary recruitment for clerical professionals, qualified professionals and executives. Through organic growth, it has become a FTSE 250 company with more than 6,000 employees globally. In the first half of 2018, the company delivered an increase of 14.2% in gross profit and 18.8% in operating profit, and factors in this success may be the company's long-term relationships with clients and candidates as well as a unique approach to managing its employees. For, inclusive leadership, as we have seen, can be regarded as being a generic leadership style that brings *internal* enhancements to employee productivity, motivation and well-being, *external* enhancements to customer-centricity as well as being a style that boosts the diversity mindset and diversity density of organisations. It is this latter aspect that this case study largely addresses.

The challenges faced

PageGroup's biggest asset is its people. Understanding, embracing and operating in a multicultural world is fundamental to both its success as a business and that of its employees. It strives to nurture an inclusive working environment internally and works closely with its clients to support its diversity and inclusion strategies, sourcing from a diverse talent pool and ensuring that the environments that it recruits into are inclusive. The concept of inclusivity embraces both a generic leadership style that helps people feel involved and appreciated – for example senior leaders work alongside employees and not from large offices – and also includes initiatives that build greater diversity within the organisation.

2. Value placed on inclusive leadership

Innovative actions

In order to drive efficiencies across its operating structure, historically the group offered its business leaders the freedom to implement their own business processes and support functions. Although it achieved great success, it was clear from a business and employee engagement perspective that there was a great deal more that it could do to reach its full potential.

In 2012, the businesses came together under a single brand and management structure, creating one focused and unified business, PageGroup ('the Group'). Since then, the Group has evolved into an international business with a global Human Resources function driving key initiatives to gain greater synergy and alignment and a common environment for success. Moreover, as a result of losing talented women, the Group made a strategic decision in 2012 to shift its culture and become a truly inclusive business with the key drivers being moral, ethical and commercial. The Group has always prided itself on leading from the front and is totally committed to supporting and promoting an inclusive environment and culture in which all its employees can feel valued and realise their full potential.

Being inclusive is not just an item on the Group's to-do list, since it is an integral part of its culture and business. In essence, PageGroup's mission is closely tied to the people that work for the Group, the companies that it does business with, the candidates whose lives it changes for the better on a daily basis, and the communities and individuals it helps by giving back to others. As a recruitment company, the Group focuses on people, and the Group believes that this focus begins with its employees.

The main priorities? The Group prides itself on ensuring that the well-being and work-life needs of its employees are all provided for. Today, the Group aspires to provide its employees with the best working environment and conditions so that it can attract and, most importantly, retain the type of people that can contribute to the success of the organisation.

It is the Group's view that an inclusive and diverse team can bring different perspectives and insights to the business, generating a level of creativity, problem-solving capability and sustainability that might be less easy to achieve were it not for the inclusivity and diversity within the business. For PageGroup, being an inclusive workplace means understanding the needs of employees and making them feel valued and respected and this involves using an considerate, generic style of leadership as well as encouraging its people to bring their true selves to work so that they feel comfortable, valued and supported. It considers that this approach helps the company attract and retain good people and also helps them perform to the best of their ability through a better understanding of the Group's diverse clients and candidates.

Tools for inclusive leadership

The starting point for greater inclusivity and diversity was in 2012, the year when CEO Steve Ingham (who has personal D&I objectives linked to his remuneration) launched 'Women@Page – where women succeed at work' – to create a more inclusive working environment. The specific objectives were to create more gender balance, increase the number of women at senior leadership level, and support, develop and retain talented women. Pivotal to this has been its global female mentoring programme which grew from 40 UK participants in 2012, to 200 in 2016. According to one female mentee, the programme provided "invaluable advice and coaching, making me more confident in board meetings and facilitating a subsequent promotion".

Following the initial focus on women, the Group set out to make the business open for other groups. This produced the OpenPage initiative, an expression of PageGroup's belief in inclusion and diversity recognising that all individuals are different and are appreciated for this. It incorporates the Group's core values – 'we work as a team'; 'we make a difference'; 'we are passionate'; 'we value determination'; 'we enjoy what we do' – into a clear diversity and inclusion programme. The OpenPage framework includes the seven strands namely: are Ability@Page, Age@Page, Parents@Page, Pride@Page, Unity@Page, Women@Page and most recently 'Dynamic Working@Page' – ensuring that the Group embraces all people irrespective of disability, age, caring status, sexual orientation or gender identity, race or gender.

At the time of writing, the aim of OpenPage was to remove barriers, promote inclusion and ensure that all employees feel valued, respected and supported with a strong sense of belonging. The OpenPage strategy sits with the Executive Board and is owned by the Group's Global Diversity and Inclusion (D&I) director, with each Board member appointing a Regional OpenPage lead. All these are highly visible, inspirational people with a passion to drive positive change.

It should be noted that OpenPage has strategic, not just tactical, objectives and has clear leadership and support from the CEO and Main Board (44% female) and so full business engagement. There are also high levels of ownership and accountability with OpenPage regional steering committees and a global communications programme and global dashboard to measure, track and analyse all programmes. So the D&I strategy is supported by clear metrics and management systems as well as alignment with key business and talent requirements, something that requires collaboration across HR, Marketing and Operations.

Internal recruitment: PageGroup is one of a small number of organisations in which the vast majority of directors are promoted from within the organisation, with 87% of all directors falling into this category.

Work-life balance: feedback from the Group's Global Engagement Survey and Exit Interviews revealed that one challenge facing women had been juggling work and family, so at the end of 2013 the Group launched Maternity@Page. This includes a maternity timeline; maternity guidelines for line managers; signing of the Working

Forward Pledge; and launching pre/post maternity workshops in partnership with 'My Family Care' (see www.myfamilycare.co.uk/). The Group has a portal with 'My Family Care' that includes free emergency back-up child/elder care as well as affiliation with the P3 network for its LGBT parents, or parents of LGBT children.

Moreover, since parenthood relates to men as well as to women, and with the increase in dual working parents/adoption/carers/same-sex parents, the Group felt the need to be *truly* inclusive to all. This led to the launch of 'Parents@Page – where families and carers come first', a special interest group that acknowledges how hard the balancing act can be and offers resources fo parents and carers. Moreover, mindful of the fact that there has been a 23% increase in men/women working felxibly in the UIK since 2012, the Group introduced flexible working so that, from 2013, 75% of operational directors returned to work on a different work pattern, with options to work from home.

To underpin these initiatives for more flexible working, the Group launched 'Dynamic Working' in January 2017 in order to change the way that people work together and as individuals. It is a commitment from the Group's senior leadership team to embrace a more flexible and effective way of working, helping to meet the changing needs of its employees as well as the business. By giving employees balance and choices to deal with drivers inside and outside of work, the Group has moved from a focus on presenteesim to one of outputs, placing trust 1in employees' ability to perform at their best whilst away from the workplace. In fact, facilitating and enabling the development of different work patterns has in fact boosted people's performance.

Moreover, as part of initiatives in the area of work-life balance, the Group launched a new Flexible Benefits portal in January 2017 allowing employees to buy and sell benefits to suit with the offering including Health, Financial and Emotional benefits.

Communications: the aim of achieving effective communications is a critical part of the Group's inclusion strategy, aspiring to embed an inclusive approach reaches all employees, enabling them to feel respected and able to fulfill their potential.

Mechanisms for listening to people's views includes 'The Times Top 100 Best Companies' Survey, its global 'Have Your Say' employee engagement survey and PageGroup's internal 'Ideas Group'. Many of the initiatives helping to refine its Employee Value Proposition (launched 2015) have come from employee feedback, and its campaign 'You Said, We Did' regularly reports back to employees on current and planned changes. Moreover, active networks operate across all of the Group's OpenPage strands, each supported by a Senior Business Sponsor and Network Champion. PageGroup considers that this network has helped open up communication channels, provide excellent peer group support and bring about policy and behaviour changes.

Other forms of communication include podcast interviews on 'Page Radio', profiles of returners, Q&A's with senior business leaders, Best Practice guidelines, case studies, Real People/Real Stories, social media across Facebook, Twitter and LinkedIn, and half-yearly progress reports and awards.

Training and development: PageGroup provides information and guidance on diversity and inclusion training to all employees and prides itself on the work that it has undertaken to embed this into the organisational culture. As the Group's Director of Diversity and Inclusion says,

> If you want to have an inclusive culture with inclusive leadership, you need to support your leaders with the cultural shifts needed. Then, the more you can change the internal culture, the more you can drive change.

In 2016, the Group enhanced its comprehensive training and development framework by starting the roll-out of a global digital learning platform known as 'Boost!' which includes online inclusion learning modules in a blended learning format. Its Global Performance Toolbox enables employees to drive their own progress, development and careers with, for example, online courses on unconscious bias, inclusive leadership and mindfulness. These courses complement other mandatory training from the Group's legal team regarding discrimination, acceptable behaviours and appropriate language.

PageGroup's vision going forward is to build upon these foundations and accelerate the effectiveness of the Group's OpenPage programme, a key enabler of the inclusive culture that underpins the Group's business strategy. This inclusive culture has a generic element that creates an environment in which employees feel known and accepted as individuals, listened to and given the confidence to grow. There is also an element concerned with diversity which is investigated in the next section.

Diversity

The Group is working on many fronts to achieve an inclusive worksforce. In terms of recruitment, the Group achieved 'Proud to be Clear Assured' status by the Clear Company that offers recruitment software for diversity recruitment (www.the-clearcompany.co.uk/p/who-we-are). Details regarding progress on particular fronts are as follows:

Male/female ratio: since 2012, in the UK, PageGroup's female-to-male manager ratio has moved from 42:58 to 48:52 with UK female operational directors increasing from 25% in 2012 to 39% in 2016. In 2016, 67% of the net increase in operational directors in the UK were female. In the 2016 graduate scheme, twenty-eight of the intake were female and fifteen male.

Parenting: The Group has run parenting seminars for more than 200 employees and expanded in 2017 to allow parents globally to dial-in via webinars. There has been a 322% increase in the number of paternity leavers since enhancing paternity pay, and there have been seminars for fathers.

LGBTA: Pride@Page: the Group launched its 'sexual orientation and gender identity don't matter' initiative in 2015 with a LGBTA (lesbian, gay, bisexual, transgender/transsexual and allies) network the goal of which is to embrace a culture of acceptance without exception. As Stonewall's first recruitment company to be a Global Diversity Champion, the Group feels passionate about its employees bringing their whole selves to work and, since its launch, it has seen employees able to come out to family, friends and colleagues. In fact, the group celebrates 'Pride Month' (June) as a concentrated way of raising visibility across the business.

Moreover, the Group has increased its ranking in Stonewall's workplace equality index rising from 374th place in 2015, 258th in 2016 to 153rd in 2017. It is featured in the annual Stonewall 'Starting out Guide' and runs CV and interview skills sessions for LGBT students in London and the North West, updating all of its policies and benefits to be inclusive of all LGBT employees.

Disability: Ability@Page was launched in 2016 with the strapline 'where disability doesn't hold you back'. Initiatives include inviting employees on Disability Awareness Day, to share their personal stories of living with a disability as well as making reasonable adjustments for employees for example, providing adjustable desks for people with bad backs, or special pens and ear pieces for the hearing impaired, all of which have which led to higher levels of engagement. The Group partners with the Business Disability Forum, having attained Disability Confident Level 2, and has devised factsheets for employees when interviewing candidates with a range of disabilities.

Mental health: PageGroup was the first recruitment business to sign the 'Time to Change' pledge (see www.time-to-change.org.uk/). It participated in the 'Time to Talk' Day in February 2017, has undertaken 'Time to Change' mental health champion training and has appointed volunteer mental health champions. The Group offers UNUM (www.unum.co.uk/) confidential Employee Assistance Programme in cases of hardship and ran CV and interview skills workshops in conjunction with the National Autistics Society.

3. Definitive outcomes

Earlier, we saw the financial success achieved by PageGroup in the first half of 2018 and while there may be many factors involved, the strongly inclusive culture in the Group is likely to have played a major role. The evidence for this inclusive culture came from the results of a survey together with in-depth interviews with employees, both of which revealed strong evidence of inclusive leadership in PageGroup and high levels of satisfaction on the part of employees at all levels. More information on this important evidence follows in the next sections.

Survey evidence

In 2016, PageGroup participated in cross-industry research (Moss *et al*, 2016) sponsored by the Employer's Network on Equality and Diversity (enei) and by industry examining:

i   the degree to which inclusive leadership (IL) is perceived in a range of organisations as measured through a survey (completed by first-level managers and those with no management responsibilities) as well as interviews with employees at all levels of the organisation

ii   the extent to which the presence or absence of inclusive leadership might be
mirrored in employees' perceptions as to their own productivity levels, motivation and well-being.

It should be noted that PageGroup was one of eleven large organisations
participating in this research described in more detail in Chapter 5. Interestingly, PageGroup was perceived by employees as having an unusually high level
of inclusive leadership with employees also producing high ratings in respect
of their self-perceptions of their individual productivity, engagement and work
satisfaction.

Some interesting differences emerged between the responses of PageGroup and
those of the other ten organisations. Firstly, most respondents in PageGroup were
from the millennial generation, with most having worked in the organisation for
under five years and only 16% having any caring responsibilities (in other organisations most respondents were 35–53 years of age and had worked in the organisation
for over ten years, with 59% having caring responsibilities outside of work). Since
68% of PageGroup respondents were female, this difference would appear to reflect
the younger age of PageGroup personnel participants rather than any factor relating to gender.

Secondly, in terms of opinions, employees who had worked for PageGroup
for up to five years provided the same IL rating scores and positive ratings for
their own work outputs as employees who had been there for under a year.
By contrast, in the remaining ten organisations, there was a tendency for new
employees to offer considerably higher leadership ratings than employees who
had been in the organisation for over a year. This shows that the perceptions of
PageGroup employees regarding leadership styles and their own individual per-
formance/motivation/well-being changed less over time in PageGroup than in
other organisations.

Interview evidence

The positive survey findings were supported by responses from nine interviews conducted with managers and non-managers. For example, when asked
about whether IL was practised in PageGroup, 89% of non-manager responses
indicated that IL was practised 'to a great extent' and, in a further question
about trust in leaders, 100% of non-managers indicated trust in leaders. These
responses back up the positive survey findings regarding the presence of IL in
the Group.

In terms of positive outcomes, the largest percentage of responses highlighted
IL's role in retention (36%). Here, for example, are the *verbatim* comments of a
manager:

> If you improve retention, you have a happier and more engaged workforce.
> People feel valued and are more likely to want to be successful for the
> company

Moreover, according to a senior manager,

> One of the by-products of IL is a shared vision and there are massive benefits to this since if everybody knows what the vision is, it's much easier to organise the direction that things take. For example, you can propel any decision made at an executive level and it can reach the lower tiers very easily.

One non-manager described a by-product of IL as being greater trust, saying,

> Since you are taking people's views into account, you build up trust between people. This is a massive benefit in a large company since everyone feels that everyone is on the same page and everyone trusts what everyone is doing.

Negative outcomes of IL

Half of the responses did not perceive any negative impacts.

IL and its impact on a diverse talent pool

One senior manager took the view that IL results in a wide range of people and talents flourishing. In his words, it

> brings a mix of personalities and experience for the business which means different tasks/jobs match different types of people. If different people feel valued, you're more likely to have a range of people to choose from who are better suited to certain tasks. If you need creativity, you need people with creative skills; if you need somebody to deliver a project, you need more of a process-driven task oriented person.

Whether there is trust in leaders

All of the non-managers to whom this question was exclusively addressed admitted to having trust in the leadership. Here, by way of example, are two of the comments:

> I have 100% trust in leaders since they communicate with employees and I have very strong relationships with the leadership of the Group. They have made it clear that if there is something wrong, we can talk to them. They will make time as soon as you need to speak to someone about something.
>
> The inclusive nature – regular updates and shared vision – creates a culture of being part of the same team. When a team does particularly well, a weekend away can be organised.

Delegating power and sharing decision-making

Of the sample of managers and non-managers, 54% considered that there was a great deal of emphasis on delegating power, with 85% referring to 'some' or 'a lot of emphasis' on delegating power. Where non-manager responses were concerned, here are typical views:

> There is a big culture of delegation of power because of our structure. The structure we have means that managers managing the team can make decisions for their teams. There is a massive delegation of power to teams.

To what extent are a diversity of people valued?

This question was put to non-managers, 100% of whom agreed that a diversity of people are valued within the Group.

To what extent is change needed?

Interestingly, more managers than non-managers considered that change in leadership style was needed, with 75% of managers holding this view and only 25% of non-managers. Here is what a senior manager said,

> Because we're an organically grown business, there are a number of people at the top who are quite old school in their thinking but younger people are coming through, it's changing the balance meaning that there's more inclusive behaviour. This is a move in the right direction.

Is IL rewarded?

This question was addressed exclusively to managers, all of whom indicated that IL was rewarded. Here is a comment from a senior manager:

> We promote based on success and you can't build a successful business if you don't show IL. Without it, you don't get the financial targets; you don't get an engaged/happy workforce; you don't get the results. If you don't get the results in our company, you won't get promoted so I believe that you do get rewarded for IL because you'll get the results with it.

Developing employees

This question was addressed exclusively to non-managers, all of whom said that existing personnel are developed and trained for new roles. Here is a comment from two non-managers:

> The ethos of the company is to grow organically, hire graduates but every other management task is filled from within. Have never seen a manager brought in from the outside.
> The perception is that about 90% of roles are filled internally (bar roles where entry is at graduate level). 90% of managerial positions would be filled by someone already working in the company.

Positive outcomes of IL

Strategy

To what extent is there an emphasis on new products, services and markets as against cost control?

This question was addressed exclusively to managers, and just over half (60%) considered there to be an emphasis on both elements. Here, for example, is a view from a senior manager:

> There is quite a focus on the new rather than the existing; we are always having to look for new things – that's how we grow.

To what extent is there a strategic emphasis on new products, services or markets or improving procedures?

This question was again addressed exclusively to managers, and 80% considered there to be an emphasis on both improving existing products and developing new ones.

Extent to which tasks are highly structured

Most respondents considered the tasks to be highly structured. Here is one non-manager response, for example:

> A lot of the processes are very structured but because you're dealing with people, you can't always follow the structure.

To what extent is there a strategic emphasis on being adventurous or focused on being careful and reluctant?

Almost half of respondents (44%) described PageGroup as 'adventurous and keen to develop new ideas' and no one described it as 'careful and reluctant'.

4. Discussion and conclusions

It is clear from both manager and non-manager responses that PageGroup is perceived as having an inclusive culture, something described as creating a strong vision, a sense of teamwork and buy-in from the staff. It is also perceived as encouraging staff retention, facilitating senior appointments to be made from within the Group.

Key factors thought to have contributed to this culture include the willingness of managers to listen to others, the value placed on diversity and the strong emphasis on teamwork and a caring, inclusive culture. As part of this last point, the MD in the UK makes a point of having no office and spending every day with a different set of employees, something that facilitates an appreciation of the work being undertaken as well as building relationships with employees. This arrangement, in turn, allows employees the opportunity to get to know the MD and pose questions about the business.

Running through many of the respondents' views is reference to the presence of strong teamwork. This is interesting since it was suggested earlier in the book (see Chapter 2) that a collectivist culture was likely to be a pre-condition for the flourishing of an inclusive style. So, consciously or unconsciously, PageGroup has moved away from individualism and high power distance and has established the optimum conditions in which an inclusive culture can take root. Of course, inclusive leadership will then bring all the multiple benefits that we have seen associated with it, which is why we say that it may be a major factor in the Group's excellent results.

In terms of the elements of inclusive leadership that are most evident in Page-Group, you can see these summarised in Table 9.1.

TABLE 9.1 The main attributes of IL referred to by PageGroup respondents

IL attribute and whether Tf or SL	Definition of attribute	Words of respondents/facts
Inspirational motivation (Tf) and conceptualisation	Having a vision about possibilities and articulating that vision to followers	"One of the by-products of IL is a shared vision and there are massive benefits to this since if everybody knows what the vision is, it's much easier to organise the direction that things take."
(SL)		"The inclusive nature – regular updates and shared vision – creates a culture of being part of the same team. When a team does particularly well, a weekend away can be organised."
Unqualified acceptance (SL)	Being inclusive in considering followers; being non-judgemental and accepting each follower as a unique individual	"The Group embraces all people irrespective of disability, age, caring status, sexual orientation or gender identity, race or gender".
Listening (SL)	Actively listening to followers that involves not only listening to the content but also the underlying meaning and emotional significance	"The leadership of the Group have made it clear that if there is something wrong, we can talk to them. They will make time as soon as you need to speak to someone about something."

(Continued)

TABLE 9.1 (Continued)

IL attribute and whether Tf or SL	Definition of attribute	Words of respondents/facts
Growth (SL)	Encouraging followers to reach their full potential by providing opportunities for them to make autonomous and unique contributions	"Existing personnel are developed and trained for new roles."; "The ethos of the company is to grow organically, hire graduates but every other management task is filled from within." This implies training and growth.
Healing	Helping followers cope with any burdens or personal troubles in their lives	The Group's portal 'My Family Care' offers free emergency back-up child or elder care.

As we can see, five attributes are the focus of the inclusive leadership style in PageGroup, and this is consistent with the finding in Chapters 5, 6 and 7 that the fifteen attributes used to define IL are unidimensional and coalesced into a single construct. So, the fact that most of the emphasis in PageGroup appears to be on the five attributes in Table 9.1 is a good example of the way that a selection of IL attributes may be the focus of IL in any one organisation.

How does the strong presence of inclusive leadership at PageGroup relate to the contextual and strategic factors mentioned earlier in Chapter 2? Taking context first, it will be recalled that Fiedler considered the conditions necessary for participative leadership to be the following:

– Moderate relations between leader and subordinate
– Moderate task structure
– Moderate power (i.e. some delegation takes place).

If we consider the perceptions of managers and non-managers, we can see that the middle condition ('moderate task structure') is in place but that the two other conditions are not, since relations between leader and subordinate are good rather than 'moderate' and since substantial rather than 'moderate' power is delegated. So the instance of high inclusivity at PageGroup appears to be at odds with the conditions predicted by Fiedler, suggesting perhaps that Fiedler's conclusions need to be revisited. This conclusion is particularly strong since the moderate talk structure and good leader/subordinate relations and strong delegation appear to be present in the three other case study organisations as well.

What of the strategic context? PageGroup appears to meet the conditions in which a 'prospector' organisation can flourish by virtue of placing an emphasis on high exploration (remember the strong perceptions of the Group as adventurous?)

and low on uncertainty avoidance (Håkonsson *et al*, 2012). Moreover, this conclusion is reinforced by the strong evidence for shared decision-making in the Group, with more than half of respondents perceiving decision-making to be shared, something associated with an 'explore' strategy. More detail on the links with the strategy literature can be found in Chapter 2.

In terms of leadership style, the interview responses pointing to high levels of delegation and high levels of uncertainty avoidance would seem to favour a 'producer' style of manager, with a long-term focus and much decision-making passed to subordinates. So, in this sense, the strategy literature helps predict the type of leadership practised at PageGroup. By the same token, it shows that the style of leadership in place at PageGroup is a best fit solution.

Conclusions

PageGroup's success owes much to the inclusive leadership strongly evidenced by its directors, managers and non-managers. This leadership style creates a culture which transmits a vision and inspires a strong work ethic as well as loyalty to the Group.

References

Håkonsson, D., Burton, R., Obel, B. and Lauridsen, J. (2012). Strategy implementation requires the right executive style: Evidence from Danish SMEs. *Long Range Planning*, 45 (2–3), 182–208.

Moss, G., Sims, C., Dodds, I. and David, A. (2016). *Inclusive leadership . . . driving performance through diversity*. London: Employers Network on Equality and Inclusion.

10

INCLUSIVE LEADERSHIP IN SEVENOAKS SCHOOL

1. Overview of the organisation

Background: Sevenoaks School

Sevenoaks School in Kent bucks the trend in more ways than one. In the fifteenth century, when many people left their possessions to the church, William Sevenoke bequeathed his London properties to the people of Sevenoaks to establish a free grammar school and almshouses for the poor. William was believed to be a foundling, adopted by a local landowner and later Lord Mayor of London, and his bequest launched one of the oldest secular school foundations in England. In 2008 and 2018, it was named the *Sunday Times* independent school of the year, ahead of renowned institutions such as Eton, St Paul's, Winchester and Westminster.

From early times, the school flourished and in 1560, a year after she visited the area, Elizabeth I issued Letters Patent incorporating the school and granting it a seal, now used as the school logo. By the late eighteenth century, it was taking some fee-paying scholars and in the next century, new facilities and a strengthening academic and sporting record attracted increasing student numbers. A period of curricular and co-curricular innovation followed in the mid-twentieth century under the pioneering headship of Kim Taylor (1954–1968), who introduced technology classes, encouraged inter-disciplinary studies, pioneered a Voluntary Service Unit and opened an international boarding house for this all-boys school set in 100 acres in the Kent countryside. Pupil numbers expanded under his aegis, and he personally left his mark on pupils by making a point of teaching all the new boys in their first year, a memorable experience as he read Arthur Miller in a range of American accents (obituary).

More innovation followed. The school admitted girls in 1976 and just two years later adopted the International Baccalaureate (IB), being the first leading independent school to do this. In 1999, the decision was made to go all-IB in the Sixth Form, moving away from A-levels completely. Another first followed when, in 2002, the school's first female head in the school's history, Katy Ricks, was appointed to run the school. Under her leadership, innovation continued with the development of school-created Sevenoaks School Certificate examinations in English literature, drama, music, art, history of music, visual communications and robotics, all accepted by UCAS for university entrance.

The school continually innovates, opening three new institutes in September 2017: the Institute for Teaching and Learning, the Institute of Higher Education and Professional Insight and the Institute of Service and Social Impact. Moreover, in 2018, it opened a new Science and Technology block that unites four cognate sciences under one roof, allowing for more integrated learning, and there are plans to expand boarding facilities beyond those available to its current 350 boarders. This is a non-endowed school with no private foundation behind it so has literally plowed its own furrows in pursuing these developments.

Academic excellence and more

Its recognition as best Independent School in the *Sunday Times* awards was anchored in consistent academic excellence – a regular clutch of forty Oxbridge offers are achieved most years – as well as a history of innovation and strong extra-curricular activity. This last point is key in the school's vision, for example, with its marketing literature celebrating the fact that what happens outside the classroom is just as important as what happens inside. Intellectual, emotional and personal qualities are thought to be interrelated, with one influencing the other in a very significant way. Moreover, in the school document, 'Horizon 2020', setting out the school's vision, research is quoted from the University of Oxford suggesting that 47% of today's jobs will be automated within two decades, making, so the document states, creativity, critical thinking and teamwork as the skills least vulnerable to automation. Linked to this is the school's belief that success is increasingly defined not by examination results but by people's ability to create, work with others, lead, empathise and show commitment.

In the same document, other objectives are presented (see www.sevenoaksschool. org/fileadmin/user_upload/Horizon_2020_Final_high_res_version_-_low_res. pdf), including the ability to create an inspirational teaching and learning environment, widen access and diversity, remain at the forefront and secure future financial independence. In terms of teaching style, the school boasts 'unstuffy but demanding teaching' (this is taken from 'The middle school curriculum at Sevenoaks', p. 4), with a former pupil, Eliza Ecclestone, explaining that this was a school in which 'the carrot reigned supreme' and in which the power of positive reinforcement was demonstrated (Sevenoaks publication 'Continuum'). She contrasts this experience with that at a very 'academic, strict school'.

Moreover, elsewhere in 'Continuum' (no page numbers provided), it is written that 'If at first you don't succeed, fail, fail, and fail again' with a former pupil quoted as having said at Founder's Day that 'in a volatile, unpredictable and often scary world, we should experiment rather than play safe – even if that means failing our way to success'.

So much for the teaching philosophy of the school. In terms of diversity, one year 10 student writes, 'Everyone is accepted at Sevenoaks, no matter how different. And we all get the opportunity to do what we want without being judged' ('Continuum'). In fact, from an article in the *Independent* newspaper (2006), we learn that a balanced education is what the school is about. 'It runs six days a week, full-on with everything from jazz bands to the year-eight philosophy club'. All of this is supported by the school's seven values of creativity, independent learning, critical thinking, international understanding, collaboration, self-awareness and social responsibility.

2. Leadership and the challenges faced

The current head, Katy Ricks, explains how her philosophy of leadership evolved from the experiences that she had over a number of schools as a junior teacher, head of department and deputy head. Two of the schools had a whole school ethos and vision, leaving a sense of autonomy and individuality in teaching staff. She was also able to learn from those who have not had a real vision, or at least have not articulated it, reinforcing her belief in the importance of vision. This provides a focus for people's efforts and she adds that if things go wrong, the school works to try to restore things.

According to Dr Ricks, interactions with people are vital since each interaction represents an opportunity to involve people in the enterprise. She still teaches a class and will talk to students and staff when walking around the campus. She comments on how she 'hates being told what to do' and tries to remember that others may feel the same way. In fact, the model that she follows when interacting with others is very much the mental model that informed her experience teaching English. This begins by explaining why something is interesting, then allows for a period in which discussion takes place about the topic and finally leaves people thinking that they would like more. Moreover, she perceives her role as being that of facilitating the process of making decisions in the school.

3. Definitive outcomes

The initiatives taken at Sevenoaks School over a number of years and under different heads have created an inclusive culture which has assisted the school in achieving innovative outcomes. These are manifested in impressive examination results (in 2018, 55% of IB results achieved a score of 40 out of a maximum points score of 45) and in the award from the *Sunday Times* newspaper of Best Independent School in 2008 and 2018. It is likely that, given the school's long tradition of inclusive leadership and innovation that these will continue even after the current Head, Dr Katy Ricks, moves on to becoming Chief Master of King Edward's School in Birmingham in summer 2019. This follows 17 years as Head at Sevenoaks.

Meanwhile, in-depth interviews with academic staff and a student shed further light on the outcomes of the inclusive culture in the school. *Verbatim* qualitative comments follow from staff at the level of head of department and above, as well as from a student. Their views on a range of issues are shown below.

A. Interviews with academic staff

The *verbatim* views of four members of staff are presented below, with comments merged to form a continuous, seamless narrative. As before, readers can form their own views as to the type of leadership practised and compare these to the conclusions offered at the end of the chapter.

What does inclusive leadership mean to you?

"It means including other people's thinking, drawing on other people's expertise and empowering others. It also means including everyone in the decision-making process so that people feel that they have a strong say in the way that decisions go. Moreover, it involves empowering team members so that they can contribute, develop and excel either individually or as part of the organisation, and it involves making sure that people are listened to. Regular meetings take place across the school at which people can learn the rationale for decisions and feed into them as well. That way, if you make a decision that people are unhappy with, and if they understood the rationale, then it helps them accept it. Generally, there is always an opportunity to change and influence things at the school."

To what extent do you see the fifteen competencies of inclusive leadership encouraged and practiced at Sevenoaks School?

"The senior management team allow considerable autonomy to staff who are essentially allowed to do what they feel is right. That gives them the opportunity to develop meaningful schemes of work, for example, that are relevant to students."

"I see that the Head is very inclusive since she listens (a strong characteristic), inspires, encourages and creates a shared vision. Everyone in the school speaks very openly and honestly and everyone is able to challenge the Head. Even when the Head is in the minority, she really factors everyone's views into her decisions. As a leader, she is very visionary and idealistic and manages a very diverse senior management team. She reads all the minutes of meetings whether of teacher groups or pupils' councils and through that has her finger on the pulse, being aware of everything that goes on. She also meets pupils on a regular basis and communicates honestly, having a policy that anyone can make an appointment to see her."

"Her *modus operandi* runs through the behaviours of those who have progressed in the organisation. These people tend to show trust in other people, empower them, discuss things honestly and show empathy in checking whether all is well."

"On a day-to-day basis, if a young member of staff comes up with an idea, you listen and don't dismiss the idea. Doing this brings a sense of joint ownership and trust and leads to honesty and room for growth. If you trust your staff, as we do here, then it is easier for honesty to prevail. For, people tend to lie when they are worried about getting into trouble or expecting a disproportionate outcome."

"The school definitely encourages others to be creative. This is witnessed by the establishment of the Teaching and Learning Institute which encourages teaching staff to be creative. So, for example, there are projects on the classroom of the future and whether students will still sit in classrooms (and if so, would these be different in style with whiteboards on all the walls) and whether they might join up with people online locally and/or across the world. There is also a project on where people will eat on campus; whether to open up spaces beyond the current dining room; and finally a project on exams and whether candidates will still write on paper, sitting behind desks."

"Where the 'growth' element of inclusive leadership is concerned, the school has a healthy CPD budget which is available to fund personal research, develop an idea or cover the costs of training (for example if a member of staff wants to train as a rugby coach) and the Head is usually keen to offer her support. In terms of studies, departments are encouraged to engage in cross-curricular activities during 'enrichment week' with the English and History departments, for example, working together on World War 1 poems."

"In the same spirit of collaboration, a new Science block has been opened in summer 2018, replacing the separate buildings in which the sciences had been taught in the past. This new building allows for the integration of the three sciences, with project work physically facilitated across the three sciences, particularly for the non-exam year students."

"In terms of vision, the school has a very clear vision and the Head regularly gives talks on her vision to teaching and support staff. What is more, the school is always looking out for the next opportunity and threat and regularly communicates with governors, parents and teachers."

In your experience, are men and women equally likely to deliver inclusive leadership?

A view expressed by two respondents was that women may be more likely to deliver inclusive leadership than men, with men in senior leadership probably potentially less collaborative, less empathetic and less good at listening. A third view was that men within the teaching profession are likely to be more inclusive than those outside the profession on the basis that a particular type is likely to be attracted to teaching. A fourth person expressed the view that there were no differences.

In your experience, would people of different nationalities be equally likely to deliver inclusive leadership?

Most respondents did not have experiences on which to form a view but one person expressed the view that Anglo-Saxon countries (UK, US and Canada) had more inclusive instincts than some other countries.

What are the impacts of inclusive leadership?

Positive effects

"Giving people a voice ensures that they work as a team with buy-in. If you're passing ideas down without buy-in from staff, it's less effective leadership, whereas inclusive leadership is a style that ensures that everyone feels as though they are participating in the leadership, having a share of the responsibility and also a voice."

"An inclusive style really does encourage people to reach their full potential, since people tend to live up to the expectations held of them. The same applies to pupils who need to be given the opportunity to express their ideas, experiment, explore, plan and make choices. If they are not given these opportunities, they, like staff, will lose interest."

"People who are led in an inclusive way are more likely to be prepared to go the extra mile than those not led in this way. So, for example, here at Sevenoaks, a teacher will take a pupil to the Accident and Emergency section at the hospital at 1.00 am and be prepared to teach the next morning. Of course, they could phone in to say that they were tired but in practice this tends not to happen. The teacher will always receive a warm 'thank you' from the school."

"Inclusive leadership leads to everyone feeling empowered and valued, and this produces a happier staff with a greater diversity of ideas contributed. With a different style of leadership, you get a 'them and us' attitude which makes innovation very difficult since you get push-back from staff."

Negative effects

One person cited the fact that it could feel disenfranchising if your views were not taken into account in the final decisions made but there was a strong sense that the advantages of inclusive leadership far outweighed the disadvantages.

What are the impacts of inclusive leadership on a diverse talent pool?

There was possibly less diversity in the staff body than might be found in a state school, and so respondents had no strong views on this question.

To what extent do you think that your organisation places emphasis on delegating power throughout the organisation?

"We delegate a lot, especially down to the level below Head, middle management and Heads of Department levels and the Head looks at opportunities to upskill people to drive things forward and give people an opportunity to update their skills for their CVs."

"The word 'power' does not fit well with the school – the delegation of 'responsibility' rather than 'power' is a better fit with the school culture. In terms of input to strategic decision-making, the views of employees may be collected before management make a decision or a subset of staff may be asked for their views. In terms of academic decisions, academic staff, department heads and subject specialists have a lot of autonomy in their subjects. In terms of pastoral care, consistency in decision-making is key so decisions need to be concentrated in a few hands."

Are a high proportion of tasks highly structured and precisely defined? Or does much of the work involve tasks that can't be easily structured and clearly defined?

"Aims and objectives underpin the strategy but how we get there is not rigidly structured and the methods for achieving outcomes are consistently up for discussion. In terms of individual jobs, teachers' work is very structured and the day is pretty planned and for a lot of the more senior staff, work is often reactive and responsive, so not able to be planned."

To what extent does your strategy prioritise the development of new markets/services/products as against services that the organisation has had several years' experience of?

"There is a strong academic tradition at Sevenoaks School but the school knows that it has to embrace innovation. It is always seeking to encourage new ways of doing things, trailblazing and embracing new ideas that could improve provision at the school. So, there is a big CPD budget to facilitate growth in the staff."

"The 'products' in the school are exams and IT systems and change in these areas is encouraged if that produces a better outcome. For example, about 25% of departments at the school are now setting their own Sevenoaks School Certificate syllabi and assessment schedules and also conducting greater internal moderation than is customary. This initiative is unique amongst secondary schools and is borne of dissatisfaction with existing GCSEs with a sense that some GCSEs do not encourage independent and open-minded enquiry, and are not a true test of students' abilities in a subject. So, the development of new GCSE courses at Sevenoaks is a reflection of the need to make courses more stretching and challenging than regular GCSEs."

"Creating challenging courses lower down the school is also possible since teachers have the flexibility in years 7, 8 and 9 to write the curricula that they want. The school is also experimenting with removing grades lower down the school and focusing on teacher feedback."

To what extent does Sevenoaks School prioritise cost/quality control and improving procedures as against developing new products?

"There is a lot of quality control but we're not struggling financially so if an initiative will bring a lot of benefits, we'll find the money for it since it is important to get the right product."

How would you describe Sevenoaks – adventurous when making decisions and keen to develop brand new ideas or careful and reluctant to take risks?

"Adventurous and actually quite brave, a philosophy that comes from the top. The school builds on what it is good at rather than following trends and is also happy to take risks. Adventurous decisions include the following:

- building a new boarding house
- taking the decision to use the International Baccalaureate exclusively at Sixth Form
- creating the school's own Sevenoaks School Certificate (e.g. one on English literature that includes foreign literature; one on robotics)."

In what ways might the current style of leadership in your organisation need to change in future in your opinion?

"There does not need to be massive change. The Head has an outstanding leadership style and it should not change too much but perhaps communications with staff could be enhanced. Inclusivity is really important since if you have buy-in, people will work harder and so it makes sense for more organisations, including schools, to be inclusive in order to achieve success. This relates not just to employees but to students too, since students will also work much harder if they perceive that their own interests are factored in. For example, they will be more inclined to engage in charity work if they think that they will develop more skills."

Is inclusive leadership rewarded?

"Not explicitly, no. However, people's actions in creating greater inclusivity won't go unnoticed. For example, one person took on the task of organising 'Enrichment week', an initiative that brings different departments together, and he has been praised for doing this and can cite this when applying for promotion."

What is the influence of the top person and how does the behaviour and attitudes of the top person inform the responses and behaviours of others?

"The behaviour of the Head definitely informs the behaviours and attitudes of other people in the school. For example, the way that the Head treats the Senior Leadership Team (SLT) behind closed doors will affect the way that they treat other people. So, if a member of the SLT is managed in a particular way, then that person will lead in that way too (incidentally, the word 'manage' was said not to be the right word here!). If they are not treated in an inclusive way, they won't be inclusive. There is a trickle-down effect from the top."

"The influence of the top person will extend to priorities as well. For example, if the Head is not interested in the future, the other staff won't be interested either.

Our Head ticks the inclusive leadership boxes in lots of ways and this does have a positive impact on the teaching culture in the school. At the top, there is a great deal of listening and encouraging others to be creative and these characteristics appear in the rest of the workforce. For example, when the Head tells Directors of subject areas that they are doing an amazing job, it makes these people feel valued and they can then do their job better. She will attend all of the plays and then write a 'thank you' letter that will be posted on the Head of Drama's door so that everyone can read it and feel included in the thanks."

What does it feel like to work at Sevenoaks School?

"It is a great place to work and you feel that you are listened to and encouraged. What is more, it is a great place to teach, not least because students are so motivated. Compared to a grammar school that I taught at previously, this school is more forward-looking and I feel I have more flexibility here and more room to trial initiatives and take risks. Teachers can change the content of a subject syllabus and if you want to trial the use of Apple TV, because we have the luxury of more money, you will get the support to do this. In comparison with the grammar school, change is more obvious here and pretty constant."

Other views: "It is exciting, exhilarating and really stimulating. All the children are sparky and that feels very positive. Moreover, staff feel valued and we all understand where the school is going. It is a rewarding job and students will send cards to teachers to express their appreciation and leaders to their reports. This follows the lead of the Head who, from time to time, sends postcards (witty and beautiful ones!) to staff and to students."

"It feels exciting working here. You are working with bright people, both staff and students and this is exciting and demanding."

"I love working at Sevenoaks. I work within a group of like-minded people, we have great facilities, are paid well and I personally feel fulfilled. This is somewhere where you can do whatever you want and all the staff have that sense."

B. Conversation with a Sixth Form pupil

What does it feel like to be a student here?

"It feels very busy with things happening all the time and no two days the same. You feel that you are getting a lot and giving a lot. It feels focused with everyone working hard and you know about other people's interests. Everyone has their thing and teachers and students will talk about it and people are not afraid to achieve and talk about their achievements. No one feels bad about this because everyone is achieving."

"There is no division between boarders and day pupils not least because day pupils can have breakfast and dinner in the boarding house. There is freedom in the teaching since the teachers will often wander off-syllabus and stop following a strict menu. Students have lots of contact with teachers, for example you all queue together for breakfast, lunch and dinner (you can stand and chat to teachers in the queue) and you can stop and talk to teachers and the Head across the campus. So the academic staff seem very human and not scary."

4. Discussion and conclusions

Sevenoaks School is one with an enviable reputation for innovation and growth. These elements have helped the school survive and flourish in a competitive arena without the private endowments and large foundations that characterise other top independent schools. Until the 1960s, it was a relatively small school, but some brave thinking, particularly on the part of Tim Taylor in the 1960s, led to its expansion to the current size of the school. This courage characterises more recent developments, whether it be the decision to move wholeheartedly over to the IB exam system, to create their own Sevenoaks School Certificate examinations or to create a Learning and Teaching Institute, a new, integrated science block or a new boarding house. Supporting this evident streak of innovation is an inclusive leadership style that cascades down from the top of the organisation, seeping into all corners of the school's life. Interviews with staff bear witness to the extent to which this style is deeply embedded in the school's ethos and culture.

Which of the inclusive attributes are most in evidence in the school? From the conversations that the author had with academic staff and a pupil, Table 10.1 summarises the inclusive leadership attributes mentioned with the greatest frequency. Do note that, as we saw earlier in Chapters 5, 6 and 7 when reporting on the studies of IL in eleven organisations and two universities that the fifteen attributes used to define IL all evidenced a high level of unidimensionality, coalescing into a single construct So, the fact that most of the emphasis in Sevenoaks School is on the six attributes shown in Table 10.1 is a good example of the way that a selection of IL attributes can be the focus of IL in any one organisation.

TABLE 10.1 The six main attributes of IL referred to by Sevenoaks School respondents

IL attribute and whether Tf or SL	Definition of attribute	Words of respondents/facts
Inspirational motivation (Tf) and conceptualisation (SL)	Having a vision about possibilities and articulating that vision to followers	"The Head creates a shared vision." "The school has a very clear vision and the Head regularly gives talks on her vision to teaching and support staff."
Unqualified acceptance (SL)	Being inclusive in considering followers; being non-judgemental and accepting each follower as a unique individual	"Everyone in the school speaks very openly and honestly and everyone is able to challenge the Head."

(Continued)

TABLE 10.1 (Continued)

IL attribute and whether Tf or SL	Definition of attribute	Words of respondents/facts
Listening (SL)	Actively listening to followers that involves not only listening to the content but also the underlying meaning and emotional significance	"At the top, there is a great deal of listening . . . and these characteristics appear in the rest of the workforce." "On a day-to-day basis, if a young member of staff comes up with an idea, you listen and don't dismiss the idea. Doing this brings a sense of joint ownership and trust and leads to honesty and room for growth." "It is a great place to work and you feel that you are listened to."
Empathy (SL)	Putting oneself mentally and emotionally into followers' places in order to more fully understand experiences and perspectives	"Those who have progressed in the organisation tend to show empathy in checking whether all is well."
Growth (SL)	Encouraging followers to reach their full potential by providing opportunities for them to make autonomous and unique contributions	"The school has a healthy CPD budget which is available to fund personal research, develop an idea or cover the costs of training (for example if a member of staff wants to train as a rugby coach) and the Head is usually keen to offer her support." "An inclusive style really does encourage people to reach their full potential since people tend to live up to the expectations held of them. The same applies to pupils who need to be given the opportunity to express their ideas, experiment, explore, plan and make choices. If they are not given these opportunities, they, like staff, will lose interest."

IL attribute and whether Tf or SL	Definition of attribute	Words of respondents/facts
Confidence building	Providing followers with opportunities and recognition so that they see themselves as valuable contributors to the team and organisation	"When the Head tells Directors of subject areas that they are doing an amazing job, it makes these people feel valued and they can then do their job better. She will attend all of the plays and then write a 'thank you' letter that will be posted on the Head of Drama's door so that everyone can read it and feel included in the thanks."

In terms of the school's strategic perspective, it appears to have elements of an 'analyser' and also a 'prospector' strategy, with an emphasis on following procedures (for example the need to be consistent in dealing with issues relating to pastoral care) but also on being adventurous. According to the literature on organisational strategy, the best fit leadership style in this situation would be one that is high on delegation and exploration, the style that appears to be in place at Sevenoaks School so this appears to be a Best Fit solution. In fact, without this style, it is difficult to envisage how the school could have scaled the heights of academic and co-curricular success that it has since an inclusive style has fueled a drive for innovation and continuous improvement that runs right across the school.

Conclusions

The leadership at Sevenoaks School appears to be inclusive in character, with the tone of this leadership set at the top and cascading down. This style seems to be an important ingredient in the successes that the school has enjoyed, recognised by the achievement of *Sunday Times* independent school of the year in both 2008 and 2018.

References

History of Sevenoaks School, www.sevenoaksschool.org/about-us/the-school/school-history/
Obituary of Kim Taylor, www.sevenoaksschool.org/fileadmin/user_upload/Kim_Taylor_
    Obituary.pdf

11

INCLUSIVE LEADERSHIP IN APAM

1. Overview of the organisation

APAM was founded in 2010 by Executive Directors Simon Cooke and William Powell and has since expanded to a team of over forty real estate professionals. With a detailed knowledge of real estate across the UK and a proven track record of maximising value, the team identifies and delivers the most appropriate commercial real estate strategy to achieve each client's risk and return aspirations. APAM's diverse range of clients is based around the world and includes high-net-worth individuals, institutions, as well as private equity firms and banks. In the space of seven years, the firm has grown from three to over forty staff, from £0 to £1.4 billion of assets under management, and from zero to just under 500 properties under its management or ownership. It has offices in London, Manchester, Cardiff, Edinburgh and Glasgow, enabling the people in APAM to spend time on the ground rather than behind a screen.

The firm prides itself on creating value through its hands-on, energetic asset management approach where each client has a segregated mandate. It also speaks of having a deep knowledge database having analysed over £50bn of UK property assets and is trusted by clients, including private investors and institutions such as Britannia Invest and UOL Group; private equity firms such as Värde Partners, Patron Capital and Oaktree; and banks and their administrators, such as Lloyds Bank, JP Morgan and KPMG. These aspects, together with a strong internal culture and values that include leadership, trust and passion, have supported the firm's steady growth over a period of seven years.

2. The challenges faced

APAM has faced multiple challenges over the past seven years, including being a new brand without a multi-year track record and without immediate market recognition in many circles. A further challenge has been servicing global investment clients from Singapore, USA, Denmark, the Middle East, Israel and South Africa, all with different investment objectives, structures and reporting systems.

3. The innovative actions taken

The firm has developed a clear product offering, with strong tools and people skills both internally and externally, all of which have contributed to its continued success. Taking these points in turn:

Clear product offering

APAM has settled into three key business streams, maintaining a balance across (i) distressed bank workouts, (ii) high return opportunities for private equity clients and (iii) co-investment in prime assets alongside global high-net-worth individuals and institutions. Across all of these products, APAM's team provides an end-to-end service, with specialists in real estate investment, asset management, property management, financing, accounting and client reporting.

Strong tools

Expert knowledge is the firm's principal asset. APAM has built a powerful bespoke knowledge database of UK real estate over the last seven years, analysing over 6,000 properties with a value of £50 billion as part of its underwriting, due diligence and acquisition work. This information, the firm's confidential intellectual property, provides the firm with forward-looking insight into real estate trends, strategies and opportunities throughout the UK.

Moreover, the firm has invested considerable resources in the development and maintenance of a bespoke centralised database and asset management reporting system which ensures that data is validated and quality assured across all mandates. The ability to customise reports enables APAM to service each client according to their specific needs and requirements and a dedicated client reporting and accounting team works with the database.

Strong people skills for internal and external impact

People skills/culture for internal impact

APAM recognises that its success is driven by the quality of people that it recruits as well as its own culture. The firm has strong core values in relation to its leadership style and passion for its work, as well as an emphasis on strategic teamwork and collaboration.

One of the keys to the success of APAM's team lies in the quality and character of its recruitment process. So, instead of following a standard recruitment process with rigid job descriptions and defined vacancies, the firm builds on the talented people who approach the firm and then, after several conversations in which the two sides have time to consider each other, the individual is then found a role that suits their skills and will help drive the business forward.

The advantages of this kind of approach over a more standard one are twofold. Firstly, it helps identify those with exceptional talent and innovation since potential candidates can be considered holistically and not simply in relation to a specific job description. Secondly, the unrushed conversations allow mutual trust to be built between the firm and the candidate, something often lost in a more rushed recruitment process when a role is required to be filled with urgency. The additional time taken also enables candidates to learn thoroughly about the company so that there are no surprises after they start.

This 'getting to know you' aspect of the recruitment process results in a sense of commitment and deep knowledge of the firm, contributing to a much higher retention rate than might be achieved through a standard recruitment process. In fact, even where a 'standard process' is followed using a recruitment agent, whether for an administrative or management role, APAM makes sure that there is a three-stage interview process with the aim of building a relationship prior to appointment. The third interview is always less formal than the previous ones and provides an opportunity for the interviewer and interviewee to talk openly about the role and expectations on both sides. At this third interview, potential recruits are also able to meet staff across all levels of the firm, typically one of the founding directors, a more junior member of their team and also their prospective manager.

Recruiting a diversity of people with appropriate skills and personalities makes it possible to develop the enterprising and inclusive culture that the directors have aspired to create. For example, of the more than forty employees in the firm, personalities reflect thirteen of the sixteen MBTI types showing the tendency to shy away from the recruitment of any single type of person.

Structural features assist in creating this inclusive culture, with all twenty-five of the London staff, including directors, sharing the same large office and the remaining staff sharing an office in Manchester too. The close proximity of staff helps people understand how different parts of the business relate to each other and also helps develop a culture in which people of all levels feel able to freely ask questions of each other. Moreover, it creates a cohesive team and feeling of empowerment, elements facilitated also by the working styles of the management team, the open-ended job descriptions, common goals, the freedom to volunteer ideas and the absence of an individual reward-based system. In fact, there is a group bonus scheme into which 10% of profits are paid and which is distributed to staff at the end of a five-year period. This is a long-term incentive plan that encourages collective responsibility and a sense that growing the business will grow a bigger bonus pot too.

The sense of empowerment that employees feel also derives from a range of employee-led initiatives, including a Junior Board. This is formed from a rotational cross-section of staff across grades and teams and is an initiative designed to empower the team and encourage networking. Key focus areas include APAM's charitable initiatives, corporate hospitality and social committee engagements.

People skills for external impact

The firm prides itself on making a difference for its clients and, as part of its service, produces bespoke reports for clients and innovative development of the properties in its portfolio. For example, after jointly acquiring Arlington Business Park in the Thames Valley, real estate that consists of 360,000 square feet of buildings set amidst landscaped grounds and a lake, APAM transformed one of the most dated business park developments in the area into one of the most attractive and well-appointed.

How did APAM achieve this? A survey was sent to the 1,500-people working at Arlington Business Park and, the strength of feedback, the firm introduced a new café with a cashless payment system, a floating meeting room on the expansive lake, a gymnasium and an events programme, providing a range of activities including fifteen fitness classes a week, quizzes and language classes. During the summer, successful events included outdoor film showings, summer sports days and Formula 1 pit-stop challenges. In the winter, there was a Christmas Fayre, and the park was opened to the local community, schools and families.

APAM's inclusive approach at Arlington Business Park did not end there for, as Director Chris Taylor said, "Our challenge is to keep the events programme fresh and to react to tenant demand. If someone has an idea for an event, we'll consider it".

4. Definitive outcomes

Since the time that APAM was created seven years ago, it has experienced meteoric success. In terms of assets under management, these amounted to £1.4bn in 2018, and it has successfully exited almost £1bn of properties. By 2019, APAM was in a situation where clients had increasing confidence in placing repeat business of ever-greater frequency and volume, with a joint venture for example with a South African client in January 2016 involving the acquisition of five assets with a total value of about £30m. What is more, the client has retained APAM as the investment asset and property manager on all the properties purchased.

In terms of recruitment, two examples of appointments that have followed the non-structured recruitment process described above include:

- Investment manager joining from CBRE Global Investors
- Head of operations joining from PwC and being promoted to director after one year.

Staff development is also a key factor in success helping with the effectiveness of day-to-day work, ensuring that people have the ability to lead and make a real impact within the firm and also increasing retention. By way of example, an APAM asset manager has become head of investor reporting; a team assistant has been promoted within five months to the Investor Reporting Team; an analyst moved across into the Investment Management Team; and a PA's role has developed into that of the operations and marketing manager.

Where charitable initiatives are concerned, the team has selected monthly self-funded social committees and charity partners and two junior members of staff have raised over £3,000 for a single charity over a period of five months. In terms of marketing and business development, social media campaigns have led to increased brand awareness through strategies adopted by all staff across their personal profiles.

What of the leadership and culture in the organisation and their impacts on APAM's activities? Five in-depth interviews with management and non-management staff were conducted to obtain insights on the role that these have played in APAM's stellar growth. *Verbatim* qualitative comments on a wide range of questions follow with the comments of different staff melded into continuous text.

Is inclusive leadership present at APAM?

Managers emphasised the extent to which a vision is set at the top of the firm and that how people then achieve the vision is largely delegated to staff. Moreover, a team approach to work is encouraged by having an open-plan office in London in which all staff, including directors, are based. According to one manager, "this generates transparency and a team culture", and interviews with a cross-section of staff revealed that curiosity is also fostered since the directors encourage colleagues to ask questions. What is more, this open culture is complemented by initiatives such as the 'Friday note', a light-hearted summary written by a different person each week of who has done what. Each Monday morning, a staff meeting is held in the London office which staff from other offices can join virtually.

In terms of leadership style, both managers and non-managers regard APAM's leadership as inclusive since there is a strong sense that people and ideas are listened to within the firm; that people are given constructive advice and that APAM supports people and helps them grow. One non-manager, for example, mentioned that "when out at networking events, the director will sometimes say of me, '[name] is one of our star performers'. He says this in front of me and whether it's true or not, he's publicly giving support to his staff".

What are the benefits of inclusive leadership?

Managers mention that inclusive leadership "leaves room for people to be creative and to try new things with support". One, for example, mentions "the lack of a rigid job description that . . . leaves room for freedom to try out your own approach to meet end-goals". Another points to the fact, relatedly, that the absence of job descriptions has produced more inclusivity since "we've had to pick up everything when needed". Moreover, according to two of the three managers, inclusive leadership has encouraged creativity and freedom to explore, producing also team spirit, peer-to-peer respect and encouraging people to speak up. A further benefit is said to be that people feel included, which breeds loyalty and makes the firm a better place to work.

Interestingly, non-managers take a similar view. Comments from their ranks include the fact that the inclusive style "energises", "gives people a stake", by facilitating emotional investment, "provides a real incentive to move things on", "creates a sense of caring about the firm" and "creates a willingness to go the extra mile". This last point appeared in various guises, with one person talking about "going above and beyond if you feel that you've a connection to the firm".

Two further themes relate to the learning that takes place for senior and more junior people and the motivational impacts of de-emphasising with one person saying that, "You enjoy coming to work a lot more if you have a relationship with someone in a leadership role since it makes the hierarchy less obvious. Also, it's very easy to ask and double-check what you are doing so that you know it is correct, helping you to perform better". In terms of learning, one non-manager made the point that "leaders can learn too – it's not true that you can't teach old dogs new tricks since there is a trickle-up and a trickle-down effect". Moreover, "for young people who don't really know what they want to do, being in an inclusive environment helps them see which posts they are most interested in".

So, already we have some tangible indications of the impacts that inclusive leadership can make. In fact, one manager went so far as to say, "The growth in APAM could not have been achieved with transactional leadership since we would not have been thinking 'What should we be doing that we're not?' and we would not have achieved the growth without getting people on board with the vision and the end goal". Interestingly, the "getting people on board" concept appears to rely to a great extent on the fostering of teamwork, something that the firm works hard to achieve.

As one manager volunteered,

> We focus on developing a team so that people's skills complement each other and so that we do not have clones in terms of personality and styles. When we recruit, we don't look initially at qualifications and grades since we focus more on the person and how they could fit into the team since it is a combination of skills and personality that bring the best results. It is also important to encourage people with different views to speak up.

Few negative aspects were mentioned except that one manager noted the risk of being too transparent and sharing too much information. Also, that sometimes, too many voices can slow the decision-making process down.

To what extent power is delegated in APAM?

One director emphasised the importance of including others. "If people feel included, they breed loyalty and make the firm a better place to work. By de-emphasising hierarchy, you notice an energising effect with the team having a real incentive to positively force change and a willingness to go the extra mile".

This philosophy is echoed by a manager who spoke of the importance of delegating and empowering staff so that they feel responsible to deliver, with senior management defining the choices and then leaving decision-making to the operational team. In the course of this, the management team offer learning opportunities to people across the firm, allowing those people to broaden their experience, try new things, make mistakes and learn from them.

As one manager noted,

> Within my team, team-members are responsible for one complete portfolio which gives them ownership. It takes longer to bring someone up to speed to handle a complete portfolio than to give people a few smaller, separate jobs but this 'whole job' approach allows an employee to feel pride in what they have accomplished and also provides opportunities for growth. For, once a person has the confidence to handle one or two portfolios, they can then confidently run ten, and running a portfolio demands a range of related skills, for example giving presentations. A further benefit of a 'whole task' approach is that it results in one person having comprehensive understanding of a single topic, something that produces more joined-up thinking than a production line approach would do.

Corroboration of the positive impacts of this overall approach comes from the two non-managers interviewed. One, for example, while acknowledging that there is a hierarchy, recognises that "we have a very flat structure and that working daily with a director, provides a version of teamwork". As he says: "There's nothing I do that the director wouldn't do either' so you don't have completely separate tasks. In this sense, yes, power is definitely delegated".

A second non-manager took a similar view, saying that, with the exception of quarterly reporting which is a special case, staff have free rein in determining how to reach an end goal. "This is good," he says, since "if tasks are clearly defined you stop looking for solutions further afield, which is often where solutions can be found".

Nature of the tasks in APAM

APAM managers were of the view that a lot of what the firm does is structured and clearly defined with the extent to which this is the case varying across the business. At the same time, managers are frequently considering new opportunities, so there is an emphasis on new products, with business development a key focus of meetings. As part of this, a core objective is expanding the client base as well as winning new markets. In fact, the directors are adventurous in winning new work but they refuse to take unnecessary risk, never borrowing money for example.

In which ways might the current styles of leadership in your organisation need to change in the future?

Asked whether the current style of leadership might need to change in the future, one manager expressed great admiration for the directors, finding their leadership "good and fit for purpose". Another expressed the view that, further down the line, as the firm moved beyond forty people, it might be necessary to develop more processes where reports were concerned and also make changes in some of the deliverables offered might also be needed, changes that could put a halt to some of the firm's current creativity. However, in this manager's view, the style of leadership in the firm could remain unchanged.

Is IL rewarded?

One manager pointed out that

> the inclusive leadership style in the firm comes largely from the directors and my PDR process will focus on objectives for the team and the way that I manage the whole team. There's a good deal of feedback on this since I sit down every two weeks with a director for a 30-minute catch-up.

This female manager compared her experience in APAM with that of a previous organisation where she had been told to "dominate meetings more and toughen up". She contrasted this with her experience at APAM, where nobody had told her to act in a style different from her own: "They accept different people's styles even though the directors might conduct meetings in a different way from them".

How are people rewarded?

One manager explained that although people don't have KPIs, annual discretionary bonuses are awarded on the basis of whether objectives have been achieved. "We're not commission-based since rewards are more linked to the performance of the business as a whole. So, it's not about one individual doing well but about the team and whether, collectively, everyone is pulling in the right direction."

One non-manager commented on the number of internal opportunities available, pointing out that this was something that allows people to follow their interests and creates a "strong room for progression". The availability of plentiful opportunities for progression clearly serves as a powerful reward and motivator for staff.

To what extent do the behaviours and attitudes of the directors inform the responses and behaviours of other people in the organisation?

One manager had interesting views on the style of the directors describing them as "definitely influential and very passionate and motivating". He said that this behaviour affects people's mood in a positive way. As he said:

> One of the directors is very charismatic and it is palpable when he is not there. When he is there – in the open-plan office that we all share – there is a different energy level in the room and people can feed off that. I think that it is very important to be in close physical proximity with senior leaders and so would not want to manage my team remotely.

This manager went on to talk of the importance of proximity in leadership, pointing out that the importance lay not in micromanagement but in "support and discussion". He added that "in an open-plan environment, you can see how hard the partners are working and that is contagious. If my team is working hard too then I need to follow suit".

Work ethic is one thing, but work culture is another. As the manager says,

> Both directors have great influence and one has a very strong presence. The way that they interact with people is very important since if people are scared to put their hand up and get their heads bitten off, they'll crawl back into a hole. Fortunately, it's not like that here.

One non-manager corroborated this by saying how influential the directors were and that "if you don't see them on a regular basis, you feel a level of disconnect". She went on to describe how both directors work in the open-plan office space and how one of them walks around the office talking directly to members of staff, sometimes addressing the whole room with all twenty-five staff (other staff in the firm work in Manchester), sometimes giving out a single message, such as, "Why are we keeping these solicitors?". She went on to say that in another firm she worked for, the equity partners were never seen and that a divide established itself such that if you were overworked and underpaid there would be a high level of dissatisfaction. In her view, the physical presence of people is very important and, in her words, "if you are not physically present, you can't influence people very much".

In your view, do a diversity of employees tend to trust the leaders? (question for non-managers)

According to one non-manager, "Definitely. Everyone buys into the vision of the firm and we trust the leadership to produce the best solutions for the business. Everyone's livelihood depends on these decisions so if we have trust in the leaders' decision, this is very significant". Another commented, "The leaders trust me to get on with my job myself and if I don't understand something, I can just ask my manager".

What does it feel like to work at APAM?

The managers interviewed were universally enthusiastic about the experience of working at APAM, using positive descriptions such as "Enjoyable"; "Challenging";

"Exciting seeing the value of what you are adding"; and "Empowering, since I am allowed to do different things and not kept in a box". One manager commented, "both the directors are naturally inclusive in their behaviours and want to draw on the wider community of staff; one of them in particular tends to get energy from everyone being involved".

Of the two non-managers, one commented that she really enjoyed working there, saying,

> People make it a very enjoyable place to work and it has come far in a short space of time. I like the open-plan office since there is a lot of overlap between teams, and an office like this makes for good working relationships between and within teams. I've jumped desk more than anyone else in the room and I feel very much included in the energy in the room – one big team together!

The second non-manager said,

> Working in this environment influences you to work hard because you are surrounded by people who are working. Since you are given responsibility, you rise to the challenge and that raises your game. This makes me hungry to learn more. Also, having everyone around you makes it easy to ask questions.

5. Discussion and conclusions

It is manifest from the responses of managers and non-managers alike that APAM is regarded as having inclusive leadership, with the elements in this thought to be a major factor in the firm's success. Key manifestations of this style include the working behaviours of the directors, the open-plan office in which people of all levels sit together, the open-ended job descriptions, the freedom to volunteer ideas and questions, the opportunities to progress in the organisation and the provision of team rather than individual-based rewards.

Running through many of the respondents' answers are references to the presence of strong teamwork, with tasks shared across all levels of the company. This is interesting given the suggestion earlier on, in Chapter 2, that a collectivist culture is likely to facilitate the successful exercise of an inclusive style of leadership. So, consciously or unconsciously, APAM's move from individualism and high-power distance to collectivism and low power distance have established the conditions necessary for an inclusive culture. With this comes, naturally enough, all the benefits that we have found to be associated with inclusive style of leadership.

A summary of the main elements of inclusive leadership practised at APAM are shown in Table 11.1 with evidence coming from the *verbatim* comments of interviewees. Incidentally, we saw earlier in Chapters 5, 6 and 7 when reporting on the study of IL in eleven organisations and two universities, that the fifteen attributes used to define IL were unidimensional and coalesced into a single construct.

TABLE 11.1 The six main attributes of IL referred to by APAM respondents

IL attribute and whether Tf or SL	Definition of attribute	Words of respondents/facts
Inspirational motivation (Tf) and conceptualisation (SL)	Having a vision about possibilities and articulating that vision to followers	"A vision is set at the top of the firm and how people achieve that is largely delegated to staff." According to one manager and one non-manager, "Definitely. Everyone buys into the vision of the firm". One manager described the directors of APAM as "Definitely influential and very passionate and motivating". Speaking of one of the directors, he said that he "is very charismatic and it is palpable when he is not there. When he is there – in the open-plan office that we all share – there is a different energy level in the room and people can feed off that".
Individualised consideration (Tf)	Showing individual interest and offering one-to-one support for followers	"You enjoy coming to work a lot more if you have a relationship with someone in a leadership role since it makes the hierarchy less obvious."
Unqualified acceptance (SL)	Being inclusive in considering followers; being non-judgemental and accepting each follower as a unique individual	One female manager compared her experience in APAM with that of a previous organisation, pointing out that she had been told to "dominate meetings more and toughen up". She contrasted this with her experience at APAM where nobody had told me to act in a style different from her own: "They accept different people's styles even though the directors might conduct meetings in a different way from them".

IL attribute and whether Tf or SL	Definition of attribute	Words of respondents/facts
Listening (SL)	Actively listening to followers that involves not only listening to the content but also the underlying meaning and emotional significance	The interview respondents indicated that people and ideas are listened to within the firm.
Growth (SL)	Encouraging followers to reach their full potential by providing opportunities for them to make autonomous and unique contributions	Senior management defines the choices and then leaves decision-making to the operational team. In the course of this, the management team offer learning opportunities to people across the firm, allowing them to broaden their experience, try new things, make mistakes and learn from them. One manager noted, "Within my team, team-members are responsible for one complete portfolio which gives them ownership. It takes longer to bring someone up to speed to handle a complete portfolio than to give people a few smaller, separate jobs but this 'whole job' approach allows an employee to feel pride in what they have accomplished and also provides opportunities for growth. For, once a person has the confidence to handle one or two portfolios, they can then confidently run ten, and running a portfolio demands a range of related skills, for example giving presentations".

(Continued)

TABLE 11.1 (Continued)

IL attribute and whether Tf or SL	Definition of attribute	Words of respondents/facts
		One non-manager noted, "Since you are given responsibility, you rise to the challenge and that raises your game. This makes me hungry to learn more".
Confidence building	Providing followers with opportunities and recognition so that they see themselves as valuable contributors to the team and organisation	There is a sense that APAM supports people and helps them grow. One non-manager, for example, mentioned that "when out at networking events, the director will sometimes say of me, '[name] is one of our star performers'. He says this in front of me and whether it's true or not, he's publicly giving support to his staff".

So, the fact that most of the emphasis in APAM appears to be on the six attributes in Table 11.1 is a good example of the way that a selection of IL attributes can be the focus of IL in any one organisation.

Turning now to strategy, how does the strong presence of inclusive leadership at APAM relate to the contextual and strategic factors mentioned in Chapter 2?

Taking context first, it can be recalled that Fiedler considered the conditions necessary for participative leadership to be the following:

– Moderate relations between leader and subordinate
– Moderate task structure
– Moderate power (i.e. some delegation takes place).

If we consider the views offered by managers and non-managers, then we can see evidence of the central condition ('moderate task structure') but no evidence of the two other conditions since relations between leader and subordinate are in fact good rather than 'moderate' and, where delegation of power is concerned, 'substantial' rather than 'moderate' power is delegated. So, the instance of high inclusivity at APAM would seem to be at odds with the conditions predicted for this by Fiedler.

What of the strategic context? APAM seems to fulfil the conditions for an 'analyser' type of organisation, since the firm places an emphasis on high exploration as well as high exploitation (Håkonsson et al, 2012), as well as having 'producer'-type managers offering high levels of delegation and high levels of uncertainty avoidance (avoidance of risk is present in reference to a director's preference for borrowing money and taking unnecessary risks). So, in this sense, the strategy literature, with the exception of Fiedler's theory, can be said to predict the type of leadership that is practised at APAM, making the presence of inclusive leadership in the firm a 'best fit' solution.

Conclusions

The success that APAM has achieved over a period of just seven years appears to owe much to the inclusive leadership that is strongly in evidence in the firm. This style of leadership creates a culture that inspires creativity, discretionary labour and a sense of well-being and loyalty, all factors that have contributed to the firm's success.

Reference

Håkonsson, D., Burton, R., Obel, B. and Lauridsen, J. (2012). Strategy implementation requires the right executive style: Evidence from Danish SMEs. *Long Range Planning*, 45 (2–3), 182–208.

12

INCLUSIVE LEADERSHIP, CUSTOMER CENTRICITY AND DESIGN

Customer centricity

The past few years have seen a growing interest in understanding how organisations can increase their connections with customers. The reader may recall the Deloitte report that identified the factors driving inclusive leadership, one of which is the drive to cultivate more customer-centric mind-sets (Bourke and Dillon, 2016). The buzzwords of 'empathy' and 'connectedness' are, according to Deloitte Australia, taking hold as organisations strive to better understand their customers' worlds with inclusive leadership as an essential part of achieving this.

Deloitte Australia cite the instance of telecoms company, Telstra, as one that illustrates customer centricity and certainly, Telstra's annual report for 2016 shows the priority placed on improving the customer experience:

> Improving customer advocacy remains our number one strategic priority. By providing great customer experiences, we can change the way that customers talk about us.
>
> *(https://telstra2016ar.interactiveinvestorreports.com/strategy-and-performance/improve-customer-advocacy/)*

How did the company set about this? Ostensibly, the company launched a transformational programme to orient the entire company around the customer and to connect everything to everyone. This approach was driven by the view that, to remain competitive, organisations must be customer-centric and understand the changing needs and wants of their customers. So the transformation journey was designed to influence how the company structures its business, how it develops leaders and how it enacts diversity and inclusion.

Unfortunately, the Dreoitte document discussing the way that Telstra went about creating greater customer centricity (Deloitte, 2015) has little in the way of detail regarding how Telstra embedded customer centricity in its organisation and how inclusive leadership helped it achieve this. Yes, there is reference to the aim of achieving "connectivity" within the organisation, with leadership as a central part of this; there is reference to the appointment of a "director of customer advocacy" with a brief to orient the entire organisation around the customer; and there is reference to embedding a style of leadership capable of creating an internal landscape that can relate to the customer and their needs. However, there is little here on the specifics of how a new type of leadership can drive external connectivity and little on what customer-centric goals the company has set itself.

If this is disappointing, so too are the examples offered up elsewhere by supposedly customer-centric companies. The French company L'Oréal, for example, is frequently quoted as customer-centric, but this accolade relies almost exclusively on its 'True Match' foundation range which is billed as matching the skin tones of 98% of UK women rather than the usual 39%. Similarly, in the UK, the supermarket giant, Tesco, is quoted as customer-centric by virtue of piloting a "relaxed lane" at the checkout in order to take the pressure off customers with dementia and those who do not want to feel rushed. Are we really seeing here, in these two cases, the pinnacle of customer centricity, or is the concept of customer centricity just narrowly defined?

The sense of disappointment does not end there. According to a survey conducted by The Economist Intelligence Unit and SAS in 2012 amongst 389 global marketing and non-marketing executives, only six in ten senior business leaders view their companies as customer-centric (Nanji, 2013). This makes for depressing reading since in 1954 Drucker famously wrote that "there is only one valid definition of a business purpose: to create a customer", and that "marketing is . . . the whole business seen from the point of view of its final result, that is from the customer's point of view" (1954, p. 37). Then, in 1995, Michael Hammer, former Professor of Computing at the Massachusetts Institute of Technology (MIT), stated that business survival depends on shaping products and services around the "unique and particular needs" of the customer (Hammer, 1995) a view that launched the initiative known as 'Business Process Engineering' (BPR). Many consulting firms embarked on a BPR process with their clients and so you have to ask what happened to these initiatives and Drucker's important thoughts.

Fast forward twenty years to 2015, and you find Deloitte explaining that customers expect greater personalisation and a voice in shaping the products and services that they consume, something that they say is important in an age of choice facilitated by digital devices (Deloitte, 2015, p. 1). Deloitte goes on to suggest that the challenge for companies is to deliver a personal touch with individualised insights and efficiencies of scale following operating models that put the customer at the heart of everything they do.

With so many voices putting the customer centre-stage over so many decades, you would expect organisations to be drowning in customer-focused initiatives of ever-increasing levels of complexity. Is this the case? In fact, the three examples of Telstra, L'Oréal and Tesco show a somewhat superficial understanding of the customer, and one has to wait for the unfortunate Cambridge Analytica debacle (Moss, 2018), in which the 'likes' of Facebook users' were extrapolated to personality type and advert preferences, to see any sophistication in organisations' understanding of their customers.

Personality is one important segmentation variable and another is gender. Currently, 83% of consumer purchases are made by women (Moss, 2016) but as we have seen only a tiny proportion of *executive* board positions are held by women in many industrialised countries. In the UK, for example, the proportion of executive board positions in FTSE companies held by women is currently under 10%, showing that only this small proportion contribute to the talent pipelines of organisations. By contrast, female representation at the less significant *non-executive* board level is 31% (Kollewe and Hickey, 2015) and one can well question the extent to which these non-executive board members, parachuted in from the outside, can realisticallty influence customer-facing strategies and organisational cultures. For those interested, Table 12.1 presents those figures showing the slow pace of change of *executive* places on FTSE boards in recent years.

In fact, the paucity of female input to decision-making – and design and marketing decision-making in particular – has been a recurring theme in my own publications on design and marketing since the 1990s (Moss, 2016). For decades now, I have been beating the drum concerning the need for an 'outside-in' perspective that allows congruent attitudes to develop between the external customer and internal personnel but the tiny proportion of female *executive* members on boards shows the small percentage of women influencing senior decision-making, even in sectors - retailing, furniture, groceries, domestic real estate and pharmaceuticals - where the majority of purchasers are women.

Not surprising then perhaps that many male-dominated organisations and sectors pay lip service to customer centricity, with L'Oréal and Tesco offering examples of initiatives that do not affect the customer offer in any profound sense. Given

TABLE 12.1 Figures showing the percentage of executive and non-executive females on the boards of FTSE 100 companies

%	2010/11	2012	2013	2014	Oct 2015
Female non-executive directors	15.6	22.4	21.8	25.5	31.4
Female executive directors	5.5	6.6	5.8	6.9	9.6

Source: Davies Review, cited in Kollewe and Hickey (2015)

what we see of the products, websites and retail interiors currently on display, we can well ask whether the visual and linguistic preferences of the majority purchasers, women, are being factored into design and marketing decisions and whether these organisations seek out information on women's preferences. The dissatisfaction that women and other consumers express in customer satisfaction studies suggests that their views are not guiding product and service design (Moss, 2016) and this is where inclusive leadership can step in to help.

Customer centricity and inclusive leadership

As we have seen, the report by Deloitte Australia (Bourke and Dillon, 2016) proposes an all-important link between inclusive leadership and customer centricity, and one could second-guess the reason even though it is not set down in this report. For IL, according to the definition used in this book, places an emphasis on 'empathy', 'unqualified acceptance' and 'foresight', and these three competencies alone will facilitate a focus on the diversity of people within and outside the organisation.

This process whereby interactions internally and externally mirror each other is exemplified by an anecdote in the book *How to Lead across New Borders* (Gundling *et al*, 2015) describing how a high-tech company found a link between employee innovation and the way that people were managed. They also found that involving people who knew the company's target markets could produce better products with the authors speaking of the need to: "bring diversity into our product development cycle in order to be relevant" (Gundling *et al*, 2015, p. 132). This echoes a comment from a non-manager at one of our case study organisations, Royal Mail Sales, who suggested that,

> You need to keep up with the customer who is increasingly knowledgeable. We in Sales need to adapt and speak to customers in different ways so companies need to treat employees in such a way that the team can adapt. If everything was tightly structured, you couldn't be so adaptable with customers (in other words, you might focus on making several phone calls rather than focus on being flexible with one customer).

So here we have the all-important link between inclusive leadership (IL) and customer centricity (CC). Not only does IL deliver superior productivity, motivation, well-being and diversity, but it also enhances innovation and CC. Here, for example, is Virgin's CEO Richard Branson speaking of the importance of a strong focus on employees in order, then, to create positive communications with customers (Kissmetrics blog): "Everything trickles down from your staff"). As he says:

> If the person who works at your company is 100% proud of the job they're doing, if you give them the tools to do a good job, [if] they're proud of the

brand, if they're well looked after, [and] they're treated well, then they're going to be smiling, they're going to happy, and therefore the customer will have a nice experience.

If the person [who's] working for your company is not given the right tools, is not looked after, is not appreciated, they're not going to do things with a smile, and therefore the customer will be treated in a way in which they don't want to come back for more. So my philosophy has always been, if you can put your staff first, your customers second, and your shareholders third, effectively in the end the shareholders do well, the customers do better, and your staff are happy.

So, Branson provides his experience of the link between IL and improved customer communications, and one wonders whether IL could touch other aspects of CC as well. In fact, at the time of going to press, (February 2019), the author was involved in qualitative research to understand the connections, if any, between IL and CC. This research involved interviews with four Norwegian organisations of which two were design firms (one a software SME and one focused on sustainable design) and two were Big Four global consultancies with those involved in this research consisting of the author of this book, Benja Stig Fagerland of South Eastern University in Norway and Alan David of the University of Westminster.

What did we find? The findings were exciting since they showed a clear association between IL and CC and a clear finding that if you did not want to produce a standard deliverable but instead a tailored or creative product, then IL was the leadership style of choice. For curious readers, it may be of interest to know that CC embraces the four elements identified in an excellent overview paper (Lamberti, 2013) as being:

(i)   interactive customer relationship management: the explicit and hidden needs of customers are understood and there is decision-making interactivity with the customer

(ii) internal integration: coordinated structures are available for gathering and sharing information about the customer

(iii) customer integration: the customer is involved in the value-generation process

(iv) external integration: customer management processes are available and these can include suppliers and partners in the supply chain

The twelve semi-structured, in-depth interviews conducted by the team with go-ahead organisations in Norway showed that embedding inclusive leadership in organisations not only produces flat structures, trust and openness but also facilitates all four aspects of CC mentioned here. What is more, it fosters a 'diversity mindset' (David, 2010), ensuring that organisations have a high proportion of heterogeneous employees, producing a high level of 'diversity density' within the organisation (*ibid*).

That is not all, however. For, the interviews with these go-ahead Norwegian companies showed that IL also delivers the behaviours that facilitate *design thinking* (Rowe, 1991), a mindset that not only encourages people to question their personal assumptions but also to learn from end-user input (*ibid*). Since design thinking relies on 'market orientation', in turn linked to CC, IL will bring about design thinking as well as CC. So, even if a lot of the detail passes you by, just remember that IL can bring about greater design creativity and overall CC, delighting customers in the process. These connections are modelled in Figure 12.1, which shows the relationship between the various elements touched on above.

There is insufficient space here, unfortunately, to provide a full description of the research findings, but one of the main findings, expressed by the female CEO of one of the two design companies interviewed, this one a software design company, was that: "To be customer-centric, you need to be inclusive and have a 'growth mindset' as well as a 'diversity mindset'".

The head of marketing at the same SME was equally emphatic, saying that "Inclusive leadership helps you put the emphasis on thinking about people internally and this extends externally too" and she expanded on this point, saying, "So, you transfer the leadership values used internally to the client, externally". In this way, IL definitely supports CC with the main elements in IL facilitating CC being: consideration, motivation, listening, growth and empathy.

Interestingly, a female head at the second design firm, this one specialised in human-centred design, expressed the view that

> An inclusive management style is the best if you want to develop this kind
> of design. It is necessary because you develop things for people and people
> are different. You need IL if you want to be people-centred in your design'.

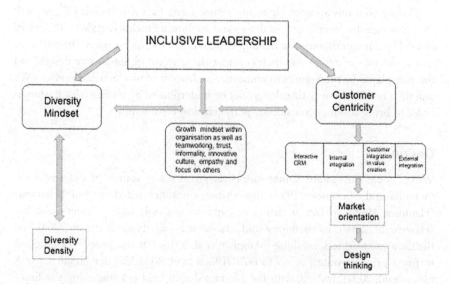

FIGURE 12.1 Summary of findings regarding the impact of IL on CC

Moreover, echoing and expanding on these thoughts, a respondent from a Big Four consultancy expressed the interesting view that having a bureaucratic system of management would not produce CC:

> Bureaucratic leadership . . . produces the ability to deliver standardised services as against diversified, tailored services that will bring delight to customers. I am one hundred per cent certain that there is a link between inclusive leadership and producing a more diversified service. If you follow this way of thinking, you need to give a lot of freedom to your employees to think about the best solutions for the client.

He was vocal, going on to say,

> If you are to be really successful in performing, you must have people working for you who are self-motivated and who are trusted so that you can delegate to them. To do this, you need to create a safe, open, warm environment. You need to delegate a lot and give empowerment.

We can leave the final word to an interaction designer from another Big Four consultancy:

> Agencies that exhibit the competencies of listening and empathy have more creativity and produce lovable products. Without these skills, you only produce 'viable' products so you need to make your employees feel safe because sometimes you need to fail before you find the right solution.

Having seen this array of views suggesting a link between IL and CC, we will now focus on the specific case of design and see how an inclusive style of leadership can deliver 'design thinking' in making design more customer-centric. We will look first at the role of design and then consider the concept of 'interactive design' and the part played by preferences in consumer evaluation of products and services. We will then review the way that design can be underpinned by inclusive leadership in order to bring about an 'outside-in' perspective in organisations.

Design

Why a focus on design? Quite simply, design is a key source of differentiation (Schmitt and Simonson, 1997) that shapes consumer reactions and behaviour (Hammer, 1995). In fact, it shapes perceptions not only of a product's usability (Hassenzahl, 2007), its usefulness and ease-of-use (Van Iwaarden et al, 2004) and the time attended to something (Maughan et al, 2007), but also people's willingness to pay a price premium of up to 66% (Bloch et al, 2003; Van der Heijden, 2003; Hassenzahl, 2007). Indeed, with the product design field encompassing the functionality, ergonomics and aesthetics of a physical product (Schmitt and Simonson,

1997), one well-respected researcher has described design as replacing nature 'as the dominant presence in human experience' (Buchanan, 1995, p. xii).

An important aspect of design is of course a product's appearance, whether its materials, proportions, colour, ornamentation, shape, size or reflectivity (Lawson, 1983) and companies today, in a competitive environment, need to reflect on consumers' aesthetic preferences (Creusen *et al*, 2010, pp. 1437–1438). This interaction of product and customer aesthetic leads Buchanan (2001, p. 11) to speak of "interaction design", an approach that seeks to understand the "experience of human beings that make and use [products]" assisting a new understanding through "an investigation of what makes a product useful, usable, and desirable".

'Interaction design', in turn, could be viewed as a way of implementing what is known as 'market orientation', a concept that is one of the most researched in the strategic marketing literature (Talke *et al*, 2011). This orientation allows an organisation to achieve "Design Thinking, an approach that encourages designers to question their personal assumptions and learn from end-users through end-user input" (Rowe, 1991). Ultimately, market orientation has a positive impact on radical innovation, performance and new product development (*ibid*) but it relies on having designers who can relate to the concerns and aesthetics of the target market. Realting in this way is not simple since research has demonstrated a design preference for designs produced by those with the same gender and personality as the designer (Moss, 2016 and 2017) so, as a UX designer has written, "we cannot just hire from our bubble, we can't just design for our bubble" (Braga, 2017). This leads him to speak of the need to have "diversity in our mindsets, in our day-to-day" (*ibid*), thereby ensuring the appeal of design for a diversity of customers. The alternative is to hand-pick designers for particular markets.

Since the notion of aesthetic people is all-important, we will now provide a brief overview of the psychology of preference, reviewing the earlier literature on design and marketing preferences and then moving on to the part that gender and personality play in this.

Interaction design

The concept of 'interaction design' fits within an 'interactionist' philosophy (Mischel, 1997) which acknowledges that the evaluations that individuals make of physical settings may differ, producing different 'life-spaces' and consumption behaviours (Gehrt and Yan, 2004). Given this and the fact that purchases offer a vehicle for self-expression (Karande *et al*, 1997), this philosophy of 'interaction design' is consistent with the marketing notion signalled earlier of shaping products around the 'unique and particular needs' of the customer (Hammer, 1995). Just how a range of desirable designs can be produced, ia open to question with one view being the need for a heterogeneous designer population (Dell'Era *et al*, 2010) and another, as we have seen, on the need for diverse thinking. Then there is the question of which elements constitute 'desirability', a question that remains one of the "weakest topics of design research today" (Buchanan, 2001). There are also gaps in our understanding of how the look of a product affects preferences (Veryzer, 1993) and how preferences relate to educational background, gender and race (Nixon, 1997), with all these questions, reinforcing a sense that deeper knowledge of product differentiation and preferences is lacking (Noble and Kumar, 2010).

So, for some period, research commentators have lamented the absence of empirical work on the interactive effect of design. By contrast, there is no shortage of theoretical information on the contrasting 'universalist' or Kantian approach, which views aesthetic tastes as universal rather than differentiated. In this way, research identified non-conscious design processes, so-called 'internal processing algorithms' (IPAs), that were believed to underlie positive design reactions (Veryzer, 1993), with follow-up research efforts to encode the universal rules governing aesthetic preferences (Creusen *et al*, 2010). Regrettably, the empirical work of these researchers was not segmented by demographic variables despite the view that research should examine the role of biology and culture in the formation of IPAs (Veryzer, 1993). In fact, a similar deficiency applies to many studies of web design aesthetics, which propose a universalist aesthetic paradigm without testing the appeal of different web design paradigms for different audiences rooted in a universalist paradigm (Veryzer, 1993; Creusen *et al*, 2010; Schmitt and Simonson, 1997). This failure to allow for interaction design leads to the production of design guidelines that are presumed to apply universally across all demographic groups with examples including Maeda's *Laws of Simplicity* (2006) and Nielsen's design guidelines for web design and homepage usability (2012).

In order to have a better understanding of the role that an interactionist approach could play in a customer-centric approach, this chapter looks at the findings of research on the part played by personality, gender and nationality in design creations and preferences. It then goes on to propose a systematic approach to customer centricity and ends by linking this process to inclusive leadership.

Design creations and preferences

Elsewhere, I have written fairly extensively about the links binding the creator to the visual work that they create and the way that a person's gender, personality and nationality can leave their mark in design (Moss, 2012, 2016, 2017). If you like, this research shows how a visual design provides a *quasi* x-ray of the person who has created it, revealing the imprint of the creator's personality, gender and nationality. This process is in part summarised by Deyan Sudjic, Director of London's Design Museum, when he writes of design as a "reflection of emotional and cultural values" (2009, p. 49). Of course, in the case of gender, it may reflect physical factors too, such as visuo-spatial skills.

In fact, there is a large body of earlier research on the impacts of personality, gender and nationality, some of it quite fascinating, and so we sketch the main findings below.

Personality

How does personality influence graphic expression? Research has been conducted for over one hundred years in many parts of the world revealing how a person's personality can leave an indelible mark in many forms of graphic expression, whether drawings, paintings, digital drawings or handwriting. Particularly interesting studies are those by Waehner (1946), Alschuler and Hattwick (1947) and Harris (2017) with the conclusions of Waehner's study on the links between personality and graphic expression shown in Table 12.2 below.

A year after Waehner's research, a book appeared (Alschuler and Hattwick, 1947) which is interesting because of what it suggests about the relationship between the art work of children aged 2 to 4 and what is known of their behaviours from progress records, teachers' daily logs and full-day diary records. For, in the course of analysing 150 paintings, the authors discuss the significance of the use of colour, line and form, arguing for a link between colour and strong emotional drives and between line and form and self-control, concern with external stimuli and higher frequency of reasoned (in contrast to impulsive) behaviour (Moss, 2017). Their work is qualitative and, as we shall see in a little while, their conclusions mirror those of Waehner's more quantitative research.

To provide a flavour of Alschuler and Hattwick's work, they note that where shape is concerned, children whose drawings emphasise straight lines tend to stand out for their relatively assertive, outgoing behaviour, with length of line corresponding with control and less impulsive behaviour. By contrast, they suggest that

TABLE 12.2 Interpretation of generic features in drawings and paintings

Generic feature	Example	Interpretation
Size	Small size	Anxiety, depression, reduced energy, tendency to control
Distribution	Central distribution	Immature, depressive
	Symmetrical distribution	Conventional/depressive, controlled/constricted
	Wide distribution (over 50% of area)	Free imagination, relaxed mood, creative
Curved/sharp edges	<50% curves and many sharp edges	Aggressive/offensive
	>70% curves and few sharp edges	Introverted, creative, restrained, preoccupied with self
Colour	Greater colour than form variety	Energy, impetus, initiative
	Greater form than colour variety	Intellectually better developed than emotionally controlled

Source: Waehner (1946)

those with curved, continuous strokes are more dependent, withdrawn, submissive and subjectively orientated than those forming vertical, square or rectangular forms. Applying this understanding of colour and shape, Alschuler and Hattwick conclude that children tend to express through creative media the same feelings expressed in overt behaviour:

> almost every drawing and painting made by a young child is meaningful and in some measure expresses the child who did it (p. 5) . . . children tend to draw and paint what they are feeling and experiencing rather than what they see.
>
> *(p. 8)*

As mentioned, their conclusions mirror those of Waehner and other researchers as you can see in our earlier book, titled *Personality, Design and Marketing* (Moss, 2017).

Finally, a word about the more recent study by Judy Harris (2017), Professor in Educational Technology at the College of William and Mary which, this time, involved ten gifted fifth-grade boys. The methodology was interesting since each of these was asked to produce three images: the first, a freehand picture used with crayons, magic markers or coloured pencils; the second using a touch-sensitive graphics tablet; and the third produced using digital drawing software. These thirty pictures were then shown to fourteen teachers without the three pictures produced by a single individual being grouped together in any way. Then the teachers were asked to provide two types of information concerning the creators of the pictures, firstly demographic data (age) and then impressions of the students' behaviour patterns, learning styles, school subject preferences and any other information that occurred to the viewing teachers. These responses were then rewritten as lists of statements about the student artists.

Meanwhile, semi-structured interviews took place with the children, their parents and current classroom teachers, all of whom were asked to describe the children's most and least favourite school subjects, problem-solving methods, social interaction patterns, personal 'life philosophies' and activity preferences. These interviews were audiotaped and transcribed *verbatim*, and the content subsequently analysed by theme. These themes were then compared with the statements of the viewing teachers.

What did the comparison reveal? A large 69% of viewers' comments about the children's art corresponded with the interview data, with only 21% of teacher comments disagreeing with interview data and only 10% of teacher comments not mentioned in interviews. Interestingly, in terms of the accuracy of comments on the three types of drawing media, there was only one percentage point difference in terms of accuracy with the highest level of agreement with interview data (70%) being to drawings produced with the drawing tablet; a 69% level of agreement for drawings produced using digital drawing software and the lowest figure for drawings produced using hand-held drawing tools. Not surprisingly with such dramatic results, Harris concluded that digital as well as non-digital creations encode and communicate aspects of the personality and behaviours of their creators.

So, based on these studies and others, one can reasonably assume that the per-sonalities of designers will be projected into their work, notwithstanding the effects of their training. This is significant since the evidence presented in *Personality, Design and Marketing* (Moss, 2017) suggested that in selecting between different designs, people tend to prefer visuals created by those with similar personalities to their own. This is an important addition to the relatively novice but important field of interaction design, since it suggests that, where design is concerned, customer centricity can best be achieved by matching the personality of the purchaser with that of the designer.

Gender

We now move into the somewhat controversial and choppy waters of gender. I say this since the 'nature/nurture' argument is still alive and well, with many arguing for the irrelevance of gender as a variable, and some arguing for the impacts of social and/or biological factors. We do not need to engage with this debate since we are in the relatively safe waters of design and comparing male and female visual crea-tions and preferences.

What do we know about male and female visual creations? There is in fact a large body of research comparing the drawings, paintings and designs of children and young people – some of this research being my own – and the conclusions point to gender leaving its imprint on visual productions. You can find detailed information in my book *Gender, Design and Marketing* (2016) which summarises much of the research conducted in many parts of the world. The studies discussed here compared the drawings, paintings and designs of children, adolescents and/ or adults, with attention focused on a variety of visual elements, for example col-our, detail, shape and dimensionality, and on thematic elements (such as whether the subject matter was rooted in animate or inanimate themes; organic or non-organic; male or female).

The findings? It may or may not come as a surprise to learn that consistent differences appeared in cross-study studies comparing the visual and thematic ele-ments in male and female-created drawings, paintings, graphic, product and web design.

Now comes the $64,000 question. What of male and female preferences as between the designs of males and females? The same or different? In fact, in study after study, the research highlights a statistically significant tendency for people of one gender to prefer designs created by those of the same gender across a number of design media, ages and cultures (Moss, 2016).

In order to give a sense of this, we offer a glimpse into the findings of two studies involving graphic and product designs. The first of these (Moss and Horvath, 2014) presented six pairs of designs to men and women in five countries with a request that they indicate a single preference from each pair, with each pair focused on a similar genre of design (e.g. children's chairs; Christmas cards; underground inte-riors; drink cans; cushions) and Table 12.3 shows the extent to which people were drawn to designs created by their own gender. In actual fact, across the six pairs

TABLE 12.3 Preference test results across five nationalities with an indication of the statistical extent to which male and female responses differ

Designs	Significance (tendency of men and women in five countries to prefer designs created by those of their own gender)
Pair 1–2	.536
Pair 3–4	.000
Pair 5–6	.000
Pair 7–8	.003
Pair 9–10	.009
Pair 11–12	.000

Source: Moss and Horvath (2014)

of designs, the tendency to do this was at the 0.001 level of significance which, in statistical terms, is highly significant since it shows the probability of this being a chance result as being just one in a thousand.

In 2017, a very similar study was conducted using the same pairs of stimuli but with respondents aged 11 or under (Moss and Horvath, 2017). This time, a total of 111 responses were received with the proportion of girls and boys being similar (although slightly more boys than girls) and spread across four year groups: twenty-seven Year 3 respondents aged 7–8 (fifteen boys and thirteen girls); twenty-six Year 4 respondents aged 8–9 (sixteen boys and ten girls); twenty-seven Year 5 respondents aged 10–11 (twelve boys and fifteen girls) and thirty Year 6 respondents (fifteen boys and fifteen girls). The nationalities of the pupils were mainly British, although four of the children were from overseas.

As in the previous study, the question focused on selecting a preferred design from the same paired designs used previously although the first pair of designs used previously, a pair of IKEA chairs, was excluded since the researchers took the view that the aesthetics of the two chairs were insufficiently different to justify their inclusion in the design questionnaire. The results? Once again, there was a statistically signigicant tendency to select designs created by designers of their own gender (see Table 12.4).

So, in both studies, there was a strong tendency for people, whether adults or children, to prefer designs created by those of the same gender as themselves. This mirrors the evidence in respect of personality with people drawn to visuals created by those with similar personalities to their own. As before, this finding in relation to gender is an important addition to the relatively novice but important field of interaction design, offering important clues as to how customer centricity can be achieved with audiences of women. In this case, the evidence suggests the importance of ensuring that the visuals targeted at them have strong elements of the female aesthetic. This means factoring in visual factors (colours, detail, dimensionality and shape) as well as thematic factors, thereby going beyond the simplistic view that colouring a product pink will endear it to women.

TABLE 12.4 The statistical extent to which children prefer designs created by those of the same gender as themselves

Pairs of designs used in the experiment	Significance (tendency of the boys and girls to prefer designs created by their own gender)
1–2	0.000
3–4	0.793
5–6	0.000
7–8	0.936
9–10	0.005

Nationality

There is perhaps a little more consensus amongst researchers of nationality than there is perhaps in the case of gender. So, there is recognition of the differences that can divide cultures (Randlesome, 1990; Adler, 2007) with Hofstede's well-known analysis (1980) of differences in management cultures, for example, producing a set of criteria according to which national cultures can be compared. Even a critic of Hofstede, McSweeney (2002), has acknowledged that "Hofstede's dimensions can usefully frame initial discussion about national peculiarities".

Despite this endorsement of Hofstede's work and despite studies relating his concepts to marketing (Kapferer, 1992; Schuiling and Kapferer, 2004; Samli, 1995), there has been relatively little research investigating the impact of nationality on design creations and preferences. One of the few studies on this topic, by the current author in fact, compared French and British life assurance literature (Moss and Vinten, 2001), finding large-scale differences between them in both concepts and imagery. For example, the French literature was more formal and more likely to portray a powerful figure (e.g. CEO) while the British literature was less formal and had no worked examples. These findings reflected differences in the relative power distance and risk aversion in the two countries, with France having a higher power distance (hence the image of the CEO i the French literature) and higher risk aversion (hence the detailed financial examples there) than the UK (Hofstede, 1980). So, these conclusions were a useful first step in exploring the impact of national culture on design.

A second step involved a comparison of personal websites produced in the UK and in France. These were compared against twenty-two features, with twelve showing significant differences between those produced in the UK and in France, and seven of these twelve reflecting web design aspects that earlier research (Moss et al, 2006) had identified as typifying the feminine aesthetic. This suggests that the French websites contained a greater proportion of feminine features than those in the British websites which, in turn, could reflect that fact that French culture is more feminine in character than British culture, with France scoring 43 on a scale of 0–120 for masculinity and Britain scoring a figure of 66 (Hofstede, 1980). The finding of more feminine features in the French than British-produced websites suggests, like the earlier research on life assurance literature (Moss and Vinten, 2001), that Hofstede's measures can provide pointers not just to management style but to marketing and design styles in different countries.

Preferences

This overview of the impact of personality, gender and nationality on visual creations and, where the evidence is available, on preferences reveals the substantial evidence of an interactive effect. In bald terms, this means that organisations need to think carefully about the diversity of their marketing and design teams, since this will not only influence the visuals created but also customer preferences. For, as we have seen when looking at personality and at gender, there is a tendency for people to prefer designs created by those of a like personality or gender.

This tendency for like to attract like reinforces the description of aesthetic experience as being "a dynamic process that takes place between object and spectator. . . [who] identifies with the object [and] becomes, so to speak, fused with it" (Crozier and Greenhalgh, 1992, p. 74). This identification seems to operate at a deep, perhaps unconscious level – as witnessed by boys and girls and men and women preferring designs created by their own gender – as well as at a more conscious one. By analogy, the literature on brand personality suggests that the probability of a purchase is increased by congruity between a brand's personality and a consumer's notions of actual or ideal self (Aaker, 1997; Karande *et al*, 1997).

Implications of an 'outside-in' perspective for organisations

So, we return now to the starting point of this chapter, customer centricity and the way that the 'outside-in' perspective can breathe life into this. Operationalising this means ensuring that the customer's perspective becomes that of the organisation so that there is congruity between the two.

How can this congruity be achieved? The challenges involved should not be under-estimated since success turns on careful recruitment, appraisal and promotion, ensuring that the personality and/or gender/nationality of the assessor does not obstruct the selection of those with a personality/gender/nationality that is congruent with that of the consumer but different from that of the assessor. This demands a high level of awareness on the part of assessors, ensuring that recruitment in one's own image does not take place (Byrne and Neuman, 1992; Dipboye and Macan, 1998). It also demands an awareness of the factors that influence congruity between product and customer self-concept (Brock, 1965; Crozier and Greenhalgh, 1992; Hammer, 1995; Karande *et al*, 1997; De Chernatony *et al*, 2004), factors that can lead to enhanced pleasure and purchasing (Groppel, 1993; Donovan *et al*, 1994; Yahomoto and Lambert, 1994). Last but by no means least, it demands a leadership style and organisational culture that is sufficiently inclusive to permit external customer success criteria to come to the fore within the organisation.

The importance of leadership in creating successful products is not in doubt, since it provides the context in which the organisation's products and designs are created (Bass, 1998; Alimo-Metcalfe and Alban-Metcalf, 2005). In reality, this influence can operate at several levels, with the values of brand managers permeating the brand (Schneider, 2001) and senior management involved either by spearheading new brand values (Driscoll and Hoffman, 2000) or by recruiting personnel involved in marketing, design and branding activities (Moss, 2007). In this last respect, senior management may unwittingly impose its own values during the recruitment process, substituting their own personal preferences for the official selection criteria contained in the job specification (Moss and Daunton, 2006). The problem for CC is that in some cases these values may be at odds with those of the customer constituency (Moss, 2007), and so there is a challenge for Human Resources in ensuring not only that selection criteria reflect customer values but also are enforced.

Underpinning these assumptions is an interactionist perspective in which aesthetic perceptions are a function of *individual* rather than *universal* values (Porteous, 1996), linking with the 'empathy principle' according to which aesthetic value is not inherent in objects but is the product of empathy between object, perceiver and artist (Dipboye and Macan, 1988). Such a focus – with the workings spelt out in Figure 12.1 – would demand a workplace culture that not only encourages diversity but also encourages everyday norms to be seen through the prism of customers rather than through the personal preferences of leaders and managers.

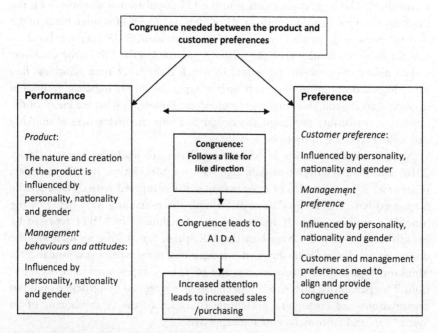

FIGURE 12.2 Normative model of links that need to exist between performance and preference to create congruence (Moss, 2007)

So, recapping the argument, we are suggesting that optimal design and marketing solutions are those which reflect the values and aesthetic preferences of the target market, providing features that mirror these (Hammer, 1995; Janz and Prasarnphanich, 2003; Moss *et al*, 2008). In order to put this into practice, organisations need to ensure that there is a match between the so-called 'performance' elements in the organisation (leadership style, products and design norms) and the preferences of the end-user. Very often, these two elements are not synchronised, and organisations need to work hard to overcome the obstacles in the way of achieving congruity between the thinking inside and outside the organisation. In the case of design, this means aligning internal and external aesthetics.

The parallels between the psychology of performance on the one hand, and the psychology of preference on the other, suggest that congruence can best be achieved by ensuring that the people creating products have ways of seeing that are as similar as possible to those of the people purchasing and consuming products. In other words, where personality and gender are concerned, they suggest that creatives employed by organisations should have personality and gender characteristics that mirror those of the target market. This view is to adopt the 'inside-out' or 'outside-in' perspective (Baden-Fuller, 1995).

Take personality, for example. According to data from the Centre for Applications of Psychological Type (CAPT), men and women score differently on the ever popular Myers Briggs Type Inventory (MBTI or 'Big Four') – a personality test used by 70% of Fortune 500 companies (Brighton and Hove Chamber of Commerce). The biggest discrepancy in the US population as a whole is on the thinking/feeling dimension, with 43.5% of men and 75.5% of women being of the 'feeling' persuasion (www.capt.org/products/examples/20025HO.pdf). Incidentally, for those not familiar with the Jungian types used in the MBTI, the thinking/feeling dimension concerns the extent to which feelings act as an additional factor to logical decision-making, with 'feeling' types able to use logic *and* feelings in decision-making and 'thinking' types logic alone. Following what we know of the impacts of personality on design, the design creations and preferences of thinking and feeling types are likely to be very different.

Now, we know that up to 83% of purchases are made by women (Moss, 2016) and that, according to Ashridge data for MBTI type in UK managers (Carr *et al*, 2011), just 11% of male managers (as compared with 24% of female managers) have the 'feeling' disposition with the remaining 89% being of the 'thinking' predisposition. If we assume the distribution of MBTI types to be broadly similar in the US and in the UK, then, for as long as men are the dominant gender in leadership and management, there will be a dominance of 'thinking' types within organisations and of 'feeling' types outside of organisations. This perceptual dissonance will challenge perceptual congruence between organisations and customers, presenting obstacles to the establishment of an 'outside-in' and customer-centric perspective.

Incidentally, if you are wondering what the current gender balance is in senior leadership globally, figures for female representation in the US on Fortune 500 company boards remained below 17% for the fourth year running (Prime and Salib, 2014). In the UK, women hold under 10% of executive directorships, up from 5.5% in 2010 (Davies, 2013, p. 6) and across the European Union zone, 15% of non-executive directors and 8.9% of executive directors are women (European Commission, 2012). Internationally, in 2015, in 55% of the 128 countries surveyed by the ILO in 2015, men constituted 70% of leaders and managers with a higher average demonstrated in the remaining 45% of organisations surveyed (ILO, 2015). With figures so skewed in favour of male leaders and managers, gender parity in senior management is likely to be a long way off.

So, the reality of having a different demographic inside and outside organisa-tions is likely to be with us for some time to come. This being the case, perceptual change relies on an increasing focus on a diversity mindset and awareness of 'group think', something facilitated by inclusive leadership (Deloitte, 2012). Further steps to achieving congruence are outlined in the next section.

Practical steps to congruence

How can managers inside an organisation attune their thinking to an exterior demo-graphic? If they share demographic characteristics, the challenge should be relatively simple, but what if they do not? In essence, the ideal options involve recruiting and promoting staff whose perceptions and aesthetic preferences match those of the tar-get market and, since the majority of purchasers in many markets will be female, this approach would involve recruiting more women as managers. An alternative strat-egy would involve using training and development to bring about greater diversity in managers' thinking. In the particular instance of product aesthetics, such training would focus on the diverse nature of aesthetic preferences and possible differences in the thinking and perceptions of customers on the one hand and those in the design and marketing functions on the other.

The first option, that of recruitment, appears, on the face of it, to be the most direct method of achieving congruence with customer perspectives, but regrettably, it is not an obstacle-free option. Firstly, it may be difficult, even using personality testing tools, to find the staff with personality profiles to match those of custom-ers. Secondly, recruiting staff whose values may differ from those of the majority in any organisation may make it difficult for these people to flourish and be val-ued. Moreover, since people tend to recruit people like themselves (Lewis, 2006), succeeding in breaking out from current recruitment norms (often favouring the recruitment of men) may be difficult. Moreover, the personality profiles of those within organisations may accentuate this problem.

Why might personality exacerbate the problem? The dominant MBTI type cur-rently employed in UK organisations is the ESTJ type (i.e. 'thinking' not 'feeling' types, together with 'sensing' and 'judgement' types) constituting 22% of types in an Ashridge study of type conducted with over 22,000 respondents (Carr et al, 2011), the largest single set of types in their dataset. Moreover, the ESTJ type is the second most common personality type amongst men in the US (www.capt.org/products/examples/20025HO.pdf) so the UK and US situations are similar. The important thing to note is that the four personality predispositions that together feed into the ESTJ type create a tendency to make judgements and establish rules of behaviour to which others are expected to conform. As a consequence, the current tendency in organisations to recruit people with an ESTJ predisposition is likely to place psychological constraints on the creation of a more diverse and, to that extent, more divergent workforce.

So, given the personality characteristics of ESTJ managers, changing an organisation with a high proportion of these types is not likely to be easy. It might involve educating existing staff in the value of new ways of seeing, much as had been achieved in the public sector probation services organisation that recognised the importance of a new style of leadership and adjusted its Human Resources procedures to ensure the presence of a more inclusive style of leader (Moss *et al*, 2006). However, it must be said that doing this requires a high level of innovation on the part of the organisation, and this may be hard to achieve in an organisation with a high proportion of ESTJ managers since this personality profile may encourage *status quo* recruitment (Windolf, 1986). This type of recruitment can be "conservative, often recruiting from the same social strata and age groups" of existing staff and can lead to organisational "failure or at the very least stunted growth" (Boxall and Purcell, 2003, p. 140).

Of course, a new strategy of innovative recruitment involving the recruitment of a more heterogeneous set of applicants could help overcome these problems but this demands a shift in culture to ensure that prevailing values will not obstruct the acceptance of people whose values and ways of seeing, whilst in line with the customer, may be at odds with those of the conservative majority in the organisation. We will discuss the implications of this later while meanwhile returning to the alternative strategy, namely the training of existing staff.

What would this necessitate? Essentially, training would need to educate existing incumbents in the alternative values of the customer, particularly (given our focus on design) on the many and various 'ways of seeing', and focusing on those of the target demographic. It has to be said, however, that even if managers gain a logical understanding of the vast range of people's aesthetic preferences, they may still struggle to think their way into another set of perceptions. A further difficulty relates to the difficulty of identifying the personality types in the target market, although a knowledge of the gender balance in the market as well as an analysis of the language of customers (as seen in their contributions to chat rooms) will allow inferences to be made about their personality type.

The other option that would pave the way to the recruitment of those who share customer demographic characteristics (e.g. gender and/or personality) would be culture change within the organisation. This is an option that offers a more viable long-term solution than does training, and so is the focus of the next section.

Creating an inclusive culture that is customer-centric

Whilst training can be a stop-gap solution to influencing the way that employees respond to visual stimuli, recruiting a diverse range of people who can mirror the thinking and perceptions of the customer can be a longer-term solution. However, in many cases, the culture of the organisation will need to change to make it accepting of greater diversity.

This is where inclusive leadership can come to the rescue, since it can foster a culture that will embrace difference and acknowledge the importance of being in tune with customer preferences. Such a culture would, for example, be more able than a command and control one to allow constructive criticism of websites created by an all-male web design team for a predominantly female demographic or even, better still, train up or recruit suitable female web designers. It might additionally be one that makes it possible to undertake market research using alternative design paradigms to ensure that the website designs really do match the preferences of the target demographic.

As we saw earlier, the skills and attributes that make up inclusive leadership style consist of the twin elements of transformational and servant leadership, with the former validated by an extensive literature and the latter recognised as a valid model for modern leadership (Greenleaf, 1977; Russell and Stone, 2002). Combining the two produces the fifteen attributes that have been the focus of much of this book, with several of these concerned with interpersonal behaviours (for example empathy, listening, healing, individualised attention) and several with broader cognitive behaviours such as foresight, conceptualising and awareness.

If the reader has read the case studies, then they will have seen some of the key steps that need to be followed in developing an inclusive culture. These include setting a vision, obtaining buy-in and creating a context in which leaders become facilitators and coaches rather than autocratic figures. In Royal Mail Sales, this last point was achieved by signing all managers up to an eight-month-long coaching course and not only empowering staff (for example by giving front-line staff the autonomy to decide how they apportion their time between different customers) but also allowing people to be themselves.

The evidence is clear. According to one manager at Royal Mail Sales, "A lot of our business is about developing relationships with customers and so empowering staff and allowing people to be themselves is an important part of developing positive relationships with customers". According to another, "If employees are more positive, they'll do more, they will be more creative and the customer will see that things are progressing more quickly, more creatively". The consequences? According to Graham Davis, former Director of Sales at Royal Mail, the Sales operation was 'crashing' through its targets.

Further change processes can involve members of staff in informal gatherings at which an exchange of views with leaders can take place. Such a mechanism is a good way of breaking down barriers, with the director of Royal Mail Sales, for example, meeting with groups all around the country and spending most of the time in discussion with staff after an extremely short presentation. Another powerful example is the change in culture and turnaround of British Airways in the 1980s. In fact, so powerful an example is this of inclusive leadership and customer centricity that it is the focus of the next section.

British Airways

In the late 1970s and early 1980s, British Airways (BA) was performing disastrously against almost every indicator. Its productivity was below that of its main overseas competitors, it was beset by industrial disputes and it was recording substantial financial losses (£140 million or some £200 a minute in 1981). Staff discontent was more than matched by customer dissatisfaction, and in 1980 a survey by the International Airline Passengers Association put BA at the top of a list of airlines to be avoided at all costs (Grugulis and Wilkinson, 2002). To add to the misery, BA declared a loss of £1 billion on under £3 billion in revenue in 1983.

In that year, the then chairman of BA, Lord King, appointed Colin Marshall as the company's CEO. Marshall, previously co-chairman of Avis Cars in New York, had been "dedicated to meeting customer requirements" (*Guardian* obituary, 2012) and instrumental in surpassing Hertz performance in Europe. British born and educated – he had been a scholarship boy at University College School in London – he was "meticulous, endlessly pleasant, apparently open and rarely ruffled" (*ibid*) and, as part of his forward thinking, he stated that "the customer doesn't expect things to go right all of the time – the big test is what you do when things go wrong" (Prokesh, 1995). He realised, moreover, that the customer relationship in the airline business does not begin and end with touchdown and passport control, and so he introduced the first arrival lounges in commercial aviation history.

His interest in customer satisfaction went beyond changes to the physical infrastructure so he was soon looking at the part that employees played in this. In fact, he is on record as saying,

> We ... have to 'design' our people and their service attitude just as we design an aircraft seat, an in-flight entertainment programme or an airport lounge to meet the needs and preferences of our customers.
>
> *(Prokesh, 1995)*

With this in mind, Marshall initiated a company-wide training programme, 'Putting People First', for all 40,000 of BA's employees. Remarkably, he personally attended 95% of the training sessions which, contrary to BA's normal hierarchical and militaristic culture, were organised as cross-functional and cross-grade groups, with attendees out of uniform (Grugulis and Wilkinson, 2002). This formidable training programme helped transform BA from a loss-making public sector airline into one that, by 1986, was earning almost £500 million on revenues of around £5 billion. By that time, moreover, BA's customer service ratings routinely exceeded every single airline except Singapore Airlines and Swiss Air, and by December 1986, BA was the highest rated airline for customer service, beating even those two giant competitors. How can we explain Marshall's success at BA?

One reason is that, true to Best Practice Change Management, he set out to develop a new culture, with a clear vision for the company which placed the customer at the heart of it. As he stated in a speech (Broughton, 2012),

In a deregulated environment, where government policies can no longer fix markets and offer competitive protection, who calls the shots? The answer is obvious: the customer. It is the essential truth of the new world competitive order – of global business development – that customer choice, preference and demand are its real driving forces.

Beyond that, Marshall was a passionate advocate of inclusive leadership *avant la lettre*. So, he not only led by example, attending 95% of the 'Putting People First' training sessions and question-and-answer sessions there but also, and for two years, wore a 'Putting People First' lapel badge like other employees. Moreover, he emphasised the importance of teamwork by introducing team briefings, team-working and team targets. This is interesting since we saw a similar emphasis on teamworking in our case study organisations –PageGroup, Royal Mail and APAM, for example – with the top person in these organisations sharing office space with staff so as to boost inclusivity.

What is more, Marshall developed Total Quality Management (TQM) and autonomous teamworking and developed top/down briefings in order to ensure that mobile and isolated staff were not neglected. In fact, in March 1996, BA became the first company to make daily TV broadcasts to its staff.

It was not just a vision for customer service and improved communications that transformed operations but also a profound understanding of emotional processes, something that led Marshall to create 'families' of cabin crew so that these 'families', working shift patterns, could provide mutual support, make cabin crew feel happier about their environments and connect better with passengers. Moreover, a new appraisal and reward system was introduced that judged results not just against targets but also on *how* they had been achieved. Since bonuses could theoretically equate to 20% of salary, the fact that equal weighting was now given to quantitative and behavioural achievements elevated the importance of exhibiting desired behaviours. One can't help but be reminded of the recent shift within the British Civil Service from an exclusively objectives-based appraisal system to one now based in the *what* as well as the *how* (see the relevant interview on pages 103–104 in Chapter 4 on what it feels like to be managed by someone practising inclusive leadership).

In fact, revisiting Marshall's leadership behaviours and mapping these against inclusive leadership attributes shows a clear tendency to IL on his part (see Table 12.5). Do note that some of the actions that are attributed to Marshall in this table come from the testimony of Jamie Bowden, author of an obituary on Colin Marshall and previously customer service manager at BA at the time that the incidents marked with '★' took place (2012). In fact, if we are looking for validation of the impacts of such inclusive leadership, it could not have been better expressed by Jamie Bowden, who wrote that "those of us who were there for the ride will remember his [CM's] tenure as the best working years of our lives". This is praise indeed, but nothing short of what one might expect of someone practising inclusive leadership.

TABLE 12.5 Competencies in inclusive leadership (Moss *et al*, 2016) and the way that these map against Colin Marshall's actions as CEO at British Airways

Inclusive leadership attributes	Description	Actions by Marshall that illustrate this
Individualised consideration	Showing individual interest and offering one-to-one support for followers	CM could come into the airport at 6.00–7.00 am on a weekend to chat to front-line staff in the check-in and baggage loading rest rooms. He would chat and have a hot drink with staff ★ He always made a point of attending welcome events for new attendees if only via a video link
Idealised influence	Having admirable qualities that followers want to identify with	
Inspirational motivation	Providing an appealing vision that inspires followers	CM put staff motivation and the customer at the heart of everything BA did ★
Intellectual stimulation	Encouraging followers to develop their ideas and to be challenged	
Unqualified acceptance	Being inclusive in considering followers	He remembered the names of front-line staff, e.g. check-in agents and cabin crew, remembering them even into retirement ★
Empathy	Putting oneself mentally and emotionally into the follower's place	Many a colleague would relate stories of personal kindness by CM
Listening	Actively listening to followers	Part of BA's refocus under CM was to more actively listen to their key customers.
Persuasion	Being able to influence followers	Top/down briefings were developed to ensure that mobile and isolated staff were not neglected
Confidence building	Providing followers with opportunities and recognition	Many a high-flying executive would attribute success to his mentoring.
Growth	Encouraging followers to reach their full potential	See the comments immediately above
Foresight	Having the ability to anticipate events and where they might lead	CM reported that the most serious thing that he observed was the low morale among employees and this spread into passengers' experience, pre CM's changes, of airline employees as really lacking in enthusiasm for their jobs (Arnold and Stevens, 2012)
Conceptualisation	Having a vision about possibilities and articulating that vision to followers	He presented a vision for BA to the organisation's staff ★

Inclusive leadership attributes	Description	Actions by Marshall that illustrate this
Awareness	Being fully open and aware of environmental cues	He is reported (by an acquaintance of the author) as having personally assisted with a booking problem when the acquaintance encountered CM on board a flight. CM personally arranged for discretionary drinks for the duration of the flight and then followed up with correspondence
Stewardship	Articulating the belief that the organisation's legacy is to contribute to society	CM presented customer choice, preference and demand as the real driving forces of global businesss and this customer focus produced the memorable slogan, 'The World's Favourite Airline'.
Healing	Helping followers cope with any burdens	Once when a queue formed at the launch of a new service, he personally helped by serving breakfast to customers (Hopfl, 1993)

So, do take care to try and read through the inclusive actions that Colin Marshall took (see Table 12.5), since many of these were extraordinary by any standards.

Where has this taken us? We have highlighted the rather unique way in which Colin Marshall led BA, and he himself spelt out his underlying philosophy when he spoke of the fact that "a service business is a people business" (Prokesh, 1995) and that, as a consequence,

> Delivering long-term and consistent value in a service business begins and ends with the way employees are trained, nurtured and led.
>
> *(ibid)*

These were not just empty words, for he spoke of the importance of providing feedback on behaviour not just to cabin crew but to managers as well. In fact, in an interview he referred to plans for a new programme of 360 degree for managers from subordinates, peers and superiors, saying that "Managers who are merely paying lip-service to supporting employees will have nowhere to hide" *(ibid)*.

The success of this new culture at BA was such that, within nine years of Marshall's arrival at BA, turnover had risen from a little over £2 billion in 1981 to more than double in 1992, and profitability from a loss of £140 million to a profit of £434 million. Privatisation came in 1987 as well as a knighthood for Marshall, with a life peerage following the next year, in 1998. Of course, the contribution that he made to BA's success cannot be precisely quantified but there seems little doubt that his inclusive approach to leadership played a major part in the successes that he achieved at the airline.

Inclusive leadership enhances customer service

With Marshall's words on the criticality of leadership in a service environment, it is fascinating to see another CEO, this time Vineet Nayar of HCL Technologies – one of the most successful business leaders of his generation (Black, 2011) – recogniding the importance of employees in a service business in the title to his book "Employees First, Customers Second". In a similar vein, the head of corporate Human Resources at the successful firm Mitchells and Butler, owner of restaurant and pub chains including Harvester, O'Neill's and All Bar One, writes that staff retention, profitability and customer satisfaction are all significantly higher where managers focus on their teams than when [they do] not (*ibid*).

So, it seems that inclusive leadership holds the key to customer centricity, whether in terms of creating enhanced awareness of diversity or in terms of creating a climate which encourages empathy and a focus on the 'other'. With this in mind, it is easy to see how a transactional organisation in which managers wield the big stick will not achieve anything like the same positive results since employees will only retreat into themselves, disgruntled and not make the effort to think of ways of pleasing the customer. It seems that inclusive leadership can create the conditions in which genuine customer centricity can take root.

In the next chapter, we look at the all-important question as to the steps that need to be taken to allow inclusive leadership to take root.

References

Aaker, J. L. (1997). Dimensions or brand personality. *Journal of Marketing Research*, 34 (3), 347–356.

Adler, N. (2007). *International dimensions of organizational behavior*. Mason: Thomson Higher Education.

Alimo-Metcalf, B. and Alban-Metcalf, A. (2005). Leadership: Time for a new direction? *Leadership*, 1 (1), 51–71, www.ctrtraining.co.uk/documents/AlimoMetcalfeLeadershipTime-foraNewDirection.pdf

Alschuler, R. H. and Hattwick, W. (1947). *Painting and personality*. Chicago: University of Chicago Press.

Arnold, L. and Stevens, C. (2012). Colin Marshall who revived BA dies at 78. *Bloomberg Magazine*, 8 July, www.bloomberg.com/news/articles/2012-07-08/colin-marshall-who-turned-around-british-airways-dies-at-78

Baden-Fuller, C. (1995). Strategic innovation, corporate entrepreneurship and matching outside-in to inside-out approaches to strategy research. *British Journal of Management*, 6 (Special issues), 3–16.

Bass, B. (1998). *Current developments in transformational leadership: Research and applications: Invited address to the American Psychological Association*. San Francisco, CA: American Psychological Association.

Black, O. (2011). Think tank: Put your employees first and your customers second. *The Telegraph*, www.telegraph.co.uk/finance/businessclub/management-advice/8813996/Think-Tank-put-your-employees-first-and-your-customers-second.html

Bloch, P. H., Brunel, F. and Todd, S. (2003). Individual differences in the centrality of visual product aesthetics: Concept and measurement. *Journal of Personality and Social Psychology*, 71, 665–679.

Bourke, J. and Dillon, B. (2016). *The six signature traits of inclusive leadership Thriving in a diverse new world,* Deloitte Australia, www2.deloitte.com/insights/us/en/topics/talent/six-signature-traits-of-inclusive-leadership.html

Bowden, J. (2012). Obituary of Colin Marshall. *Independent,* www.independent.co.uk/travel/news-and-advice/lord-marshall-s-legacy-7920907.html

Boxall, P. and Purcell, J. (2003). *Strategy and human resource management.* Basingstoke: Palgrave Macmillan.

Braga, C. (2017). *The benefits of a diverse team,* 4 April, https://uxdesign.cc/the-benefits-of-a-diverse-team-c423d4a849d4

Brighton and Hove Chamber of Commerce, 79% of FTSE 100 use it: Are you? www.business-inbrighton.org.uk/blog/2016/11/16/79-ftse-100-firms-use-it-are-you, accessed on 18 August 2018.

Brock, T. C. (1965). Communicator-recipient similarity and decision change. *Journal of Personality and Social Psychology,* 1, 650–654.

Broughton, M. (2012). Lord Marshall of Knightsbridge, up to speed. *British Airways,* www.ba-touchdown.com/wp-content/uploads/2012/07/LordMarshall.pdf

Buchanan, R. (1995). Rhetoric, humanism and design. In Buchanan, R. and Margolin, V. (eds.), *Discovering design,* pp. 23–68. Chicago: University of Chicago Press.

Buchanan, R. (2001). Human dignity and human rights: Thoughts on the principles of human-centered design. *Design Issues,* 17 (3), 35–39.

Byrne, D. and Neuman, J. (1992). The implications of attraction research for organizational issues. In Kelley, K. (ed.), *Issues, theory and research in industrial and organizational psychology.* New York, NY: Elsevier.

Carr, M., Curd, J., Davda, F. and Piper, N. (2011). MBTI research into distribution of type. *Ashridge Business School,* www.ashridge.org.uk/Media-Library/Ashridge/PDFs/Publications/MBTIResearchIntoDistribution2.pdf, accessed on 9 April 2016.

Creusen, M., Veryzer, R. and Schoormans, J. (2010). Product value importance and consumer preference for visual complexity and symmetry. *European Journal of Marketing,* 49 (9/10), 1437–1452.

Crozier, W., and Greenhalgh, P. (1992). The empathy principle: Towards a model for the psychology of art. *Journal for the Theory of Social Behaviour,* 22, 63–79.

David, A. (2010). Diversity, innovation and corporate strategy. In Moss, G. (ed.), *Profiting from diversity.* Basingstoke: Palgrave Macmillan.

Davies, E. (2013). *Women on boards,* www.gov.uk/government/uploads/system/uploads/attachment_data/file/182602/bis-13-p135-women-on-boards-2013.pdf, accessed on 9 April 2016.

De Chernatony, L., Drury, S. and Segal-Horn, S. (2004). Identifying and sustaining services brands' values. *Journal of Marketing Communications,* 10 (2), 73–93.

Dell'Era, C., Marchesi, A. and Verganti, R. (2010). Mastering technologies in design-driven innovations: How two Italian furniture companies make design a central part of their innovation process. *Research Technology Management,* March–April, 12–23.

Deloitte. (2012). *Inclusive leadership: Will a hug do?* www2.deloitte.com/content/dam/Deloitte/au/Documents/human-capital/deloitte-au-hc-diversity-inclusive-leadership-hug-0312.pdf, accessed on 18 August 2018.

Deloitte. (2015). *Telstra's ambition to connect everything to everyone: Transforming business through customer-centricity,* Australian interview and case study, April, www2.deloitte.com/au/en/pages/human-capital/articles/telstras-ambition-connect-everything-everyone-transforming-business-through-customer-centricity.html

Dipboye, R. and Macan, T. (1988). A process view of the selection/recruitment interview. In Schuler, R., Youngblood, S. and Huber, V. (eds.), *Readings in personnel and human resource management.* St Paul, MN: West.

Donovan, R. J., Rossiter, J., Marcoolyn, G. and Nesdale, A. (1994). Store atmosphere and purchasing behavior. *Journal of Retailing*, 70 (3), 283–294.

Driscoll, D-M. and Hoffman, W. M. (2000). *Ethics matters: How to implement values-driven management*. Waltham, MA: Bently College Center for Business Ethics.

Drucker, P. (1954). *The practice of management*. New York, NY: Harper & Row.

European Commission. (2012). *Women on boards: Commission proposes 40% objective*, http://europa.eu/rapid/press-release_IP-12-1205_en.htm, accessed on 11 July 2018.

Gehrt, K. C. and Yan, R-N. (2004). Situational, consumer, and retailer factors affecting internet catalog, and store shopping. *International Journal of Retail and Distribution Management*, 32 (1), 5–18.

Greenleaf, R. (1977). *Servant leadership: A journey into the nature of legitimate power and greatness*. Mahwah, NJ: Paulist Press.

Groppel, A. (1993). Store design and experience orientated consumers in retailing: Comparison between the United States and Germany. In Van Raaij, W. F. and Bassomy, G. J. (eds.), *European advances in consumer research*. Amsterdam: Association for Consumer Research.

Grugulis, I. and Wilkinson, A. (2002). Managing culture at British Airways: Hype, hope and reality. *Long Range Planning*, 35, 179–194, www.researchgate.net/publication/28576417_British_Airways_culture_and_structure, accessed on 22 February 2018.

Guardian. (2012). *Obituary of Colin Marshall*, www.theguardian.com/business/2012/jul/10/colin-marshall-lord-marshall-of-knightsbridge

Gundling, E., Cauldwell, C. and Kvitkovich, K. (2015). *Leading across new borders: How to succeed as the center shifts*. Hoboken, NJ: Wiley.

Hammer, M. (1995). *Reengineering the corporation*. London: Nicholas Brealey Corporation.

Harris, J. (2017). Personality communicated in children's digital and non-digital drawings: Inferences for marketing research. In Moss, G. (ed.), *Personality, design and marketing*, pp. 64–82. Abingdon: Routledge.

Hassenzahl, M. (2007). Aesthetics in interactive products: Correlates and consequences of beauty. In Schifferstein, H. N. J. and Hekkert, P. (eds.), *Product experience*. Amsterdam: Elsevier.

Hofstede, G. H. (1980). *Culture's consequences: International differences in work-related values*. Beverly Hills, CA: Sage.

Hopfl, H. (1993). Culture and commitment: British Airways. In Gowler, D., Legge, K. and Clegg, C. (eds.), *Case studies in organizational behavior and human resource management*. London: PCP.

ILO. (2015). *Women in business and management: Gaining momentum*, www.ilo.org/global/publications/books/WCMS_316450/lang – en/index.htm, accessed on 18 August 2018.

Janz, B. D. and Prasarnphanich, P. (2003). Understanding the antecedents of effective knowledge management: The importance of a knowledge-centred culture. *Decision Sciences*, 34 (2), 351–384.

Kapferer, J. (1992). *Strategic brand management*. New York, NY: The Free Press.

Karande, K., Zinham, G. and Lum, A. (1997). Brand personality and self concept: A replication and extension. *American Marketing Association, Summer Conference*, 165–171.

Kissmetrics blog, https://blog.kissmetrics.com/mega-entrepreneur-richard-branson/, accessed on 7 April 2018.

Kollewe, J. and Hickey, S. (2015). A third of boardroom positions should be held by women, UK firms told. *The Guardian*, www.theguardian.com/business/2015/oct/29/a-third-of-boardroom-positions-should-be-held-by-women-uk-firms-told, accessed on 31 December.

Lamberti, L. (2013). Customer centricity: The construct and the operational antecedents. *Journal of Strategic Marketing*, 21 (7), 588–612.

Lawson, B. (1983). *How designers think*. Westfield, NJ: Eastview Editions.

Lewis, C. (2006). Is the test relevant? *The Times*, Career section, 30 November, 8.

Maeda, J. (2006). *The laws of simplicity*. Cambridge, MA: MIT Press.

Maughan, L., Gutnikov, S. and Stevens, R. (2007). Like more, look more: Look more, like more: The evidence from eye-tracking. *Journal of Brand Management*, 14 (4), 336–343.

McSweeney, B. (2002). Hofstede's model of national cultural differences and their consequences: A triumph of faith – a failure of analysis. *Human Relations*, 55 (1), 89–118, First Published 1 January 2002.

Mischel, W. (1997). The interaction of person and situation. In Magnusson, D. and Endler, N. S. (eds.), *Personality at the crossroads: Current issues in interactional psychology*, pp. 333–352. Hillsdale, NJ: Erlbaum.

Moss, G. (2007). Psychology of performance and preference: Advantages, disadvantages, drivers and obstacles to the achievement of congruence. *Journal of Brand Management*, 14 (4), 343–358.

Moss, G. (2012). Diversity and web design. In Moss, G. (ed.), *Lessons in profiting from diversity*. Basingstoke: Palgrave Macmillan.

Moss, G. (2016). *Gender, design and marketing*. London: Routledge.

Moss, G. (2017). *Personality, design and marketing*. Abingdon: Routledge.

Moss, G. and Horvath, G. (2017). The impact of gender on children's design preferences, Design Management Association (DMA) Conference, 8 June, Hong Kong.

Moss, G. (2018). *Cambridge Analytica: Learnings on customer-centric traits*, 10 April, www.hrmagazine.co.uk/article-details/cambridge-analytica-learnings-on-customer-centric-traits

Moss, G. and Daunton, L. (2006). The discriminatory impact of deviations from selection criteria in Higher Education selection. *Career Development International*, 11 (6), 504–521.

Moss, G., Gunn, R. and Heller, J. (2006). Some men like it black, some women like it pink: Consumer implications of differences in male and female website design. *Journal of Consumer Behaviour*, 5, 328–341.

Moss, G., Gunn, R. and Kubacki, K. (2008). Gender and web design: The implications of the mirroring principle for the services branding model. *Journal of Marketing Communications*, 14, 1, 37–57.

Moss, G. and Horvath, G. (2014). The impact of nationality and gender on consumer preferences. *Design Management Institute (DMI) Conference*, 4 September, 144–167 of the Conference proceedings 'Design Management in an era of disruption', http://tinyurl.com/hgyaroe

Moss, G., Horvath, G. and Vass, E. (2017). *The impact of gender on children's design preferences*, Design Management Institute conference, Hong Kong, https://tinyurl.com/ycsjboz3

Moss, G., Sims, C., Dodds, I. and David, A. (2016). *Inclusive leadership . . . driving performance through diversity*. London: Employers Network on Equality and Inclusion.

Moss, G. and Vinten, G. (2001). Choices and preferences: The effects of nationality. *Journal of Consumer Behaviour*, 1 (2), 198–207.

Nanji, A. (2013). *Should senior marketers be the 'Voice of the Customer'?* www.marketingprofs.com/charts/2013/10938/should-senior-marketers-be-the-voice-of-the-customer/

Nielsen, J. *113 Design guidelines for homepage usability*, www.useit.com/homepageusability/guidelines.html, accessed on 3 April 2012.

Nixon, S. (1997). Circulating culture. In Gay, P. du (ed.), *Production of culture, cultures of production*, pp. 177–234. London: Sage.

Noble, C. and Kumar, M. (2010). Exploring the appeal of product design: A grounded, value-based model of key design elements and relationships. *Journal of Product Innovation Management*, 27 (5), 640–657.

Porteous, J. D. (1996). *Environmental aesthetics: Ideas, politics and planning*. London: Routledge.

Prime, J. and Salib, E. (2014). Inclusive leadership: The view from six countries. *Catalyst*, May, www.catalyst.org/knowledge/inclusive-leadership-view-six-countries, accessed on 11 July 2018.

Prokesh, S. (1995). Competing on customer service: An interview with British Airways' Colin Marshall. *Harvard Business Review*, November–December, https://hbr.org/1995/11/competing-on-customer-service-an-interview-with-british-airways-sir-colin-marshall, accessed on 22 February 2018.

Randlesome, C. (1990). *Business cultures in Europe*. Oxford: Butterworth-Heinemann.

Rowe, P. G. (1991). *Design thinking*. Cambridge: MIT Press.

Russell, R. and Stone, G. (2002). A review of servant leadership attributes: Developing a practical model. *Leadership & Organization Development Journal*, 23 (3), 145–157.

Samli, A. (1995). *International consumer behavior: Its impact on marketing strategy development*. Westport, CT: Quorum books.

Schmitt, B. and Simonson, A. (1997). *Marketing aesthetics: The strategic management of brands, identity and image*. New York, NY: The Free Press.

Schneider, R. (2001). Variety performance. *People Management*, 7 (9), 27–31.

Schuiling, I. and Kapferer, J-N. (2004). Executive insights: Real differences between local and international brands: Strategic implications for international marketers. *Journal of International Marketing*, 12 (4), 97–112.

Sudjic, D. (2009). *The language of things*. London: Penguin.

Talke, K. , Salomo, S. and Kock, A. (2011). Top management team diversity and strategic innovation orientation: The relationship and consequences for innovativeness and performance. *Journal of Product Innovation Management*, 28 (6), 819–832.

Van der Heijden, H. (2003). Factors influencing the usage of websites: The case of a generic portal in the Netherlands. *Information Management*, 40 (6).

Van Iwaarden, J., Van der Wiele, Ball L. and Millen, R. (2004). Perceptions about the quality of web sites: A survey amongst students at North-Eastern University and Erasmus University. *Information and Management*, 41, 947–959.

Van Knippenberg, D., Van Ginkel, W. and Homan, A. (2013). Diversity mindsets and the performance of diverse teams. *Organizational Behavior and Human Decision Processes*, 121 (2), 183–193.

Veryzer, R. (1993). Aesthetic response and the influence of design principles on product preferences. *Advances in Consumer Research*, 20, 224–228.

Waehner, T. S. (1946). Interpretations of spontaneous drawings and paintings. *Genetic Psychology Monograph*, 33, 3–70.

Windolf, P. (1986). Recruitment and selection and internal labour markets in Britain and Germany. *Organization Studies*, 7 (3), 235–254.

Yahomoto, M. and Lambert, D. R. (1994). The impact of product aesthetics on the evaluation of industrial products. *Journal of Product Innovation Management*, 11, 309–324.

Zahra, S. A. and George, G. (2002). Absorptive capacity: A review, reconceptualisation, and extension. *Academy of Management Review*, 27 (2), 185–203.

13

IMPLEMENTING INCLUSIVE LEADERSHIP

Conditions favouring inclusive leadership

What are the optimal conditions whereby inclusive leadership can take root? One of the best ways of answering this question is by looking at the themes emerging from the four case study organisations profiled in this book. Looking back at the cases of Royal Mail Sales, PageGroup, Sevenoaks School and the SME APAM reveals a large number of common themes. We pick up on these in the next sections and then consider the overarching impact of nationality.

A vision

According to the sales director at Royal Mail Sales, one of the first steps in growing an inclusive organisation is creating a vision. The employees in the business should ideally be involved in this process since without the vision, it is unlikely that people will think that a new process is in hand After all, if you are moving from a command and control to an inclusive environment, people will still be witnessing an emphasis on rules and processes and wondering whether change is likely. So, it is the vision that can create a new climate and with it, the belief in a new culture.

In this way, the process adopted at PageGroup began with a shared vision and once everyone in the organisation was engaged with that, it was much easier, according to managers there, to organise the direction that the organisation should take. Likewise at Sevenoaks School, there is a strong emphasis on maintaining a clear vision, with the head regularly giving talks on the school's vision to teaching and support staff. At APAM, the vision has buy-in from employees and the common goals and sense of common purpose that this provides have helped foster the firm's inclusive culture.

These views are supported by theory as well as practice. For example, Kotter (2007), the Konosuke Matshita Professor of Leadership Emeritus at Harvard Business School, famously described eight steps that organisations need to pursue in order to successfully implement change with the third step in this process involving the establishment of a vision,. Later, in a revised version of his thinking, he proposed that the vision should appeal to people's emotions and set out the strategic steps that needed to be followed with a subsequent fourth step, that of recruiting a 'volunteer army' to communicate the vision; in other words, employees need to be part of the change process and amongst its advocates. As we have seen, these ideas are reflected in the thinking of all four of our case study organisations.

Teamwork

Another theme common to many of our case study organisations is the importance of teamworking, with inclusive leaders tending to emphasise the importance of this above individual working. At Royal Mail Sales, for example, one manager reports on the way that the brand of leadership that they have there allows "everyone to feel that they're part of a team", something echoed elsewhere by another manager speaking of his experience that "you feel . . . part of a team that wants to do the best it can for the organisations, customers and shareholders that you are working for".

Similar sentiments are expressed at the real estate firm APAM, where the firm has strong core values in relation to its leadership style and passion for its work, as well as an emphasis on strategic teamwork and collaboration. There is, moreover, a sense of peer-to-peer respect across all levels of the team, something that encourages people to speak up. What is more, the presence of 'team spirit' is not just management speak, since one non-manager describes the experience of working in the firm as being "one big team together" and a second that "there is obviously a hierarchy but I work daily with a director and we work as a team".

At PageGroup, likewise, respondents describe with pride the way that, after a team has performed particularly well, the firm may organise a weekend away. Indeed, the existence and focus of the Group's energies on teamwork is corroborated by a non-manager who speaks of the extent to which there is "massive delegation of power to teams". This puts one in mind of the period at British Airways in which Colin Marshall turned around the fortunes of the organisation by, *inter alia*, introducing team briefings, teamworking and team targets. This was discussed in the previous chapter in fact.

So, we can see that across these three case study organisations and in the success story of BA's turnaround, a strong sense of teamwork is engendered, with individualist effort directed towards teamworking. This emphasis is extremely interesting since it appears that the high individualism characteristic of the UK (Hofstede *et al*, 2010) can be mitigated by teamwork to create the collectivist spirit on which one might assume inclusive leadership hangs. We will look more closely at this later on when examining the effect of nationality and the way that this can impact individualism/collectivism, together with other variables relevant to inclusive leadership. Meanwhile, however, we will look at the next key element in an organisation's journey to create an inclusive culture with inclusive leadership at its core. Empowerment.

Empowerment

The concept of empowerment is covered by two of the IL competencies, 'growth' and 'confidence giving'. That of 'growth' is defined as 'encouraging followers to reach their full potential' while the further competence of 'confidence giving' is defined as 'providing followers with opportunities and recognition', and these two competencies together appear to underpin the notion of empowerment strongly evidenced in Royal Mail.

The former director of sales there, for example, speaks eloquently of the importance of providing employees at all levels with a 'freedom box' giving, as he puts it, "freedom within a framework". He points out that when you work in a big organisation there have to be some rules/processes, but even within those processes and rules there has to be an element of fun. As he points out, it can start very narrowly with a relatively small 'freedom box' in more junior jobs but becoming larger as people move up the hierarchy. However, as he points out, even in more junior jobs it is important to leave people a 'freedom box', since unless they can operate differently, people will leave their brains at home and the organisation will not get innovation.

As he points out, when a 'freedom box' is offered to manager grades, it is amazing how much more they will contribute. For, in his view, if you raise the bar, people can end up doing more than they personally believed they were capable of. In fact, pursuing this approach may lead someone to declare, as happened to one employee in the organisation, that "this has been the best year possible and I really didn't know that I could do this".

The consequence of this way of thinking is that, in Royal Mail Sales, more and more delegated authority is being transferred to people, with employees increasingly empowered to act on decisions that affect them, and not needing to go through layers of approvals. So, the trend is increasingly moving in the direction of enhancing rather than diminishing empowerment, with one manager speaking of how "hugely empowering" it can be when you look at what you're in control of, with this particular manager having the responsibility for bringing in more than £100m in revenue.

At PageGroup likewise there is a strong emphasis on empowering people. As one non-manager says, "There is a big culture of delegation of power because of our structure and massive delegation of power to teams". A further non-manager spoke of the fact that their manager

> trusts us to get on with what we need to do and gives us a lot of room to be creative in our area. We still have to be sure that we get to the end result but there's a strong team spirit since we're not told what to do and we're not being micromanaged.

However, arriving creating a climate in which empployees are empowered will not happen overnight if the organisation has a history of transactional leadership. As a senior manager at Royal Mail Sales suggested,

> you can't change immediately from a "tell" style, one where the emphasis in on "this is how to do it" to a style where the emphasis is on asking employees "what do you think"? A coaching element comes in between these two styles that allows people to move away from a directive style, encouraging people to think for themselves. You need to let out the leash very slowly since you can knock people's confidence in the process. So, you need to lead people through this moving from a "tell" approach, to "what is the best way?" approach through to autonomy.

One way of doing this, according to this senior manager, is by listening. The type of listening involved is one where management do more than literally listen, since at Royal Mail Sales,

> we encourage reports to follow up on what they have been saying and then we feedback on the actions they have taken. Even if we can't action something, we explain the reasons – the "because" is such an important word in this whole process of active listening.

At APAM, likewise, we find a similar emphasis on delegating to and empowering staff. So, respondents talk of the way in which people of all levels can freely ask questions of each other and the way that the close proximity of staff in a single open-plan office helps everyone understand how different parts of the business relate to each other. The proximity in the office also helps to create a cohesive team and feeling of empowerment, something also linked to the range of employee-led initiatives, including a Junior Board, in the firm.

At Sevenoaks School too, we find a similar emphasis on delegation and autonomy. As one senior member of academic staff says, "We delegate a lot, especially down to the level below Head, middle management and Heads of Department levels and the Head looks at opportunities to upskill people to drive things forward and give people an opportunity to update their skills". A similar view is expressed by a colleague who speaks of the fact that "The senior management team allow considerable autonomy to staff who are essentially allowed to do what they feel is right. That gives them the opportunity to develop meaningful schemes of work, for example, that are relevant to students".

What can be concluded about empowerment? The emphasis on this in the four case study organisations quoted here puts one in mind of the leadership philosophy of Jack Welch, former CEO of General Electric Ltd in the US, who asserted that, "Before you are a leader, success is all about growing yourself. When you become a leader, success is all about growing others". Royal Mail Sales,

PageGroup, APAM and Sevenoaks School all appear to be putting this maxim into operation.

Reward system

The nature of an organisation's reward system can impact human relations, and the reward systems available at APAM and Royal Mail Sales appear to reflect this. So, at APAM, according to one manager, performance is "not about one individual doing well but about the team and whether, collectively, everyone is pulling in the right direction". In fact, the significance of a team effort leads the firm to shun individual, commission-based rewards in favour of rewards that are linked to the performance of the business as a whole.

At Royal Mail Sales, too, there is an element of this thinking, with "some teams measured not on results but on behaviour". The fact that these reward systems are not linked to individual performance may be a key factor in the ability of these organisations to foster a collective, inclusive culture.

Office layout

Three of the case study organisations, Royal Mail Sales, APAM and PageGroup, all illustrate the way in which office space can be used to enhance inclusive leadership. At both PageGroup and Royal Mail Sales, for example, the managing director and sales director, respectively, in the UK opt to be free of an office, spending every day with a different group of employees. This permits the employees to have immediate contact with the most senior person, bridging the hierarchical divide, and enabling the managing director to chat to individual employees and, through that, grasp what is going on, what is problematic, what new ideas might benefit the business and where people's talents lie.

This freedom from the trappings of high office characterises the situation at APAM as well, with all twenty-five of the London-based staff, including the two directors, sharing the same large office space. Opinions from people at all levels suggested that this arrangement enables people to freely ask questions of each other and understand how different parts of the business relate to each other. According to one manager at APAM, the proximity also helps to create a feeling of empowerment and a cohesive team with a second manager volunteering the thought, similarly, that it creates a 'team culture' as well as 'transparency'. One non-manager, moreover, considers that "working in this open-plan environment influences you to work hard because you are surrounded by people who are working. This makes me hungry to learn more".

Note also that in one of the Norwegian organisations included in the study on customer centricity (see Chapter 12), that of the software design agency, the CEO made the decision to abandon the office previously used by a CEO and share instead the open-plan area used by the rest of the company. The effect on staff has been palpable, as one staff member explains, "We now all work in the same office with the CEO and, given that she does not monitor our work, this has had a huge impact, creating more trust and making the company feel like one team".

Recruitment

Another driver is strategic recruitment, with one manager at APAM speaking of the fact that "we focus on developing a team so that people's skills complement each other and so that we do not have clones in terms of personality and styles". According to a manager at APAM, selecting people based on who they are as individuals and how they fit within a team is an excellent way of ensuring that effective teamworking is a feature of working life. As we saw earlier, staff at APAM have a diversity of personality types, reflecting thirteen of the sixteen MBTI personality types, bringing a diversity mindset into the firm. This focus on recruits as individuals in fact links to the next point relating to allowing people to be themselves.

Allowing people to be themselves and to develop

At all four case study organisations, there is a common theme of helping people to grow and to be themselves at work.

At APAM, for example, one manager mentions "the lack of a rigid job description that . . . leaves room for freedom to try out your own approach to meet end-goals". Moreover, staff development is a strategic priority, helping not just with the effectiveness of day-to-day work and ensuring that people have the ability to lead and make a real impact within the firm but also a key factor in employee retention. By way of examples, an APAM asset manager has become head of investor reporting, a team assistant has been promoted to the Investor Reporting Team after just five months, an analyst has moved into the Investment Management Team and a PA's role has developed into that of the operations and marketing manager. One non-manager in fact commented on the number of internal opportunities available, pointing out that this was something that allows people to follow their personal interests.

In fact, the ability to be oneself goes beyond movement into new job roles. One female manager, for example, compared her experience at APAM with that of a previous organisation where she had been told to "dominate meetings more and toughen up". She contrasted this with her experience at APAM where nobody had told her to act in a style different from her own: "They accept different people's styles even though the directors might conduct meetings in a different way".

This encouragement for people to be themselves at APAM has analogies with the culture at Royal Mail Sales where a manager spoke of the fact that

> up until the last couple of years, the senior team had fixed ideas on what a leader should look like. In the last couple of years, however, it is acceptable

to behave in different ways and these people who have led differently have proved that they have got results. We can be ourselves since we've proven that we can be ourselves and still get results. In fact, it has been proven that having these differences can give you more.

A similar realisation has appeared at PageGroup which is now totally committed to supporting and promoting an inclusive culture and working environment where all of its employees can realise their full potential, bring their true selves to work and feel comfortable, valued and supported. Something similar appears at Sevenoaks School with an ethos of honesty, development and growth. As one teacher there explains,

> An inclusive style really does encourage people to reach their full potential, since people tend to live up to the expectations held of them. The same applies to pupils who need to be given the opportunity to express their ideas, experiment, explore, plan and make choices. If they are not given these opportunities, they, like staff, will lose interest.

Another speaks of the fact that "Everyone in the school speaks very openly and honestly and everyone is able to challenge the Head".

Drawing on the experiences of the four case study organisations, we can see that it is not a question of making round pegs fit into square holes but rather ensuring that if the pegs are round, then so too are the holes.

Leading by example

Winning generals in the past have often not been afraid to get their boots muddy in the front line trenches and the motivation and inspiration that this provides vastly increases the chances of winning the battle. One of the most famous examples of this is Admiral Nelson who, at the battle of Trafalgar, insisted on standing on the bridge in order to be seen by his men and inspire and motivate them.

Many of the organisations that we have seen in this book have leaders who, by analogy, work closely with their people, remaining in close contact with their staff and clients. One example is Sevenoaks School where the headmistress still teaches a class every week. We have also seen the case of Royal Mail Sales and the Page-Group where directors work alongside other members of staff and at APAM, one non-manager said of the director: "There's nothing I do that he wouldn't do either' so you don't have completely separate tasks. So all case study organisations illustrate the principle of leading by example.

Strategy

Earlier, in Chapter 2, we saw the extent to which internal and external factors can influence an organisation's propensity to develop an inclusive culture in which responsibility is delegated to individuals. The diligent reader may remember that we mentioned a classic study from the late 1950s, still well regarded (Fiedler, 1994), that sought to define the contextual conditions for participative leadership, a type of leadership that has elements of IL. As we saw, Fiedler predicted that the *behavioural* conditions favouring participative leadership would include:

– Moderate relations between leader and subordinate
– Moderate task structure
– Moderate power (i.e. some delegation takes place).

Where *strategic* conditions are concerned, we saw that the extent to which there is an exploit/explore strategy (March, 1991) – reflecting a balance between the exploitation of existing options and the exploration of new ones – taken with the extent to which there is delegation of responsibility, will determine whether an organisation has a 'leader' leadership style, one involving both (i) a long-term focus and (ii) delegation (Håkonsson *et al*, 2012). These two features could be construed as the combination of five inclusive leadership attributes: those of 'foresight', 'conceptualisation' and 'awareness' which conjointly create the long-term focus; and 'confidence building' and 'growth' creating the conditions for delegation.

So, five of the factors identified in previous research as setting the scene for elements of inclusive leadership are:

– Moderate task structure
– Moderate relations between leader and subordinate
– An 'explore'/'analyser'/'prospector' strategy (rather than a 'defender'/'reactor' one)
– An approach that is low on uncertainty avoidance and high on being adventurous
– High delegation.

To what extent are these five conditions present in the case study organisations? Three of these elements are shown again in the model by Danish academics presented earlier (Håkonsson *et al*, 2012) (see Figure 13.1) and each of the five elements mentioned will be explored in turn.

Moderate task structure and moderate relations between leader and subordinate

Are tasks defined or not? According to respondents at Royal Mail, tasks are a mixture of defined and not defined. As one said,

> We need quite robust processes in place but how each team member manages their customers is different. Some will go round their customers quickly and

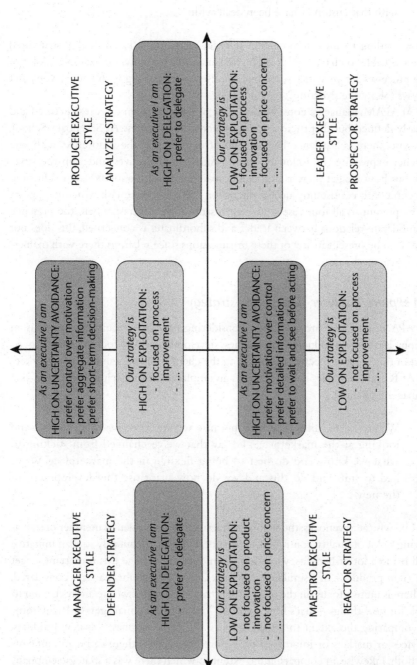

FIGURE 13.1 How leadership styles map to the strategic environment (Håkonsson *et al*, 2012)

some will not want to progress beyond the first until all the issues associated with that customer have been dealt with.

According to most respondents at PageGroup, the tasks are highly structured but amenable to change. Here is one non-manager response, for example, "A lot of the processes are very structured but because you're dealing with people, you can't always follow the structure".

At APAM, managers consider that a lot of what the firm does is structured and clearly defined but that there is variation across the business. At Sevenoaks School, likewise, there is a balance between the structured and the innovative, with one teacher expressing the following view: "Aims and objectives underpin the strategy but how we get there is not rigidly structured and the methods for achieving outcomes are consistently up for discussion". So, moderate task structure appears to be present in all four case study organisations. By contrast, where the presence of moderate relations between leader and subordinates is concerned, this does not appear to be present in any of these organisations since relations there with managers appears to be good.

An explore/analyser/ prospector strategy

At APAM, managers are frequently considering new opportunities, so there is an emphasis on new products, with business development a key focus of meetings. As part of this, a core objective is expanding the client base and winning new markets.

At Royal Mail Sales as well, there is an emphasis on an 'explore' strategy as one manager explained,

> We are more innovative now because we are listening to customers and looking at the marketplace. I'd say that we've changed from sticking to what we know and do best to being flexible in the marketplace. We've had to shift and do this and we do now prioritise the development of the new.

Likewise at Sevenoaks, the school is described by an academic member of staff as having "a lot of quality control but we're not struggling financially so if an initiative will bring a lot of benefits, we'll find the money for it since it is important to get the right product". In a similar way, at PageGroup, one senior manager considered, "There is quite a focus on the new, rather than the existing: we are always having to look for new things – that's how we grow". More widely, managers at PageGroup, in comparing the extent to which there is a strategic emphasis on new products, services or markets or improving procedures, considered there to be an emphasis on both. Likewise, in comparing the extent to which there was a strategic emphasis on being adventurous or careful and reluctant, there was a sense that the Group was all of these things.

An approach that is low on uncertainty avoidance and high on being adventurous

At Royal Mail, respondents considered the Sales operation to be a mixture of someewhere between low uncertainty avoidance and a high sense of adventure, although one manager took the view that they were closer to being adventurous with one non-manager corroborating this when he said,

> The last one or two years have been a lot more adventurous and I've put forward ideas that have been taken up. In the past, there was more red tape and it was slow to progress things. Now, we're putting forward ideas and they're being implemented more quickly. We've become more adventurous and we can now challenge how things are done, with management willing to change.

At Sevenoaks School, likewise, one academic member of staff viewed the school as "Adventurous and actually quite brave, a philosophy that comes from the top. The school builds on what it is good at rather than following trends and is also happy to take risks". A similar attitude appears in APAM, tempered by a degree of caution, with a manager considering the directors "to be adventurous in winning new work but refus[ing] to take unnecessary risk, never borrowing money for example".

High delegation

We saw earlier, when looking at empowerment, that all four case study organisations empower their employees and are therefore involved in the process of delegation.

Drawing the strands together

We have looked at the five factors that set the conditions for an inclusive culture, and, with the exception of one (moderate relations between leaders and subordinates) they all appear to be present, in different degrees, in our four case study organisations. The four elements that are present to some degree therefore are:

(i) Moderate task structure
(ii) An 'explore'/'analyser'/'prospector' (rather than a 'defender'/'reactor' one)
(iii) An approach that is low on uncertainty avoidance and high on being adventurous
(iv) High delegation.

This suggests that, where the establishment of an inclusive culture is concerned, Fiedler (1994) and Håkonsson *et al* (2012) are correct in respect of points (i) and (iv). However, where points (ii) and (iii) are concerned as well as Fiedler's point concerning moderate leader/subordinate relations, it appears that a revised set of conditions may be necessary, since a strategy that is midway between (a) prospector and defender and also midway between (b) adventurous and high uncertainty avoidance may still produce an environment that is inclusive in nature. Moreover, in terms of relations, it seems that having good leader/subordinate relations is more likely to produce inclusive leadership than only moderately good relations. So, in this sense, the conditions that favour inclusive leadership are slightly different from what one might have surmised from the behavioural and strategic literatures, with braoder conditions indicated for strategic factors, thereby extending the situations in which inclusive leadership can take root and more positive behavioural aspects favouring IL.

Do note, reader, that these findings concerning the positive behavioural aspects needed for IL as well as the somewhat modest degrees of adventurousness and exploration needed are new ones but are supported by a study of the four organisations featured in this book. Further work could usefully be conducted to test the robustness of this finding.

Of course, we also noted the conditions that facilitate the embedding of inclusive leadership and, taking our cue from the four case study organisations, these conditions include the following elements:

– a vision that staff can buy into
– teamwork, collectivist emphasis
– group-based reward system
– open-plan office layout
– careful recruitment process
– allowing people to be themselves.

There appears, moreover, to be one further factor at work, namely, low power distance, a factor that has not been discussed in the literature on inclusive leadership. Since it does appear to be a factor in the four case study organisations, we expand on this in the next section.

Power distance

As we can see also from the Royal Mail and APAM case studies, the close links between senior and more junior employees serves to blur the power differentials separating the person at the top from those lower down the hierarchy.

This mitigation of the hierarchical divide is extremely apparent at APAM where one manager, while acknowledging the existence of a hierarchy, states, "we have a very flat structure and that working daily with a director provides a version of teamwork. There is nothing I do that he wouldn't do either so you don't have completely separate tasks". Likewise, one non-manager spoke of the fact that "You enjoy coming to work a lot more if you have a relationship with someone in a leadership role since it makes the hierarchy less obvious". It is apparent also at Sevenoaks School where a pupil talks of the ease with which teachers and pupils can strike up conversations on campus or in the lunch queue. It is equally apparent at PageGroup and Royal Mail Sales where the most senior managers shun the trappings of high office by rejecting large offices and, at Royal Mail Sales, by minimising the time spent in senior management briefings, opting instead for conversations and discussions with the salesforce.

One of the effects of minimising hierarchical divisions is to increase the freedom that people perceive that they have in asking questions. At APAM, for example, one manager comments that "if people are scared to put their hand up and get their heads bitten off, they'll crawl back into a hole. Fortunately, it's not like that here". A similar sentiment comes from a manager at Royal Mail Sales who comments, "if my line manager comes to my team meetings, the way that he interacts (he is very inclusive) affects people's behaviour. For example, they will know that it is OK to ask lots of questions and to challenge".

Similarly, at Sevenoaks School, a member of academic staff speaks of the fact that "Everyone in the school speaks very openly and honestly and everyone is able to challenge the Head". Behaviour of this kind involving the challenging of senior manager opinion would be impossible in a high power distance culture but possible in one with features of low power distance. Importantly, there are studies linking degrees of power distance to national culture, with Anglo-Saxon countries generally rated as having lower power distance scores than many other countries. So, on this basis, it would be more realistic to expect to see inclusive leadership take root in the UK, US or Canada than in certain Mediterranean countries, South America or many parts of Asia, although it is important to recognise that organisations can take steps to mitigate the effects of national culture.

Speaking of national culture, there have been multiple studies suggesting other cross-border attitudinal differences that could facilitate or militate against the introduction of IL and the way that they might play out in relation to inclusive leadership is the focus of our next and final section.

Nationality

The *doyen* of cross-cultural studies is Hofstede *et al* (2010), author of the classic text on the way that variables such as power distance, individualism/collectivism, masculinity/femininity and uncertainty avoidance vary by country. One could conceive from what we have seen that the optimal conditions inclusive leadership might have a mixture of the following elements:

- low individualism
- low masculinity
- low power distance
- medium uncertainty avoidance.

A brief word on each of these four factors follows before we look at their relative incidence in different parts of the world.

Individualism concerns the extent to which people define themselves as individuals rather than members of a team or group. As we saw from our case study organisations, strong teamworking appears to provide fertile ground in which inclusive leadership can take root, and the principle of teamworking rests on collectivism, the polar opposite principle to individualism.

Masculinity relates to the extent to which the dominant values in society emphasise assertiveness and materialism as against concern for people. It is precisely a concern for people that drives inclusive leadership and so low masculine and high feminine values would assist in embedding IL.

Power distance, as we have seen, concerns the notional difference between the most and least powerful in a country or organisation, and we have seen how bridging power divides can ease the passage of inclusive leadership.

Uncertainty avoidance concerns the extent to which risks are avoided, and we have suggested that a low or intermediate score on this may facilitate IL.

So, with these constructs in mind, we can look at the extent to which they feature in different national cultures, based on the findings of Hofstede, the social scientist who did so much cross-cultural work to increase our understanding of the incidence of these constructs in different countries. In fact, his data suggests that there are huge variations between countries in the extent to which the behaviours associated with these constructs are apparent. By way of a brief insight to this, the following table (Table 13.1) shows a sample of Scandinavian, Eastern European/Middle Eastern (Israel) countries that have some of the lowest scores in the world across the four constructs that Hofstede highlighted, making them good candidates for IL.

TABLE 13.1 Assessments of the strength of power distance, individualism, uncertainty avoidance and masculinity in 10 countries

Country	Hofstede scores				
	The lower the average score, the more likely it is that IL will take root				
	Power Distance	Individualism	Masculinity	Uncertainty avoidance	Average (✓ = countries with best conditions for IL)
Denmark	18	74	16	23	33 ✓
Sweden	31	71	5	29	34 ✓
Norway	31	69	8	50	40 ✓
Netherlands	38	80	14	53	46 ✓
Israel	13	54	47	81	48 ✓
Ireland	28	70	68	35	50 ✓
UK	35	89	66	35	52 ✓
Germany	35	67	66	65	58
Brazil	69	38	49	76	58
Turkey	66	37	45	85	58
US	40	91	62	46	60
Australia	36	90	61	51	61
Japan	54	46	95	92	61
Italy	50	76	70	75	62
France	68	71	43	86	67
Belgium	65	75	54	94	72

Source: Hofstede (1991)

Are countries destined to be limited by the constraints of these profiles? The answer, based on the example of the four organisations presented in this book, suggests that in-company initiatives can successfully override some of the limiting effects of UK national culture by taking steps to mitigate the inidividualism, masculinity and power distance that may be present. In terms of successful mechanisms, these can include the encouragement of teamworking (e.g. group-based payment systems; open-plan office space); delegation down the line; and behaviours that reduce perceived power distance. As the examples of APAM and Royal Mail Sales show, these last two points can be greatly assisted by careful recruitment, a coaching style from managers and careful thought to office space.

Incidentally, for readers interested in Hofstede's methodology, his conclusions derived from a comparison of work-based norms in IBM subsidiaries from across the world and even a vocal critic, McSweeney (2002), stated that "Hofstede's dimensions can usefully frame initial discussion about national peculiarities". Of course, as we have suggested, country characteristics may just provide a backdrop within which organisations can create their own micro-climates.

Costs of implementing IL and concluding remarks

The evidence presented in this book suggests implementation of Inclusive Leadership will bring substantial benefits to organisations in terms of greater staff productivity, creativity, motivation and loyalty and enhanced relations with students and customers.

The costs? The main costs are those of achieving culture change and Best Practice Human Resources practices, so costs that an organisation is likely to bear anyway if they are aiming for excellent. So, given this, it could be said in fact that the only real cost will be the self-importance of those currently using command transactional leadership. Can we really afford, however, to maintain an outdated and uneconomic form of leadership that does not inspire, motivate and lead by example in the way that inclusive leadership does? The evidence presented in this book suggests that it is time for many organisations, in competitive and knowledge-based sectors, to make the move to IL. This is a tried and tested form of leadership and it is to be hoped that the organisations that have already trodden this path will give you the confidence and the logistical tools with which to take the next steps. You are unlikely to be disappointed as exciting new vistas appear for staff, customer engagement and profitability.

References

Fiedler, F. E. (1994). *Leadership experience and leadership performance.* Alexandria, VA: US Army Research Institute for the Behavioural and Social Sciences.

Håkonsson, D., Burton, R., Obel, B. and Lauridsen, J. (2012). Strategy implementation requires the right executive style: Evidence from Danish SMEs. *Long Range Planning,* 45 (2–3), 182–208.

Hofstede, G., Hofstede, G. J. and Minkov, M. (2010). *Cultures and organizations: Software of the mind.* 3rd edition. New York, NY: McGraw-Hill.

McSweeney, B. (2002). Hofstede's model of national cultural differences and their consequences: A triumph of faith – a failure of analysis. *Human Relations,* 55, 89–118.

INDEX

Note: Page locators in *italics* indicate figures. Page locators in **bold** indicate tables.

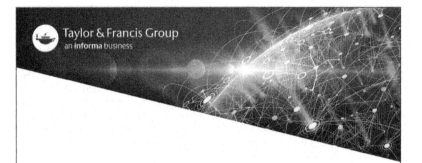